Consensus or Coercio

The State, the People anc Post-war Britain

Lawrence Black, Michael Dawswell, Zoë Doye, Julia Drake, Andrew Homer, John Jenkins, Mark Minion, Glyn Powell and Louise Tracey

New Clarion Press

© Lawrence Black, Michael Dawswell, Zoë Doye, Julia Drake, Andrew Homer, John Jenkins, Mark Minion, Glyn Powell and Louise Tracey 2001

The right of the above named to be identified as the authors of this work has been asserted in accordance with the Copyright, Designs and Patents Act 1988.

First published 2001

New Clarion Press
5 Church Row, Gretton
Cheltenham GL54 5HG
England

New Clarion Press is a workers' co-operative.

A catalogue record for this book is available from the British Library.

ISBN paperback   1 873797 31 1
     hardback   1 873797 32 X

Typeset in 10/12 Times New Roman by Jean Wilson Typesetting, Coventry
Printed in Great Britain by MFP Design and Print

Contents

Contributors

Lawrence Black is Peter and Jane Ricketts Research Fellow in History at Bristol University.

Michael Dawswell is a doctoral student at University College, London, working on return migration to the Caribbean, 1960–2000.

Zoë Doye is a part-time doctoral student at Birkbeck College, London, working on Labour, the London County Council and housing policy in the 1950s. She works on e-government for the London Borough of Waltham Forest and teaches at the Open University.

Julia Drake is currently a doctoral student at University College, London, studying Black Caribbean migration and community formation in Brixton and Notting Hill, 1958–81.

Andrew Homer is Senior Administrator in the Directorate of Lifelong Learning at the University of Luton. His Ph.D. thesis was entitled: 'Administration and social change in the post-war British new towns: a case study of Stevenage and Hemel Hempstead, 1946–70'.

John Jenkins is a research assistant on the BP history project, based at the BP Archives in Warwick University.

Ross McKibbin is a Fellow and Tutor in Modern History at St John's College, Oxford.

Mark Minion is a Research Officer for English Partnerships, the government agency for regeneration. He maintains a research interest in Labour's relationship with European socialism.

Glyn Powell received his doctorate from University College, London. His research and teaching interests include British left-wing and Communist Party history and post-Second World War European history.

Louise Tracey is a research student in the School of History at the University of Leeds. Her research interests include gender, social policy and twentieth-century social history. She is currently researching mothering and the maternity and child welfare services, 1945–60.

Foreword

Ross McKibbin

The chapters in this book are all concerned with questions central to any social system: how does a society hold together? How far does social cohesion occur spontaneously and how far by coercion? And if by coercion, how far is the state responsible for that? There are also two conceptual questions. How do we define 'cohesion' and how do we define 'the state'? For practical purposes, we can offer three 'models' of social cohesion. The first is an 'inclusive or pluralistic' cohesion, one where everybody is included, where there is an almost universal agreement about norms, and where social differences are accepted as legitimate. The second is a form of 'exclusive cohesion'; a society where most people are included, but where cohesion is secured at the price of excluding a minority – often an ethnic one. In such a case, social cohesion is racial. The third model is not unlike the first. Here a society is cohesive, yet poorly integrated: a society where there is a wide consensus about fundamental values and the legitimacy of the state in the broadest sense, but where there is much less agreement about subordinate values and a good deal of social conflict. Britain throughout much of the twentieth century probably better fits the third model than the other two.

The definition of 'the state' employed in this book is the sensible one: that it represents the governing elites, both political and bureaucratic, but is distinguishable from (say) the ruling party and has an interest which, although influenced by party-political competition, stands above such competition.

The state and cohesion

The British state's practice since the Second World War, on the whole, closely resembles the model of inclusive cohesion and is (or was) a continuation of policies thought to have procured very high degrees of social solidarity during the war itself. The best expression of that belief is

vii

probably Edward Shils and Michael Young's famous article ('The meaning of the coronation') on the present Queen's coronation, published in the *Sociological Review* (1953). Here the high degree of inclusive cohesion – higher, it is argued, than in other major industrial nations – is provided by the remarkable social integration of the working class. Whatever we think of that argument, it was the predominant 'official' view of British reality. Another expression of the same thing – appropriate to Michael Dawswell's and Julia Drake's contributions – was the 1948 British Nationality Act, which gave right of entry to Britain to virtually all citizens of the British Empire/Commonwealth. In retrospect, that seems an extraordinary piece of legislation, not just in its scope but also in its ignorance of British history.

From the 1940s to the 1970s it was this kind of social cohesion which, I think, the state attempted to promote, although several of the chapters in this book would not altogether agree with that. Such a policy was not always successful or complete, but the state nonetheless rejected a strategy (except in one respect) of exclusive cohesion. And it was particularly reluctant to do anything that might un-integrate the male industrial working class. There is, however, one important respect in which this view was significantly modified: race. The 1948 Act was never likely to survive any large-scale immigration. Historically, the state has always buckled in face of large-scale immigration. History suggested that the increasingly restrictive immigration legislation that began in 1962 was inevitable. What was not inevitable was the anti-discrimination legislation, whose scope has steadily widened under successive Labour governments. The assumption of the state was that those who are here should have the same formal rights of citizenship as anyone else – even if, in fact, those rights have not always been recognized. In order to promote inclusive cohesion within British society, the state has practised a kind of double coercion. It is coercive at all ports of entry – keeping people out – but, via anti-discrimination legislation, it also attempts to coerce the (white) host community into forms of behaviour that might not come naturally.

We can compare this with the state's attitudes to Irish migration, particularly before 1939. Their entry could not be stopped and it was accompanied by no anti-discriminatory legislation: almost the reverse. Given the Conservative Party's quite open political exploitation of anti-Irish feeling (see Merseyside), the state's passivity in the face of this was probably the closest thing we have had to a strategy of exclusive cohesion. This is in marked contrast to 'coloured' migration. The crucial variable is that the first could not be controlled, while the second could. The price that the host community had to pay for controlling 'coloured' migration was anti-discrimination legislation.

The people and cohesion

The third model of cohesion implies a society where, as I have suggested, there is an agreement on fundamental values, but a much less wholehearted agreement on others. The British, for instance, have not traditionally had a socially solidaristic attitude to industrial relations. Unlike the state, this is the way the 'people' have probably seen British cohesion. For the people there is much less commonality of experience and behaviour – illustrated, for instance, in Zoë Doye's and Andrew Homer's chapters – than the state would have liked. Here one gets group cohesion, which is not necessarily based upon class and race, even though it often is. Equally often it takes the form of associational cohesion – schools, regiments, clubs, sporting associations, etc. become the basis for social loyalties. There have also been profound cultural differences within British society. Indeed, these differences, the absence of commonality, have historically been so wide as to make problematic historical assumptions about Britishness and the almost unique cohesion of British society.

Since the late 1970s, however, traditional forms of cohesion have unquestionably decayed. Why?

1. Partly in reaction to what was thought to be social disintegration in the 1970s, as in the widespread fear that Britain was 'ungovernable', the state, or important elements of it, changed its mind about inclusive cohesion. There was an increasing tendency, especially in the 1980s, to eject people deliberately – to marginalize social failure – and to attempt to unite all winners against all losers. This was undoubtedly a kind of 'exclusive' cohesion. 'Social failure' did have obvious class and racial implications: but that was never made explicit. This policy was not aimed specifically at the 'working class' or at 'immigrants'. There was, in fact, some attempt to co-opt important elements of both, although most of those marginalized were undoubtedly working class and/or immigrants.

2. Secular social changes have had consequences for traditional forms of cohesion. The decline of the industrial working class and the simultaneous decline in trade union membership have significantly weakened group or associational cohesion. The unions were actually quite good at encouraging cohesion, with loyalties grouped around occupation or class rather than race – the Transport and General Workers' Union being a good example.

3. Related to these changes is the fact that British society is now more 'democratic' than ever before. This was partly inevitable, and partly

an unintended consequence of Thatcherism. As it has become more democratic, as people have become less willing to perform traditional roles or obey traditional authorities, British society has become less cohesive. It is very unclear, however, what new forms of cohesion will emerge.

4. There are also other important secular changes, of which the most important has probably been the disruption of the post-war family. This increasing family instability is not confined to Britain – it is common to much of northern Europe as well; but the British welfare state is now not well equipped to deal with it. How far this process will continue is, again, very uncertain.

5. The state under the Blair government is trying to restore older forms of inclusive cohesion; with, however, mixed success. The survival of governmental strategies conceived under Thatcherism and the strength of individualist ideology within the Blair government have made reversion very difficult. Furthermore, older forms of cohesion depended, more than is now recognized, on a large industrial working class and a broadly accepted social hierarchy. Both of these have now gone.

6. Finally, there has been a decline in the legitimacy of the British state itself, of which the successful campaign for Scottish devolution is the best example. Once again, it is hard to know how far this will go and what are its consequences for national cohesion.

The British state and British society are thus at a moment when the future of both is difficult to predict. The chapters in this book are intended to reflect on this and to suggest, thereby, how our future might look.

Introduction

What is 'the state'?

The term itself has several different, but closely related meanings. The contributors to *Consensus or Coercion?* refer to the British state and the role it has played since the Second World War. Given that the term is used widely – and often loosely – within historical discourse and the social sciences, it is useful to discuss the way in which it is used in the chapters of this book. The term's various connotations are all intimately related to the fact that most of the world's population is now divided into nationally administered political communities. 'The state' describes such communities in ways synonymous with modern ideas of 'the nation'.

The nation state is an administratively defined community that exists in spite of traditional and alternative considerations about people's community identities. People have always identified themselves with communities, usually determined by ethnic, cultural, class or religious considerations, but also linguistic ones, and often a combination of all of these. What defines the nation state, however, is that, although it may reflect some of these considerations, it nevertheless both encompasses and cuts across all of them.[1]

Britain's national identity, in part for geographical reasons, has until recently appeared to be both natural and historically permanent. For other areas of the world, particularly those of the so-called Third World, where the boundaries of their various administrative communities have been either imposed by post-colonial settlement or artificially drawn in the interests of the foreign and economic policies of the West, the situation is somewhat different. Even Britain, however, has existed in its present form for only a comparatively small period of its history. For example, although the crowns of England and Scotland were united in 1603, it was not until 1707 that the Act of Union constitutionally united the two nations. Wales was subject to considerable administrative confusion until Acts of Parliament in 1536 and 1543. As recently as 1921, the creation of the Irish Free State suggested that the United Kingdom was not so united. Since the 1970s, closer economic and political relations with Europe, nationalism and devolution in Scotland, Wales and Ireland – and discussion about even English identity – have combined to put this short-lived history into some theoretical doubt.[2]

Nations often appear to have come about either by accident or through 'natural' processes. A closer study, however, even of an island nation like Britain, reveals that most have been created through a process that has served the interests – particularly the economic interest – of powerful groups and individuals. As Karl Marx and others have pointed out, nations are never equitable, either economically or socially, and there is always, therefore, the potential for conflict.[3] Whether it was Britain, created and administered in the interests of first Tudor, then Restoration power, or whether it was the Middle Eastern states, created and administered on behalf of rich rulers and western interest in oil, the nation has existed, often in opposition to other interests of class, religion and even language. For Marx, the most important of these potential conflicts was between the class in whose interest any particular society was run, and those who, either through bondage or economic necessity, were forced to labour on their behalf. More recently, largely due to the collapse of European empires on the one hand and the disintegration of Stalinist communism on the other, conflict has taken the form of challenges to the administratively defined nation on the basis of ethnicity, religion or language.

Whether through calls for a different set of economic relations within any nation or through calls for change, secession or independence on the basis of ethnicity or language, there have always been pressures on the integrity of the nation state and upon the hegemony of those in whose interests it appears to exist. The state has played both a coercive and a harmonizing role in this situation. In order to legitimize itself, the state has attempted to harmonize potentially conflicting ideas about community. It has encouraged the idea that identification with the administratively defined community is more significant than identification on the basis of class, culture, language or ethnicity. Such harmonization, of course, implies a level of consensus. The state also has recourse to military and judicial coercive force when an apparent consensus has broken down. It is this dual role on behalf of a particular type of administratively constructed community with which the following chapters concern themselves.

Whether nations appear relatively stable like Britain or under constant and devastating review like those of the former Yugoslavia, the apparatus that has been used against potential opposition has been a system of military, bureaucratic and judicial paraphernalia. For some nations and at different periods in history, the role of the state appears more as one of harmonization than one of control. In post-war Britain, for example, successive governments have applied coercive state power comparatively sparingly. On the other hand, the experience of striking miners, Greenham Common protesters and Irish republicans suggests something quite different. The following chapters attempt to address this balance between the harmonizing and controlling functions of the state in post-war Britain.

How people relate to the state

People's perception of the state is conditioned in two main ways. First, in circumstances of economic and social disequilibrium, it is conditioned by how people perceive their position in society. So while it is often the case that the state is administered on behalf of the most powerful members of society, many who do not belong to this group nevertheless see their interests as being broadly synonymous, especially in societies that promote ideas of equality and opportunity. Those who do not see their interests as being synonymous with these powerful economic and social groups will perceive the state differently. As much as how perceptions of interests alter in different circumstances, this volume is alert to the importance of how people conceive of their circumstances. Some contributors – particularly in discussions of new towns and cultural provision (television) – also emphasize how the relationship between people and state was contingent upon how the people were imagined and regarded by those projecting a role for the state in their lives.

People's perception of the state also depends upon the circumstances in which they encounter parts of it, its representatives and administrators, in the course of their daily lives. Besides being the main upholder of law and order, the state is experienced in other ways: as an employer of large numbers of people and as an administrator of welfare provisions. The state is represented, in many people's lives, by employees who are hardly different from the people to whom they administer. In this sense, the state constitutes part of the social fabric of people's lives. This can obscure the fact that such relationships are with the state at all. The pensioner collecting a pension from the local post office, for example, engages not with a faceless bureaucrat, but with a counter clerk, whose life experience may well be similar to their own. The state is now such an integral part of most people's lives that much of its activity does not appear to be fulfilling a harmonizing or controlling function at all. Doctors or nurses are rarely perceived as arms of the state and yet most are employed by the state-financed and administered National Health Service.

Another example of the ambivalent, even contradictory, nature of the state in Britain is the role of local councils. In one sense, these bodies are a vital part of the civic democratic process. In another, they are an executor of various services and types of welfare provision. In another, however, they can act as a coercive arm of the state. In the 1980s, for example, some local councils were at the forefront of battling for the political and social as well as economic rights of deprived or oppressed groups. Some councils developed a record of administering on behalf of women through a range of social justice initiatives directed towards such groups as single parents, lesbians and black and Asian women. Such initiatives, however, did not prevent these same councils from voting through redundancies for school cooks and cleaners (mostly women), instituting privatization packages that often amounted to wage cuts and worsening conditions for women workers, and imprisoning non-payers of the poll tax – many of whom were women.

This apparent contradiction begs the question: are these institutions an arm of the state, both as administrators of welfare provision and as a coercive force in the execution and maintenance of certain laws, or are they a democratically instituted safeguard against the potential abuse of centrally administered state power? Such devolving of state power, of both its welfare and its executive functions, is not confined to local authorities. Charities, voluntary groups and even trade unions have acted as 'subcontractors' of devolved state power and provision. Does this mean that such institutions, in accepting devolved power, have become part of the state?

The relationship between people and state is complex and is made more so by an evolving interaction between people and the state's executors. The relationship itself relies, to a large extent, on the state's ability to legitimate itself continually as a beneficent force in society. When it appears to people as a negative force, when it is perceived to have overstepped the vaguely defined limits of its power, such legitimacy can be called into question.

Perceptions of the state as a coercive power

The state as (in Lenin's phrase) 'armed bodies of men' rarely impacts upon most people's lives. In a modern context, even the armed forces can be seen as fulfilling an apparently benign role, such as providing humanitarian aid under the auspices of the United Nations. In general, people become conscious of the state as a repressive force only when they seek to challenge the prevailing economic and social conditions in society. Thus strike activity has had a tendency, often surprisingly quickly, to alter people's perceptions not only of the nature of their own social and economic conditions, but particularly of the organizational structures that keep these in place. This suggests that increased awareness of the role of the state is synonymous with increased politicization. The perception of the state as a duality of ruler and provider is a balance that, for most people, alters over time and under different circumstances. For Caribbean migrants who are more likely to have experienced a more acute relationship with the state's repressive arm, although this duality may be perceived differently, it nevertheless continues to exist.

From a formal political perspective, both Marxists and the Labour left have understood the state as a repressive force, at least in theory. Marxists have differed from social democrats in regarding the apparently benign aspects of the state, such as welfare and housing provision, as ultimately fulfilling a similar function to its repressive aspect – that of maintaining capitalism. While remaining in the forefront of struggles to maintain such provisions, Marxists have, nevertheless, diagnosed illusions in them as falling qualitatively short of socialism. Social democracy, on the other hand, has seen state provision as an end to be achieved in itself and symptomatic of society's progress.

Breaking the state down into component parts may be empirically and analytically useful, and certainly resonates with how many people experience it. Bearing this variegated nature in mind, is it still possible to see the state as one homogeneous, integrated entity? Or are historians compelled to define specific aspects of the state when addressing the relationship between *it* and society? Objectifying the state might be necessary within the social sciences, but historians have to remain aware that 'the people' have not necessarily experienced the state in the same analytical terms. A delicate balance is thus required between the sort of objectivity that reduces the state to merely a repressive organ of class rule and one that collapses into apparently endless definition.

The state and 'the people'

The term 'the people' presents historians with similar problems of definition. 'The people' are, self-evidently, not a homogeneous mass and there are any number of subdivisions into which historians and social scientists choose to separate them. In an exercise that looks at the relationship between 'the people' and the state, it may prove useful to pursue the categories that the state itself appears to prefer and the formulae used to arrive at these.

Such formulae have relied upon the perception of an 'ideal type' upon which the state's relationship with people is based.[4] Material inequalities apart, in post-war Britain, this 'type' has shared economic and social aspirations and cultural norms based around concepts of home, family and a certain level of consumption, as well an acceptance of responsibilities regarding taxation, parenthood and abiding by the law. Such a type is constructed largely on the basis of the prevailing socio-economic relationships that exist within society and is culturally reaffirmed.

The criteria involved in the creation of this ideal type can perhaps be described as 'citizen criteria' and, in Britain, are particularly vague. In some tacit way, an agreement is assumed to exist between the state and those in society who fulfil such citizen criteria. This tacit agreement can be characterized as 'social cohesion'. When one or the other side in this concordat does not fulfil part of it, social cohesion is threatened. In this sense, the concept of social cohesion from the state's point of view is generally seen as consisting of a particular, if vaguely articulated, set of permissions and obligations. Those, wilfully or accidentally, falling outside of these aspirant criteria are not completely excluded, at least in reasonably civilized societies, but they are, nevertheless, regarded as a problem.

Inclusion or exclusion on the basis of such loosely defined, and shifting, criteria can be a powerful tool of social control. For Caribbean immigrants in the 1950s, adherence to perceived social norms and economic aspirations was not sufficient to obtain full inclusion into British society. Poor housing and low-paid employment were the result of colour and immigrant status rather than any unwillingness to adhere to concepts of citizen criteria.

What is social cohesion?

Is social cohesion imposed as a crucial feature of the state's general management of society? Is it something demanded by the people or voluntarily maintained by them as part of their daily lives? One might label any society socially cohesive where there is no serious challenge to the state and the loosely defined assumptions upon which its legitimacy rests. In such terms, the 1950s have been characterized as relatively socially cohesive. Harold Macmillan's oft-quoted words 'most of our people have never had it so good', the idea of a broad consensus around full employment, the welfare state and a booming corporatist economy have given legitimacy to this characterization.[5] Similarly, the 1960s and 1970s have been seen as challenging this idealized notion of social cohesion. Beginning with a questioning of established cultural norms in the 1960s, the period is characterized as developing through the student movement towards the unseating of the government in 1974 by striking miners and, finally, to the Winter of Discontent of 1978–9. Further, external challenges contained in the issue of Britain's place within a more integrated Europe added a dimension to questions of social cohesion.[6]

Both the 1950s as an age of equipoise and the 1960s as an age of radicalism are historical stereotypes, yet both may contain elements of truth. Was one decade more socially cohesive, therefore, than the other? Is it the case that groups such as black migrants or women were motivated to make the challenges they did during the 1960s because the rhetoric that had characterized Britain as socially cohesive was clearly so at odds with the reality of their lives, where racism and sexism were a daily experience? There was clearly a gap between Conservative and Labour political rhetoric and the reality of many people's lives.

From the state's point of view, social cohesion can be seen as the maintenance of a general order to which there are few challenges. For historians, however, conscientiously minding the gap, the perspective of the majority of people involves a range of class, gender, race and other inequalities.

How society is run – some perspectives

Two contrasting perspectives reflect the duality of perceptions of the state and its role in the maintenance of social cohesion. A desire for social cohesion could, potentially, be at odds with a desire for economic and social changes in a society which not only allows inequalities to persist, but which appears, in many ways, to be predicated upon such inequalities. John Locke's idea of a *pactorum unionis*, outlined in his 1690 work *Two Treatises of Government*, articulated ideas of a voluntary surrendering of individual sovereignty for the benefits of living in a socially cohesive society.[7] Locke's ideas can be seen to imply either equality or, possibly, an acceptance of existing political and economic disequilibrium. The gap between Locke's theoretical notions of citizenship and the reality of existing inequalities was studied by T. H. Marshall in 1949 in a series of Cambridge lectures.[8] Marshall was interested to discover how the persistent inequalities of capitalist development and expansion had not translated themselves into the sort of class polarization predicted by Marx. Marshall saw an 'amplification' of citizenship rights throughout the period of capitalist development as being largely responsible for this. His significantly non-economic list of such rights consisted of civil rights (equality before the law), political rights (the extension of the franchise) and social rights (housing, education). Economic inequalities could be rendered more acceptable as an increasing number of people were included as citizens within society's civil, political and social orbit.

In contrast to these ideas of the rights of citizenship, Marxism sees the economic inequalities inherent in capitalist development as fundamentally irreconcilable and leading towards class polarization within society, which such political, social and civil rights merely obscure. Is it the case that the economic inequalities felt by many in the post-war period were offset by an amplification of their citizenship? And are the two ideas as separate as Marshall implies? Increasing someone's political and civil rights may confer on them some notion of citizenship. But equally, it may provoke questions as to why equality before the civil law does not equate to equality economically.

Reform to offset revolution?

When Quintin Hogg warned in the House of Commons in 1943 that 'if you do not give the people reform, they will give you a social revolution', he was arguing (crudely) for an approach that brought both socio-political and economic reforms to people in a managed way.[9] For others, post-war reform has represented the need for any one administration to legitimate itself in the eyes of the electorate.[10] Others have gone further, and have seen this process of reform as representing the need for the system of capitalist democracy itself continually to legitimate itself. Across this spectrum of views, the state plays a crucial role.

Is it the case that social cohesion is, and was, nothing more than the maintenance of law and order so that a particular economic system can continue to expand? Is it the desired end of everybody in society regardless of their unequal position within it? And if it is not, which groups might be said to have an interest in the destruction of such social cohesion as exists? More importantly, how much is the idea of social cohesion nothing more than an idea? If, as Margaret Thatcher once famously observed, there is no such thing as society, only individuals as economic units of consumption, is it nothing more than the power of market forces and the fear of poverty that holds society in a state of more or less equilibrium?[11] Can a society be truly cohesive when economic inequalities prevail? And if not, does the state have an interest in maintaining an illusion of equality, either through welfare provision that appears to militate towards such an ideal, or through notions of equality of opportunity that require political policing across a whole range of areas? This raises questions about 'community' and to what extent historians can describe the

nation state as constituting such a thing. How far are national or administrative communities illusions constructed out of a state-driven ideology?

In post-war Britain the state has played a bigger and more important
role in people's lives than before – it has been a source of both missiles
and milk. Governments have come and gone since 1945, but the state has
continued to evolve. Such evolution has continued as a response to changing circumstances, such as the collapse of empire, shifting social
hierarchies and almost revolutionary changes in cultural norms. While
successfully evolving over this period, its imprint has remained re-
markably consistent and an identifiable 'British state' has persisted
throughout. Not only does it appear to have persisted in spite of changing
administrations, but it has sometimes owed its continuing existence to
such changes.

The following chapters argue that the British state's ability to represent
itself as the crucial factor in the maintenance of some perceived idea of
social cohesion has contributed to its continuing existence. *Consensus or
Coercion?* undertakes an examination of post-war Britain with particular
reference to questions of: race and immigration, political activism, 'affluence' and popular culture, local government and planned social change,
voluntary organizations, gender and the welfare state. It aspires to add to
the renewed interest in the question of the state, partly stirred by New Labour's attention to devolution and the constitution, and evident in
scholarly studies like Whiting and Green's *The Boundaries of the State in
Modern Britain*.[12] It also adds to the burgeoning literature that discusses
post-war Britain by refracting its history through a particular lens.
Collections of essays such as Conekin, Mort and Waters' *Moments of
Modernity*, Beach and Weight's *The Right to Belong*, Kandiah and Jones'
The Myth of Consensus?, Tiratsoo's *From Blitz to Blair* and Catterall and
Obelkevich's *Understanding Post-war British Society* have encouraged
new approaches and provoked new debates.[13] This collection attempts to
address some of the questions raised and to consider some of the
omissions.

In Chapter 1, Glyn Powell assesses the role of the Communist Party of
Great Britain (CPGB) in relation to social cohesion. Created as a revolutionary party, by the post-war period it saw itself in opposition to the
two-party consensus which dominated a 'quasi-corporatist' British
economy. However, this opposition remained, both industrially and politically, comfortably within the framework of British political culture and,
as such, never constituted a threat to the British state. Its continued use of
Marxist discourse and revolutionary language, moreover, actually had the
effect of co-opting much of the militant aspiration existing throughout
British trade unionism and the wider society. In this way, Powell argues,

the CPGB can be seen to have made a contribution to social cohesion in the post-war period.

Lawrence Black, in Chapter 2, examines popular culture and particularly the role of television as a culturally cohesive force in the 'affluent society'. He considers how the political left depicted 'the people' and the popularity of television, arguing that the left's perception of low moral and cultural standards attributed blame not only to the shortcomings of television providers, but also to those of the audiences. The Labour Party's articulation of social change, and the moral and prescriptive language with which it addressed televiewers and popular affluence more generally, illustrates a tension between it and the people. Labour's *dirigisme*, it is further argued, was increasingly at odds with the popular attitudes and culture emerging as post-war social and cultural change began to undermine the traditional authority of the state.

In Chapter 3, Mark Minion considers the attitudes of different groups within the Labour Party towards issues of European integration during the first Attlee government (1945–50) and in particular the search for a new political and economic locale within Europe, by a sizeable minority of party members around the pamphlet *Keep Left* and the MP R. W. G. Mackay. Minion suggests that Labour's debates point towards an ideological vitality, further indicated by the three paradigms of European unity supported by various groups within the party – functional, federal and fundamental. Such deliberations suggest, in turn, a contested and evolving conception of the nation and a common national identity. Ultimately, the party's European conflicts were subsumed within the wider concerns of the Cold War. However, many of these issues retain contemporary relevance.

In Chapter 4, Michael Dawswell focuses on the racialized reconstruction of Britishness after the Second World War. He argues that immigration and race relations legislation is one example of how the state uses it power in a coercive way, by alienating certain groups from its national community, while promoting and maintaining the myth of a socially cohesive society.

Julia Drake's 'From Colour Blind to Colour Bar' (Chapter 5) considers the impact upon local communities of the arrival of Black Caribbean migrants. This chapter examines the role of the state and local inhabitants as well as the black Caribbean population in the process of residential separation. It goes on to consider the relationship between residential and social separation through factors such as home and organizational developments.

In Chapter 6, Zoë Doye evaluates the flow of finance in and out of three London boroughs and the London County Council. Concentrating on the housing sector, she discusses the impact on various groups and communities affected by local authority decisions.

Andrew Homer, in Chapter 7, questions the actions and assumptions of the new town planners, particularly their use of planning concepts intended to develop socially cohesive communities. He discusses the social population's reaction to, and ultimate rejection of, the attempt to encourage a more socially cohesive and classless society.

The family unit is often regarded as an integral element in the maintenance of social cohesion, and in Chapter 8, Louise Tracey explores education for parenthood, maternity and child welfare. She discusses constructions of the household and the family through the maternity and child welfare services, in which education for parentcraft played a significant role. Tracey questions the extent to which this represented a new family form, examining the interaction of gender and class.

John Jenkins, in Chapter 9, explores the changing intellectual framework of civil society represented by the voluntary organizations in the 1940s and 1950s. His case study of the thinking of George Haynes, General Secretary of the National Council of Social Service, reveals a blurring of the distinction between the state and the voluntary sector during the post-war years.

1

Controlling the Fire: British Communism and the Post-war Consensus

Glyn Powell

'When you come down to it, the Communists are no different from the bourgeoisie.'
　'What makes you say that?'
　'They're not revolutionaries. They're for order, work, the family, reason.' [1]

The enemies of Communism accuse the Communist Party of aiming to introduce Soviet Power in Britain and abolish Parliament. This is a slanderous misrepresentation of our policy.[2]

The Communist Party is largely composed of people who aren't really political at all, but who have a powerful sense of service.[3]

This chapter looks at the Communist Party of Great Britain (CPGB) and its objective role in the maintenance of social cohesion in Britain after the Second World War. The British Communist Party numbered around 35,000 in the early 1950s and, despite the fact that it returned two MPs at the 1945 general election, it was never a serious threat to the British state or to the two main legislative parties.[4] The chapter argues that, furthermore, by co-opting and neutralizing the most militant and revolutionary-minded individuals in trade unions and communities, the CPGB contributed, albeit unwittingly, to the preservation of social cohesion within post-war British society. The Party co-opted these individuals through a combination of revolutionary Marxist rhetoric and association with what it identified as a model socialist society, the Soviet Union. It neutralized their revolutionary aspirations through a concentration on electoral practice and non-political trade union activity but, most crucially, through an all-absorbing identification with the ideological sophistry that had underpinned and justified the brutal project of enforced industrialization associated with Stalinism. In contrast to Britain, many of the nations that were to constitute western Europe had powerful Communist Parties. This was particularly true in France and Italy. In France, the PCF commanded the majority of seats in the constituent assembly elected in 1945.[5] In Italy, the PCI had 1,760,000 members and, despite the opposition of both the Vatican and Washington, won 19 per cent of the vote for the constituent assembly in 1948.[6] However, in a post-war situation dominated by the diplomatic and nationalist imperatives of Moscow, Yalta and Potsdam, rather than those of international Communism, neither party made an attempt to take power. The priority for both Thorez in France and Togliatti in Italy was to work with de Gaulle and di Gasperi respectively, rather than to mobilize their parties, either for revolutionary or for constitutionally sanctioned power. The experience of these Communist Parties suggests that, even had the CPGB been sufficiently large, Soviet foreign policy would have taken precedence over residual and now nominal considerations about spreading international revolution.

The Party's electoral programme, *The British Road to Socialism*, was not just the culmination of a twenty-year drift away from revolutionary theory and practice, but had been suggested by Stalin and was modelled upon the so-called 'People's Democracies' of eastern Europe.[7] The Party's trade union practice was a combination of two strategies: first, activity and leadership at shop-floor level, often successful within the non-political areas of wages and conditions, and having the potential at least, in 1957 and 1969–70, for example, to translate into political leadership;[8] and secondly, a leadership strategy that sought to place Communists into official positions within the unions in the belief that such office-holding equated to the socialist leadership of the working class.

The Party's association with Stalinism and the Soviet Union was twofold. It was both an association with the nation state of the USSR in opposition to the 'hostile capitalist forces in the world' and also, more damagingly, an association with what Edward Thompson described as 'the Monolith' which 'has droned on in a dogmatic monotone'.[9] Whether as the Comintern (Third International), Cominform or its organ *For a Lasting Peace for a People's Democracy*, this was an association with Moscow as the ideological Jerusalem of world Communism. Both the Party and the various factions that emerged from splits in the 1960s never lost this habit of adhesion, which presented members and potential members with the Soviet Union, China, Yugoslavia, Cuba or Albania as models of 'actually existing socialism'. The ideological absorption of Stalinism led the CPGB towards replicating the distorted interpretation of Marxism which, in the USSR, had justified the ruling regime's excesses in the name of a propagandized invention called Marxist-Leninism.[10]

The British state's response to Communism

Peter Wright recalled that, in 1955, MI5 initiated 'Operation Party Piece', when agents invaded the Mayfair flat 'of a wealthy [Communist] Party member' and recorded 55,000 files over the course of a weekend.[11] This typically absurd operation to obtain already available information, however, while Wright claimed it as 'proof of MI5's post-war mastery' over its rivals, reflected a misconception within the detached minds of the secret services, about the nature of the relationship between the CPGB and the Soviet Union.[12] Within the atmosphere of paranoia that the Truman Doctrine and Andrei Zhdanov's 'two camps' formulation had engendered in 1947, the Attlee government began an anti-Communist offensive, both at home and abroad.[13] Domestically, this expressed itself in a purge of the civil service in 1948, which, between 1948 and 1955, resulted in 135 civil servants being investigated.[14] Apart from this, the most energetic campaign against Communism was that which Gaitskellite politician Woodrow Wyatt and Communist renunciant Les Cannon launched against the Communist leadership of the Electrical Trades Union (ETU) between 1955 and 1961.

Do these efforts by, and on behalf of, the British state indicate that the Communist Party of Great Britain constituted a threat? As with the perplexing capers of Peter Wright and his chums, the civil service purge was predicated upon false assumptions about the conspiratorial nature of the relationship between British Communism and Moscow. Within the context of the Cold War, the British state appears to have perceived the threat from British Communism in terms of a Soviet 'fifth column' rather than as a party with the potential to confront British capitalism by inspiring and organizing the self-activity of workers. Even the campaign against Communist ETU leaders was based upon similarly hypersensitive assumptions about the role of the CPGB within the bureaucratic leadership of British trade unionism. With characteristic hyperbole, Woodrow Wyatt accused the Communist ETU leadership of 'methods of seizing and maintaining power . . . that have worked so well in Czechoslovakia and other eastern European countries'.[15] He continued with the warning that if Communists were in charge in enough unions, then 'the trade union vote at Labour Party conferences could be controlled by the Communist Party to decide Labour Party policy'.[16]

Communist trade union leadership, however, did not necessarily equate to that union's block vote being used for socialist or progressive policies or even to elect left-wing figures. The National Union of Mineworkers (NUM), for example, despite being led by Communists Arthur Horner (General Secretary), Abe Moffat (Scottish President) and Will Paynter (Welsh President), remained one of Hugh Gaitskell's key supporters in the fight with Nye Bevan for both Treasurer and later leadership of the Labour Party.[17] Bevan, himself an ex-coalminer, complained bitterly to Sam Watson, the Durham miners' leader, 'how can you support a public schoolboy from Winchester against a man born in the back streets of Tredegar?'[18] Similarly, at the 1960 Labour Party Conference, when Will Paynter had become President of the NUM, it fell to Labour left-winger Frank Cousins of the TGWU to lead the battle against Gaitskell on unilateral nuclear disarmament. In May, the miners' union had voted against supporting unilateralism by 470,000 votes to 201,000.[19] This mandated the NUM's Communist leadership to vote against Cousins' unilateralism and meant that Communists at the conference voted with, rather than against, the Labour leadership. Despite the overwhelmingly Communist leadership in the ETU throughout the 1950s, it was 1960 before such influence 'swung the Electrical Trades Union's 140,000 votes against the official policy'.[20] These examples may, of course, indicate the strength of rank-and-file democracy in these unions in opposition to their bureaucracies, but nevertheless clearly demonstrate that there was no correlation between Communist trade union leaders and opposition to the established Labour leadership.

From revolutionary to oppositionist party

The CPGB formed, at Lenin's suggestion, as a direct result of the Bolshevik Revolution. Lenin wrote in 1920, 'In my opinion, the British Communists should unite their four . . . parties and groups into a single Communist Party.'[21] Crucially, the Party formed itself on the basis of adherence to the Comintern, whose second congress was taking place at the same time. At its inauguration, the Party made two other important decisions. One, by 100 votes to 85, was to attempt affiliation with the Labour Party 'as a revolutionary tactic'.[22] Secondly, the new party agreed to participate in parliamentary activity, on the advice of Lenin, who suggested that the 'political experience of the masses' of a Labour government would make them 'disappointed in their leaders and . . . begin to support communism', while making it clear that the task of 'our "soviet" politicians' should be 'disrupting parliament from *within* . . . preparing the ground . . . for the success of the soviets' forthcoming task of dispersing parliament'.[23]

Despite CPGB General Secretary Harry Pollitt's poignant remark, while in Moscow, following Khrushchev's denunciation of Stalin at the 20th Congress of the CPSU in 1956, that 'all our problems always came from here', the Party persisted in its support for, and association with, the Soviet regime.[24] This was an adherence born from the Party's initial identification with the Comintern and it continued throughout the CPGB's existence, at least until 1968. By 1929 and the victory of Stalin's faction in the Politburo and Central Committee of the CPSU, the Soviet regime had already begun to jettison all traces of socialism. While Stalinism was revolutionary in the narrow sense that it enforced rapid industrialization on an overwhelmingly peasant society, it not only achieved this on the basis of coercion and terror, but along the way dispensed with the inconvenient social gains of the revolutionary period.[25] Although the idea that Stalin's regime constituted a socialist or even a workers' state is now self-evidently absurd, during the 1950s both eastern and western propaganda reinforced the idea to such an extent that the Soviet Union remained perceived as such by nearly everyone on the political left.[26]

In the polarized conditions of the Cold War, it is perhaps not surprising that many socialists supported the state of the Soviet Union in opposition to what it characterized as western imperialism and western capitalism. The CPGB, however, did not just support the Soviet Union as the perceived opponent of 'world capitalism', it allowed itself to be dominated by its ideology and practice, right up until Stalin's death in 1953 and beyond. Notwithstanding Harry Pollitt's acknowledgement that the association had been one fraught with problems, later in 1956 he stressed that 'The Soviet Union is and remains the greatest Socialist power in the world . . . [where] . . . the exploitation of man by man has been abolished.'[27]

The biggest exodus ever, in percentage terms, in the Party's history has been laid at the double doors of Nikita Khrushchev's denunciation of Stalin in February 1956 and his subsequent invasion of Hungary later that year. There had, however, been a steady decline in Party membership since the war from a claimed figure of 43,000 in 1948 to 33,236 for 'those registered at or about March' 1956; a fall of 23 per cent.[28] Following the twin blows of 1956, another 7,000 or so left, reducing membership to 26,742 by February 1957. CPGB historiography has emphasized the dramatic impact of 1956. This has had the effect of minimizing the reality of the Party's previous decline, as writers like George Matthews, for example, have characteristically described 1956 as a 'Watershed Year'.[29]

Most writers and commentators have also characterized the events of 1956 as being the cause of the subsequent protracted decline of Communism. Historically, however, it is more useful to view the events of that year as an effect of Stalinism's irreconcilable contradictions, culminating in a particularly acute crisis within the Party's long-term decline. Analyses that view 1956 as a political bombshell reflect the response of members such as Eric Hobsbawm, for whom Khrushchev's revelations had come 'absolutely out of the blue'.[30] This may, in turn, reflect the fact that much of this historiography has emanated from within the CPGB and, on the whole, represents a biographical perspective that has tended to concentrate upon how Party members reacted to events, rather than focusing upon longer-term causes.

In a broader periodization, Willie Thompson in *The Good Old Cause* applied the epithet 'Watershed' to the period between 1951 and 1957.[31] This spanned the life of the first edition of *The British Road to Socialism*, which was superseded by a less explicitly Stalinist programme written in 1957 and published in 1958.[32] The period 1951 to 1957, beginning with the loss of the two Communist MPs in 1950, ending with the Special Congress and a temporary revival of the Party's fortunes during the increased strike activity in 1957, marks an important period of crisis. However, while Thompson's extended perspective has merit, it probably does not go far enough in identifying the long-term continuities within CPGB history that contributed towards its decline.

The major discontinuity within this history was the Second World War rather than 1956. The war, at least after 1941, represented an unprecedented and unique set of circumstances, where arguments about Marxism and revolution became secondary to all-out support for the Soviet Union and anti-Nazism. Morris Schaer recalled that, during this period, empathy for the Soviet Union among many British people was such that they used to say 'Joe Stalin for King'.[33] For the only time in its existence, the Party cut with, rather than against, the grain of public political sentiment. This had an enormous impact upon the Party's popularity and credibility: in this period, for example, many Communist trade union leaders acceded to their various offices. Perhaps it was the experience of the war years and the sweet taste of relative popularity that encouraged the Party to mitigate its revolutionary position with an appeal to the more comfortable and familiar concepts of parliamentary representation and reform.

Many writers, including Willie Thompson, have echoed Pollitt in diagnosing the relationship with the Soviet Union as the reason for the Party's decline. Noreen Branson, for example, wrote that 'the main mistakes which the party made arose from its attitude to the Soviet Union'.[34] Similarly, Thompson wrote that 'the binding element which tied together all the political and organisational strands was less the Party's vision of a socialist Britain . . . than its relation to the existing homelands of socialism and most importantly the USSR . . . which ultimately determined its policies, its practice and its standing among the British public'.[35] While undoubtedly true, this emphasis on the external pressures of the Soviet Union has minimized the British Party's own contribution to its internal contradictions between Marxist discourse and Stalinist ideology, Bolshevik structure and reformist practice.

Stalinism, in its ideological guise of Marxist-Leninism and with its highly bureaucratic organizational structure, exerted a powerful, if sometimes only vaguely perceived, influence over British Communism. Stalinism, as the foundation upon which British Communism had developed since 1929, not only determined its ideology, discourse and practice, but had a determining effect upon the political consciousness of its members. This ideological determining, however, is not the same as saying that the Soviet Union was an ever-present feature of members' lives. Members defended, excused or justified its practices as and when they needed to, but their day-to-day activities as Communists were dominated by national and local circumstances. Stalinism determined the particular species of British Communist political consciousness. The true nature of this consciousness, however, can only be understood when such a species is seen in relation to its own political environment.

Many members remained only dimly aware of events within the Soviet Union itself. As Morris Schaer remarked about the initial reports of Khrushchev's secret speech in 1956, 'we were worried about this, the ordinary Party member didn't like what he was hearing, but he was so involved in his own struggles, that it didn't have much effect on them'.[36] Dennis Ogden agreed, saying that while it was not the case 'that all Communists supported the Soviet Union unconditionally and unreservedly . . . many spoke with two voices . . . one voice for the public . . . but in private there were all kinds of doubts'.[37] Ruth Fisher had been a telephonist at the *Daily Worker* until she left the Party after Hungary. She wrote of the period before Khrushchev's secret speech, saying 'prior to that all stories people tried to tell about what might be happening in the Soviet Union were discounted as part of cold-war propaganda'.[38] She went on to speculate about how if members like *Daily Worker* editor J. R. Campbell 'had what might be called "hostages to fortune" it's more understandable that they might put the personal safety of friends and family before coming clean about what they knew'.[39] Ruth Fisher was referring to Campbell's stepson William, who had become a Soviet citizen in 1939 and performed around Soviet theatres as Villi the Clown. In the years preceding Stalin's death, William was banned from performing because of his British origins.[40] Ruth Fisher believed that Campbell's silence about Soviet anti-Semitism, for example, may, not unnaturally, have been connected to these circumstances. Lastly, Bob Leeson, who joined the Party in 1949, wrote that 'my concerns were only indirectly with the Soviet Union and Eastern Europe. What troubled me was the departure of the Labour Government from the policies of 1945 as I understood them. My focus, essentially, was this country.'[41]

Association, firstly with the Bolsheviks and then with what, to many, appeared a socialist superpower, gave the British Party a credibility without which it would have been nothing more than a Marxist-Leninist sect. It encouraged, within the Party, an over-inflated perception of its own institutional importance, both within British society and in the world. Max Morris recalled that the Party 'became involved in Chinese affairs and all that, and I often used to think the Party a bit absurd, what the hell could we do about it? But you'd talk and talk about it . . . which made you feel important. Your effect on Britain at this time was minimal.'[42] This perception went along with what Bert Ramelson, Yorkshire District Organiser, described as the twin problems of 'sectarianism' on the one hand and 'liquidation . . . tending towards minimising the role of the Party' on the other.[43]

Sectarianism, a danger for any small organization wishing to preserve its political integrity, was exacerbated by an arrogance born of the Party's association with important Communist Parties abroad. The same arrogance, however, encouraged many members to underestimate the extent to which the imperatives of operating within the institutional processes of trade unionism and electoralism eroded that very Marxist integrity. The Party was so weak, both politically and theoretically, that in general and local elections and within the stiflingly bureaucratic world of trade union leadership, its members sometimes found it easier to ignore political arguments about socialism and concentrate upon local issues or wages and conditions. Wolf Wayne said, for example, that the pressure on shop-stewards when union issues would arise on a daily basis was such that 'you had no time and you had no thought for the higher ideas of Marx, Engels and Lenin . . . I think basically the Party gave up on that stuff . . . we just made a nod in that direction, but that's about it'. This, he continued, 'was common to the Party right the way through from the top to the bottom'.[44] An ex-ETU Communist, Jim Layzell, recalled that there were 'about 20 members of the Communist Party' in his union branch, but they were 'not all political'.[45] Layzell added, 'This was the peculiar thing about the CP . . . a lot of people in it are not political . . . they might manoeuvre a bit on different policies.'[46] Wolf Wayne also emphasized that for 'industrial comrades . . . it was union affairs, it was factory affairs they argued about'.[47]

This was also a result of what was generally acknowledged as the 'undisputed . . . low level of our theoretical understanding'.[48] Stalin, in whom Trotsky observed a 'contemptuous attitude towards ideas', described himself and his cohort in the CPSU as 'we Bolshevik practical workers' as opposed to those 'litterateurs' who now constituted a dying breed.[49] This was in opposition to Lenin, who had stressed that 'without revolutionary theory there can be no revolutionary movement' and emphasized secure theoretical analysis as opposed to 'an infatuation for the narrowest forms of practical activity'.[50] Harry Pollitt admitted in 1956 that 'We are too prone to concern ourselves with immediate problems and insufficiently with questions of principle' and talked of 'the reluctance to consider new ideas which did not seem to fit into practical day to day work'.[51] Ralph Russell said of Pollitt that he 'felt for a long time that he was anti-intellectual and anti-theory for that matter'.[52] Similarly, Brian Pearce said, 'We were, looking back on it, most of us, a bit superficial and . . . prepared not to pursue a question very deeply, to accept rather easy answers to difficult questions.'[53] Morris Schaer said of himself, 'I was never strong on theory . . . these people that call themselves Marxists, I can't believe them', and he continued, 'Stalin . . . if you read any of his stuff, it made sense.'[54] Alison MacLeod summed up how she perceived the Party's attitude to theory, saying, 'oh they'd forgotten all about Marx – who's he?'[55]

Raphael Samuel wrote that 'the CPGB may never have been in any meaningful sense a revolutionary party'.[56] Similarly, Mike Power, a 'member for 32 years', said, 'we weren't really a revolutionary party at all . . . we had the rhetoric . . . we were part of the anti-Tory movement'.[57] Certainly, by the 1950s, the Communist Party was no longer revolutionary. It had become an oppositionist party. This was important, especially within the framework of this book, which seeks to understand the forces that militated towards and against the British state being able to contain dissent during the 1950s within a consensual framework.

Communist leadership and the threat from below

For Communist trade union leaders, of whom Wolf Wayne suggested 'there was no question of enlightening the people about the aims of socialism', the imperative was remaining in office.[58] Jim Layzell went so far as to suggest of the ETU leaders that 'they were so eager for power . . . they just didn't want to give it up'.[59]

Just as Communist trade union leadership did not equate to left-wing or progressive policies, neither did Communist leadership necessarily mean any sort of threat in terms of shop-floor militant activity. According to Michael Jackson, 'in the post-Second World War years up to 95 per cent of all strikes . . . were the result of unofficial stoppages'.[60] This was on the increase throughout the 1950s and much of it was led by Communist shop stewards. In terms of the Communist leadership of these unions, however, it is doubtful that the Party's leadership strategy made any impression at all upon the façade of social cohesion that characterized 1950s Britain.

The ETU, for example, had always been considered a 'left-wing' union. In the post-war period, right up until 1961, after which Communists were banned from holding office, the union was dominated, at leadership, Executive Council and Full-time Officer level, by Communists and Communist Party sympathizers. Despite this, 'electrical engineering' accounted for just 2.6 per cent of all strike activity between 1953 and 1959.[61] The ETU was involved in 16 strikes over this period with the loss of 138 days. Shipbuilding, by contrast, lost 594 days in a series of 77 strikes over the period.[62] Notwithstanding *The Economist*'s protestations about 'some of the guerrilla strikes called by the Communist Electrical Trade Union', the proportion of strikes involving electrical workers was unremarkable.[63] Morris Schaer even recalled that 'as an active shop-steward there were some occasions when I had a struggle to discourage strike action'.[64] In 1956, the union's Communist General Secretary, Frank Haxell, urged Mr Penwill, the employers' negotiator in the National Federated Electrical Association, to accept that 'individual companies or area JICs [Joint Industrial Councils] could pay site or company bonuses', a drift away from the unifying principle of nationally negotiated wages.[65] At the 'ballot rigging' trial of the ETU's Communist leadership in 1961, under cross-examination from George Gardiner, Frank Foulkes, the union's Communist President, accused Dick Reno, saying that 'our members have lost a lot of money through Mr Reno's activities, and one of them is that he supports what we now popularly call "wild-cat strikes"'.[66] Reno was one of an emerging group of Trotskyists in this union who, according to John Lloyd, 'gleefully chased after the executive for lack of *real* militance in wage bargaining'.[67] ETU Trotskyists also exposed Frank Foulkes, who had condemned the siting of US rocket bases in Britain in line with CPGB policy, but had refused to call for strike action by electricians to stop them being built.

The Communist Party's leadership strategy was not a marginal part of its trade union activity. The gaining of official positions within the bureaucracies of leading trade unions was pivotal to its overall strategy. As Wolf Wayne recalled when discussing Communist Party fractions within unions, 'nearly every industry had its own advisory committee', but they 'had nothing to do with politics . . . they were to do with internal questions of the union . . . about standing for elections within the trade union movement'.[68] While there was a perceived, if unfulfilled, threat from Communist leaders in terms of the Labour Party block vote, as the experience of the ETU suggests, they never constituted a challenge to the hegemony of existing institutions such as the TUC or the Labour Party. Neither, more crucially, did the existence of Communist leaderships mean that such unions necessarily comprised any sort of threat to the productivity and profitability of British industry. Communist-led unions rarely seem to have impacted upon the cosy relationship between industry, state and the TUC, which constituted the prevailing 'quasi-corporatism' of the post-war period.[69]

The CPGB and elections

Another area to which the CPGB devoted huge amounts of its members' time and energy was general and local elections. The Party occasionally achieved success in local elections, but it is not clear whether this was because of the high regard in which individuals such as Annie Powell in East Rhondda were held, or because the electorate supported Communism. Similarly, in 1945, it is not clear whether or not Willie Gallacher and Phil Piratin, elected in West Fife and Stepney, respectively, owed their success more to their individual reputations than to the fact they were Communists. As the general election results in Table 1 indicate, their successors were certainly less successful, but this may be due to the exceptional year of 1945 and the subsequent ebb, throughout the 1950s, of the 'left-wing' vote generally. For the Communist Party, 1945 represented possibilities in terms of gaining power electorally. The belief in such possibilities accelerated a drift away from the Party's revolutionary genesis towards a theory and practice that was dominated by its success and failure at local and national elections.

With the publication of *The British Road to Socialism* in 1951, the CPGB replaced the idea of 'Parliamentary action as means of revolutionary propaganda and agitation' with a model that explicitly repudiated 'Soviet Power' in favour of 'People's Democracy . . . as in the People's Democracies of Eastern Europe'.[71] These 'Democracies' had established themselves after 1948, once Stalinist Communist Parties were able to dominate the previous post-war coalitions. The CPGB declared that 'Britain will reach Socialism by her own road.'[72] Recent events, however, had suggested Moscow's growing intolerance of such ideas. Yugoslavia was ejected from Cominform for just such an idea. Confusingly, James

Table 1 Support for Communist Party candidates in three constituencies between 1945 and 1955[70]

	West Fife			Stepney			Hornsey	
	Vote	%		Vote	%		Vote	%
1945	W. Gallacher 17,636 won seat	42.1	P. Piratin	5,075 won	47.6	G. J. Jones	10,058 third	21.5
1950	W. Gallacher 9,301 third	21.6	P. Piratin	5,991 third	12.5	G. J. Jones	1,191* fourth	1.9
1951	W. Lauchlan 4,728* third	10.5	E. F. Bramley	3,436* third	7.3	No Communist candidate		
1955	W. Lauchlan 5,839 third	12.6	S. Kaye	2,888* third	7.6	G. J. Jones	1,442 third	2.6

*Indicates lost deposit.

Note: Phil Piratin's vote of 5,075 in 1945 was on a total vote for the constituency of 10,658. In 1950, after reconstruction, demobilization and boundary changes, the total vote had increased to 47,809. As the percentages indicate, this puts the slight increase from 1945 into perspective.

Klugmann, in a book justifying the demonizing of Yugoslavia, with the bewildering title *From Trotsky to Tito*, accused Tito of 'putting forward a theory of a smooth and peaceful transition to socialism'.[73] No one in the British Party appeared to notice that the Party's own programme contained the same message. Similarly, leaders such as Rudolf Slansky in Czechoslovakia and Wladyslaw Gomulka in Poland were either executed or imprisoned as 'bourgeois national leaders', their trials 'to discredit the concept of a national path to socialism'.[74]

The British programme emerged from an analysis that had viewed the 1945 election as proof that 'the people of Britain were determined that there should be a change'.[75] In 1950, on the basis of a belief 'that Tory governments were a thing of the past', the CPGB stood 100 candidates.[76] It was a disaster. The Party, with a membership of 38,853, managed to capture fewer than 92,000 votes.[77] At this election, it also lost its only two members of Parliament: Willie Gallacher and Phil Piratin. In 1951, the CPGB reined in its ambition, standing just ten candidates; and in 1955, it stood seventeen. The Party was still wholly committed to the parliamentary road, however, as the following notes towards a report from a CPGB Electoral Commission (EC) suggest. The notes related to the 'Executive Council Resolution on Electoral Activity', discussed by the EC meeting in September 1953, and were probably Harry Pollitt's.

> EC dissatisfied slow growth and stagnation Party But no aspect so unsatisfactory as Electoral. Party existed 33 years – advanced many respects . . . But no voice today in H of C. – smaller no. of Councillors. British Road quotes. If these mean anything – that we must be in Parliament. Discussed many time next step re Programme. Shd have led to

big advance our electoral work . . . our work last Local Elns at lowest possible ebb . . . Impossible to think of any adv. into Parliament without big development local elections activity. If can't win Council seats – never win Parliamentary.[78]

The notes went on to state the overwhelming importance of elections for the Party saying, 'Don't win because don't regard Elns, as vital as TU' and concluded with: 'In the end the vote that counts . . . cannot allow to go on.'[79] As the notes imply, the Party's results in local elections were similarly disappointing. As the Party's Political Committee reported in October 1953, 'in the county of London 78 Communist candidates stood in 22 wards, receiving a total vote of 14,751, an average of 189 per candidate'.[80]

The crucial strategic difference between the early 1920s and the 1950s was that in 1920 the objective for parliamentary activity was to 'reduce it to absurdity'.[81] Standing for Parliament, as the Party's inaugural message to the Comintern stated, was to be 'action as means of revolutionary propaganda and agitation'.[82] By 1955, however, the Party saw 'Parliament . . . the elected representation of the people' as the means 'to make socialism possible'.[83] Parliamentary action for the remainder of the CPGB's existence had changed from a revolutionary tactic to the means by which the Party would lead the British people to socialism. The correctness or otherwise of this strategy is not at issue here. It was, however, in opposition to Marxism's central idea that 'the emancipation of the working classes must be conquered by the working classes themselves'.[84]

For members, the CPGB's electoralism evolved into something like an article of faith. As one of Doris Lessing's Communist characters said, 'we have to fight the election as if we were convinced we were going to win it (But we know we aren't going to win it)'.[85] Referring to a later period, Phil Cohen remembered his own childhood, when his father stood for local elections in London in 1968. Cohen wrote, 'Dad got very nervous' near to the election as he hoped to increase his vote 'from the 200 odd . . . anyone . . . got when they stood for the CP. On the night of the count we . . . were woken . . . and they were all shouting something about 303 . . . the next day I realised the Labour candidate won with over 5000.'[86] Max Morris recalled that he had 'fought two elections as a Communist candidate. What a bloody waste of time. Oh God!'[87] By the mid-1950s, with a Conservative government comfortably ensconced and with Hugh Gaitskell's victory over Aneurin Bevan in the Labour Party signalling the continuation of a virtual biparty consensus over what Leo Panitch called 'a contemporary expression of corporatism', the realistic prospects for the CPGB's electoral strategy meant that it constituted nothing less than the politics of despair.[88] In truth, *The British Road to Socialism* was, as Morris Schaer said, 'our get out in a way', an argument more easily accepted at work and on the doorstep than the one about revolution.[89]

The conservative nature of British Communism

In 1938, two years before his death, Trotsky attempted to build an organization of revolutionary artists from his home in Mexico. These included people such as Diego Rivera, Frida Kahlo and the French modernist poet André Breton.[90] This was a conscious attempt 'to counterbalance the "cultural" activities of the Stalinists', to allow, in the words of the resulting manifesto, 'mankind to raise itself to those heights which only geniuses have achieved in the past'.[91] In contrast, Polish writer Czeslaw Milosz wrote of writers and painters who worked 'in accordance with "socialist realism" [that] they are automatically and inescapably enrolled among the followers of Stalin'.[92] Milosz later recalled a conversation with a young Polish poet who 'admitted to me "My own stream of thought has so many tributaries . . . I get halfway through a phrase and already I submit it to Marxist criticism. I imagine what X or Y will say about it, and I change the ending".'[93]

The attitude to culture implied within these examples reflects a conservatism within Stalinist Communism. This conservatism left the CPGB unable to confront the rapid cultural changes of the 1960s and, more crucially, unable to organize meaningfully around the political activities with which such changes have become associated. Michael Rosen characterized a party failing to come to terms with what, at the time, appeared as profound cultural changes, as he described one of his parents' friends 'who led a constant battle with her kids and people in the Woodcraft Folk against rock music, dope, sex, drugs and rock and roll; basically – she regarded this with an absolute puritan fervour – all this was a betrayal of the working class'.[94]

As the Party moved into the 1960s, it was forced to confront not only these shifting cultural patterns, but also new and avowedly revolutionary political formations. Daniel and Gabriel Cohn-Bendit described French Communism's response to 1968, writing: 'Now, though the French Communist Party generally speaks with two voices, combining Leninist ideological phrases with electoral and reformist practices, during May and June, its practice and language became as one.'[95] They continued, saying that 'try as they might, the Communist students were unable to isolate the Leftists' and, as a result, 'they themselves became completely isolated in the universities'.[96] The process that the Cohn-Bendits described, summed up the degree to which the Communist Party had lost touch by this stage, but also how its traditional sectarianism and arrogance about its hegemonic position continued to dictate its strategy. As Ralph Russell said of student activity at the School of Oriental and African Studies, 'generally the attitude of the Communists was "you buggers aren't under our leadership, therefore it's not a revolutionary movement"'.[97]

The Party's conservatism had been expressed in a number of different ways during the 1950s. Anne Palmer, for example, writing in 1953, dismissed as 'the very height of absurdity . . . the various "new", "progressive" methods for the teaching of reading'.[98] Communist teachers at this time also ran a campaign against children's comics, expressing 'great concern at the decline in moral values associated with the spread of children's reading matter . . . we ask all public bodies to stigmatise such publications'.[99]

The CPGB had begun as an attempt to institute socialism within Britain through the 'adoption of [the] Soviet system'.[100] It began as an explicitly revolutionary organization, which challenged both the established parliamentary system and the British state. By the 1950s, however, the Party preferred a line and practice which, while calling for change, did not call for the overthrow of any of British society's existing governing institutions. Despite this, it retained a Marxist discourse that continued to appeal to those who aspired to revolutionary change rather than the reforms with which the Labour Party in Parliament had become identified. The unconscious co-option of such revolutionary aspirations was compounded by a more conscious process whereby such aspirations were exposed to the debilitating counter-ideology of Stalinism and an identification with one of the world's most oppressive regimes.

Apologists for British Communism have attempted to break the British Party down into separate perspectives and to judge each of these on its merits, in order to avoid confronting the political realities that the Party represented. Much Communist Party history, for example, has stressed the socialist credentials of individual members and has focused, in Doris Lessing's words, on these people's 'powerful sense of service'.[101] Such service within communities is undeniable. Similarly, 'the assiduity' of Communists within trade unions is a section of Communist activity which meant that many 'honest Labour men . . . respect individual Communists' even while they continued to 'mistrust the CP as an organisation'.[102] The intellectual contribution of people like E. P. Thompson, Eric Hobsbawm and A. L. Morton, for example, was also a significant factor within British life.

Breaking down and judging the actions of these various groups and individuals, however, has obscured more about the political reality of the Communist Party of Great Britain than it has revealed. There is no doubt that the work of many such members represented a significant contribution to what might broadly be termed progressive life within Britain. By themselves, however, such contributions could only be said to have advanced the cause of socialism in Britain in a piecemeal way. In order for them to have had a significant impact in this regard, such activities needed to be co-ordinated into a political whole, within an organization that provided those moved or inspired by such contributions with a vision and a strategy for a new kind of society. It was here that the Party's limitations rendered it a negative, rather than a positive force for change. As the organized expression of British socialist aspirations, the Communist Party constituted a great deal less than the sum of its parts.

2

'Sheep May Safely Gaze': Socialists, Television and the People in Britain, 1949–64

Lawrence Black

Socialists were wary of a social cohesion built around the values of the 'affluent society'. They disapproved of much of what they saw in social change in 1950s Britain. Yet this had as much to do with the ways in which socialism imagined these changes (the 'socialist gaze') as with anything intrinsically anti-socialist in the consumerism, suburbanization, televisions and washing machines that constituted 'affluence'. In short, such social changes were invested with an overwhelmingly negative meaning by socialists who, this chapter contends, can be seen to a large extent to have brought upon themselves their alienation from popular affluence.[1]

This 'gaze' was fashioned by the political culture of socialism: the informal reflexes, traditions and language that disclose much about both how the left saw social change, the people and 'culture', and why it saw them as it did – and thus also about the relationship between party and people. This chapter is therefore an exercise in both the history of cultural politics (the politics of television) and a more cultural approach to the history of politics.

It was primarily the values of the 'affluent society' that chafed with the ethical instincts of socialism. The latter juxtaposed cultural quality and commercial interests, and firmly rejected notions of material salvation. In tones of R. H. Tawney and William Morris, Labour's widely distributed 1958 policy primer, *The Future Labour Offers You*, closed with an exposition of what it saw as 'the full life': 'True happiness does not come from material prosperity (but poverty causes an immense amount of human unhappiness). Happiness comes from a full, free satisfying life – a decent home, a secure job that you like doing, leisure richly filled with the good things of civilisation.'[2]

This was a warning and vocabulary that socialists often issued against popular consumerism, hire-purchase, advertising, youth culture and suburban living – the changes it witnessed as Britain moved from post-war privation to affluence. This chapter sees affluence in terms both of new consumer goods and of changing social attitudes and values. It examines the fears that socialists entertained about affluence and a society convened around its perceived values – a society like the USA, a dread presence in many socialist minds, for fear that its materialistic lifestyles as much as its foreign policy were taking a hold over Britain. Specifically, the left's uneasy relationship with 'affluence' and prescriptions for a better society will be viewed through television, one of the most apparent social changes of this period.

Affluence and the left

This disposition against 'affluence' was not hegemonic on the left. But even those whose take on it was more positive, notably Labour's revisionists (who posited that Labour might profit from the recession of immediate economic needs, by appealing to the 'quality of life' issues that now concerned voters), operated in a recognizable framework. Works such as *Must Labour Lose?* and writers like Tony Crosland detected in affluence a cohesion around middle-class values, registered in support for the Conservatives. And, while less convinced of the moral wickedness of affluence, they too shared the distaste for its cultural standards and accent on private gain.[3]

Most, however, were loath to grant that 'affluence' was anything other than illusory or transient. Where it was discussed in Communist literature, prosperity was invariably preceded by adjectives such as 'so-called' or 'apparent', denoting its merely discursive status. Labour's left was also apt to think this a virtual affluence, bought not from economic advance but 'on the "never-never"'. At best, Nye Bevan was prepared to recognize in his speech to the 1959 Labour conference that this was 'a temporarily affluent society', but also 'an ugly society . . . a vulgar society . . . a meretricious society . . . in which priorities have gone all wrong'. For its moral deficiency and anticipated economic demise, Dick Crossman argued in 1960 that socialism should not taint itself by association and that 'the Labour Party should hold itself in reserve, refusing in any way to come to terms with the affluent society'.[4]

Another concern was that rather than a social cohesion to which the left was simply unwilling to subscribe, 'affluence' was actually socially disintegrative. The acquisitive ethic of 'I'm Allright Jack' and privatism of suburban living – socialists referred to 'the spiritual vacuum that exists on so many new housing estates and in New Towns'[5] – were held to be promoting individualism and undermining the left. J. K. Galbraith's critique of *The Affluent Society* was that it sustained private gain at the cost of public squalor. Interviewed in 1962, Labour's leader Hugh Gaitskell ascribed his sense that 'people nowadays are more family and less community conscious than they used to be' to living standards having 'risen in ways that especially affect people's homes – televisions, kitchen gadgets'. Ideas of '"keeping up with the Joneses" . . . people wondering all the time whether they can do better for themselves alone', had, he confessed, 'created problems for the Labour Party'.[6]

Acquiring consumer goods was, then, to endorse the 'affluent society' and become a stakeholder in it. Mervyn Jones has recalled, 'the washing-machine took on a symbolic significance in the debate and was deplored as a nefarious agent of corruption'. Hire-purchase involved buying into capitalist values. A delegate at the 1960 Labour Women's Conference objected that women who 'bought things on hire-purchase . . . were playing the Tory game when they did so'.[7] It was this process of social integration that Crosland observed, albeit less critically. Labour might celebrate rising consumption, he proposed, since it meant 'the working class no longer feels to the same extent "outside" society'.[8]

In a more theoretical vein of such thinking, the New Left stressed how, far from the tamed beast of revisionist legend, capitalism was a more pervasive presence. Its spots had faded, making it a more opaque foe, but via consumerism, advertising and television, it was sinking its claws deeper into everyday life. Raymond Williams held that 'the patterns of thinking and behaviour it promotes have never been more strong'. Raphael Samuel agreed that individual opportunity was greater in the 1950s, but was 'distorted by the supremacy of commercial standards'. Business was increasingly shaping Britons' 'quality of life', giving 'society a tone more . . . vulgarly commercial than would have seemed possible in 1945'. In an 'increasingly . . . business civilisation', Samuel feared 'the stronger the ruling class looks, the more people, like working-class Tories . . . are going to defer to them'.[9]

Where capitalism in the 'affluent' 1950s was 'inhibited now from ensuring the "degradation" of the masses economically', Richard Hoggart suggested it was 'ensuring that working-people [were] culturally robbed'. For Stuart Hall the very categories 'consumer' and 'prosperity' were complicit with capitalism. Modern society had come 'to think of prosperity almost entirely in terms of the things which it could purchase, possess and enjoy as private individuals' and 'had entered as separate consumers, directly into the mythology of prosperity'. 'Affluence' was then a trick of the *zeitgeist*, whereby 'the consumer goods industry did not to any significant extent give us the goods: instead it gave us a definition of the good life'.[10]

The argument has historical followers. Sassoon argues that in the 1950s, through televisions, cars and so forth, 'ideology was not imposed, it was purchased'. Blackwell and Seabrook see the 1950s as the moment when 'capitalism succeeded in imposing through its version of prosperity, what it had been unable to impose through its version of poverty'. The question they posed of durables like the television was 'how a growing dependency on the necessarily rising income, without which such fragile gains are snatched away, involves us all in a deepening acceptance of capitalism?'[11]

'Affluence' in the 1950s, as this mode of thought mapped it, also involved a questioning of the condition of the people. Much as socialists felt that television, advertising and mass, commercial and popular culture, such as rock'n'roll, lacked moral and cultural value, so they took an equally dim view of those who indulged in such lifestyles. Their assessments of the popular mood tended towards the conservative. As *Tribune* saw it after the 1959 election: 'millions of our people have been subtly acclimatised to . . . the casino society, the "I'm Allright Jack" society . . . nobody has taught them to do otherwise than . . . scream their applause and envy at the catchword "double your money"'. The low standards of popular culture, but also the shortcomings of its participants, were leitmotivs of J. B. Priestley's derisive concept 'Admass' – a complex of advertising and mass culture. Labour MP (and bow-tied television personality) Woodrow Wyatt deduced 'all that most electors care about is what will happen to them personally'.[12] The people, then, fell short of socialist hopes and requirements and were seen to represent a barrier to building socialism.

The notion that too much of the population suffered from a 'poverty of desire', as Ernest Bevin famously put it, was a longstanding socialist concern and accounted in part for the often prescriptive, improving attitude that socialists took towards popular lifestyles.[13] Social change in the 1950s clearly agitated such reflexes. Often they were manifest in outright elitism. But in part, this sense of disappointment transpired through the narrative (already pervasive by the 1950s) of the lost 'spirit of 1945'. Socialists, while not believing it themselves, feared that many Britons had forsaken socialism for an interest in consumer or popular capitalism.

Television

Socialists were not implacably opposed to the main agent of mass culture
– television. They recognized, as with radio, that there was a danger of
'cultural standardisation', but also the potential for greater cultural choice
and access. Of the BBC's 'long exercise in educating public taste',
Labour heartily approved.[14]

Commercial television, broadcasting from 1955, was an altogether
different matter. From May 1952, when the Conservative government's
white paper proposing the ending of the BBC's monopoly was published, socialist hackles were raised. This was not least because it was
felt the case for commercial television was being foisted on the nation in
the absence of popular support and contrary to the report of the
Beveridge Committee on Broadcasting (1949–51), by a concerted
commercial lobby and a cabal of Tory MPs exploiting the government's
slender majority.[15]

Commercial television, its advent, structures and output, was the site of
sharp political contestation in 1950s Britain. The Labour MP Christopher
Mayhew, one of commercial television's most enduring opponents, suggested that this politicization was due to the feeling of consensus in other
policy areas. 'Tories who found themselves having to take over Labour
policies' found 'television was one area in which . . . [they] could encourage a bit of private enterprise', and so pressed the issue.[16] Labour too, by
this logic, found an issue on which they could more wholeheartedly
oppose the government.

But this chapter contends that the debates about television in British society were more than an exception demonstrating the veracity or otherwise
of the routine historical story of political consensus. Not least, the divisions
provoked did not fit easily into party lines. When Conservative Central
Office issued a leaflet supportive of competition for the BBC – *There's
Free Speech, Why not Free Switch?* – the Prime Minister, Winston Churchill (no particular fan of the BBC), demanded its withdrawal.[17]

Labour's hostility to independent television (ITV) and televiewing
(while not connected to Mayhew's later move to the Liberal Party) evince
the extent to which it was heir to nineteenth-century liberal traditions of
cultural thought, improvement and 'rational recreation'. Through television can be viewed debates about the quality and organization of cultural
provision and about how Britons spent their leisure time, the role of the
state and the course of social change in post-war Britain. At a philosophical level, some have seen in the exchanges over television in this period a
conflict between Benthamite liberalism (the choice offered by ITV) and

the BBC's more Platonic ideals. For Peter Black this was akin to a debate between roundheads and royalists, about whether Britain should be free or sober.[18]

Coverage by American channels of the Coronation in June 1953, with adverts using slogans like 'Queen of the Road' to sell cars and featuring the TV chimp 'J. Fred Muggs', gave warrant to socialist scruples about commercialization. Attlee cited this as evidence of the 'vulgar' content of commercial television and warned that, should the government introduce it into Britain, Labour would 'have to alter this when we get back into power'. Hugh Gaitskell reassured a constituent who feared that commercial television would prove 'harmful to educational and cultural interests' that she could 'rely on me to do everything I can to oppose the introduction of commercial television'.[19]

Opposition was not confined to socialist voices – the majority of elite and moral opinion, from churches to the TUC, and from universities to most in the Tory ranks, was outraged at the prospect. Lord Reith, architect of the BBC's public service ethos, compared commercial television with the arrival of the Black Death. Even commercial concerns expressed unease – ABC cinemas were worried at rivalry from television, and some British advertisers were concerned that the need for a new expertise would open their market to American infiltration.[20]

Mayhew, MP for Woolwich East, was among the foremost critics. On one occasion, aping the American networks' use of 'J. Fred Muggs', Mayhew made the case against commercial television at an Oxford Union debate while cradling a chimpanzee in his arms. He was the driving force behind the founding of a catholic, cross-party lobby group, the National Television Council (NTC) shortly after the Coronation. To counter this the pro-commercial Popular Television Association (PTA) was formed. Backed by Conservative Central Office and the advertising industry, it raised some £20,000 at its first meeting, whereas the NTC received donations of less than £1,000. Mayhew compared the two propaganda campaigns to their respective broadcasting causes – the PTA was 'populist, mendacious, mercenary and rich', while the NTC, 'like much public service broadcasting, was weighty, honest, public-spirited and poor'.[21]

While Mayhew's *Dear Viewer . . .* – 'a brilliant piece of pamphleteering', according to one observer – sold some 40,000 copies, there is scant evidence that the rival campaigns, even at their peak in the summer of 1953, sparked much popular interest. The nine who turned up out of the 600 invited to Chingford Youth Community Centre by the NTC were of the view that they wanted an additional channel, but 'did not care' who provided it. Similarly, an address by historian A. J. P. Taylor, one of the

PTA's more left-wing advocates, drew an audience of five. Indeed, there is rather more evidence pointing to a dislike of politics interfering with television. That an estimated 80 per cent of viewers turned channels when a party-political broadcast was transmitted quickly led in 1956 to the parties making both channels show party broadcasts simultaneously.[22]

Mayhew was certainly no die-hard, shy of television's modernity. A documentary-maker for the BBC in the 1950s, he presented Labour's first party-political telecast in 1951 and co-presented its 1959 election series with Anthony Wedgwood Benn. His pamphlet *Dear Viewer . . .* outlined Labour's objections. It concluded on the quite Reithian note that if television was 'going to be a dominant force in our national life' then it was necessary to 'make sure it has ideals and integrity, or it will ruin us'. Commercialism would ruin standards, the viewer was told, because 'the wishes and interests of the advertisers would be paramount' and 'broadcasting firms . . . would have neither the motive nor the means to resist the advertisers' "demands"'.[23]

In countering this argument, the PTA inadvertently endorsed Mayhew's (and the NTC's) charge that advertisers would prevail over artistic/creative matters, programme-makers and ultimately viewers. Its pamphlet argued that 'the advertiser will want as many viewers as possible' and would 'therefore . . . put the interest of the viewer first'.[24]

Mayhew rebutted the argument that advertisers needed popular programmes and that the audience's interests and taste would thus predominate, suggesting that for advertisers it was not 'the enjoyability of a programme, but . . . the universality of its appeal' that mattered. This distinction – that programmes with a mass audience were not enjoyed as keenly (or did not register as highly on the BBC 'appreciation index', by which Mayhew put great store) as those with more discriminating viewers – was also the essence of socialists' case against mass culture. 'To get a maximum audience', Mayhew argued, 'a TV programme must appeal to everyone at once, even if this means appealing keenly to no-one.' It had to 'appeal simultaneously to the 15 year-old and 50-year-old . . . the highbrows and lowbrows; Scots, English and Welsh; Swing fans and Beethoven fans; male and female.' In short, 'it must play down to the lowest common factor in us all'.[25]

For evidence Mayhew turned to the experience of the USA, where, as he viewed it, television too often tended towards sensationalism, crime, sex or horror to attract viewers. He cited the instance of his own play *Those in Favour*, based on experiences of dealing with the Soviets at the United Nations. Sold by the BBC to the American ABC series *Robert Montgomery Presents*, its length was cut by one-third, adverts were inserted at critical moments and its ending was altered. 'American TV',

Mayhew argues was 'horrible' and 'made these changes, not because it [was] run by Americans, but because it [was] dominated by commercial motives'.

Nonetheless, Mayhew regarded both American imports and British productions for the American market as a danger 'not only to our TV standards, but to our whole national culture and way of life', and considered 'it would be an excellent thing if we British asserted ourselves a bit against the colossal cultural impact of America'. Ultimately, he rejected commercial television on the ethical grounds that there were 'already enough things in our national life which are commercialised; and because a great weakness of our whole Western Civilisation is the way we put things on a commercial basis which might be done for their own sake'.[26]

Cultural elitism here merged with a belief in public ownership, aimed not at economic democracy and accountability, but at cultural control and benefit, and to promote non-commercial values. The state, in Labour's mind, could (and should) act as a source for cultural good. As Labour's major cultural statement of the period, *Leisure for Living*, made clear, it was 'the duty of the state to provide something of the best in the arts as an example or inspiration to the whole of the country'.[27]

Also evident was how Labour resembled and was prepared to defend the BBC's gentlemanly and 'very British' ethos of public service. This was disclosed in Patrick Gordon Walker's support for an amendment to the 1954 Television Act that sought to bar 'aliens' from positions within the regulatory Independent Television Authority (ITA). Their employment was acceptable 'in the case of the BBC', he argued, because 'we are dealing with a public service, but in this case we are dealing with people broadcasting for profit . . . a completely different state of affairs, which needs control'. Commercial broadcasters, he continued, were 'people who cannot be trusted in any way, but the BBC can be trusted'. In particular, Gordon Walker identified a 'special danger of domination by American interests' and balked at the idea of 'the Authority . . . be[ing] exposed to a great deal of American influence and flooding'. Mayhew denied anti-Americanism, but it was clearly a spectre in Gordon Walker's mind.[28] Likewise in 1955 his fear of a change in the fourteen-day rule (barring broadcasts on matters to be discussed in Parliament within a fortnight) was that whereas the BBC could be trusted to abide by 'a gentleman's agreement . . . with commercial television we are, by definition, not dealing with gentlemen'. It seemed that the opposition between cultural quality and commercialism in the socialist outlook was related to the notion that being engaged in commercial trades precluded behaving as or being a gentleman.[29]

Communist thinking was of a kind with Mayhew and Gordon Walker.

Harry Pollitt replied to a request for an interview on the question of commercial television made by Ed Murrow's CBS network show *See it Now*, by informing them that 'commercial television would not hesitate to indulge in the vilest forms of pornography and the portrayal of crime, murder and sadism if the advertisers thought this would achieve their aim'. This, Pollitt continued, was 'what happened in the United States' and television was 'too great a potential educational instrument to be put at the mercy of private profit-making interests . . . only interested in securing greater sales and profits for their particular brand of commodities.'[30]

Labour's campaign against commercial television was based on the premises that 'all responsible and disinterested opinion condemns commercial television', that 'the standard of programmes will slump when the commercialisers get busy on the TV screen' and that 'the public is opposed to sponsored television; it revolts against the very idea'.[31] The viability of these assumptions very much remained to be seen. In the last instance, it was evident soon after ITV started broadcasting that its programmes were far from unpopular. By the summer of 1957 it was drawing 73 per cent of the growing audience, compared to the BBC's 27 per cent.[32] There was then, as Crossman feared in 1954, not only a certain cultural (or class) irony, but a political flaw to Labour's espousal of 'high' culture contra-ITV, for there were 'far more Conservative voters who object to commercial television than Labour voters'.[33]

The campaign evoked a wartime spirit – 'what have **you** done to save us from commercial television?' *Labour Woman* asked in July 1953. And Mary Allen, in obdurate mood, confessed to its readers that she was 'chilled . . . by the prospect . . . that in ten years time there will be eight million TV sets in this country, with half the adult population "looking-in" on the average night – the thought appals me!'[34] The left had a certain antediluvian streak. Tony Benn despaired of one member of the Public Information Group of Labour MPs and die-hard opponent of commercial television, the Crewe MP Scholefield Allen, because he did 'not even have a television set'.[35] As Doris Lessing later commented, many progressives and socialists simply 'refused to get one' and television became a sort of litmus test whereby 'one could more or less work out someone's political bias by the attitude he took towards television'.[36]

Doubtless, then, many socialists were to be found among the social group Tom Harrisson identified in his 1960 survey of Bolton, 'who either ostentatiously do not have television or if they do have it go out of their way to explain that it was given to them or that they only look at it occasionally'. 'Such people', he observed, 'generally refer to it by derogatory remarks' such as 'the little box', and socialists were prone to disparage television as 'a modern magic box' or 'idiot's lantern'.[37]

Harrisson traced such impulses to disassociate from the television, not to hubris or aestheticism, but to the 'psychological influence in many minds and particularly those of the powerfully non-conformist North' for 'locating sources supposedly leading to unoriginal sin'. And 'at present', he suggested, 'TV fills this bill better than anything else'.[38] The socialist mind was thus possessed, imagining a host of unedifying activities – Hollywood, gambling, milk bars and especially television – to involve some moral downfall. It was in this vein that *Leisure for Living* vowed to 'not allow television to be used – as Karl Marx and Charles Kingsley said that religion had been used – as the opium of the people'.[39] Hugh Jenkins (later Minister for the Arts in Harold Wilson's 1974–6 government) talked of 'the television that drugs most of us nightly'; Priestley of being 'half-hypnotized' peering into a 'magic mirror like a 14-stone, cigar-smoking, Lady of Shallot'.[40]

Although it was applauded for keeping the family together, there was a thinly disguised contempt among socialists for televiewing. As a life-style, it was altogether too passive for their taste. 'The lifeless time-wasting of so many older people who find in TV almost their only pleasure, but are apt to be numbed rather than stimulated by much of its present output' Labour twinned to 'teenagers hanging around aimlessly in pin-table saloons'.[41] As Lindsey Mountford told *Revolt* (the Trotskyist paper of the Socialist Workers' Federation): 'a number of acquaintances of mine who before acquiring TV were perfectly normal human beings have now become morose recluses with no other interest in life but to sit in front of the TV screen'.[42]

Mary Allen told *Labour Woman* how she would 'rather read a book, go occasionally to a theatre and listen from time to time to a radio discussion'. She did not believe television was 'one of the highest achievements of man' and viewed commercial television as 'one of his lowest'.[43] Labour's agent in suburban Merton, John Heardley-Walker, saw television as a distraction. After a poor turnout for council elections in May 1959, he wondered whether 'on a hot summer night, was Diana Dors or Bob Monkhouse, more important than exercising the long-fought-for right to vote?' He also considered the television screen to be 'so powerful a magnet that it keeps people away from the bookshelf'. Mountford similarly disapproved that if you 'go into any working-class home today . . . you will find in place of a bookcase, a TV set, usually bought on the "never-never system"'.[44] Frank Horrabin agreed that the television aerial was 'the totem pole of the twentieth century'. Discussing a George Chapman sketch of a Rhondda skyline strewn with aerials, he supposed that its title, 'Sheep may Safely Gaze', referred 'to the two-legged animals gazing absorbed at their TV screens'.[45]

Left-wing voices resounded with the diehard TV-less, the one-sixth of Britons whom a 1957 *Sunday Times* survey classified as 'abstainers', in regarding television as a watchword for all that was wrong with the new society. Doctors diagnosed 'TV neck',.'TV dyspepsia' and buck teeth for children who watched from the floor, chin in hands. In the *New Statesman*, footballer Danny Blanchflower (more half-back than left-winger) blamed recent national sporting disappointments on the exaggerated expectations that television coverage created.[46]

Notwithstanding perceptions of explicit in-built political prejudice (Communists called for the BBC's 1954 televization of Orwell's *Nineteen Eighty-Four* to be cancelled),[47] the socialist press scorned television standards. Reviewing performances on *Saturday Night is Variety Night* for the *Daily Worker*, Alison Macleod was reluctant 'to mention those who sent me over to the commercial channel'. Another typically double-edged review in 1956 declared, 'all this American entertainment has made me think more favourably of Wilfred Pickles'.[48] By the first week of 1957 Macleod was urging 'all left-wingers' to 'forget whatever else you were saving up for, and save up for a television'. This was not because of a dramatic improvement in the New Year's television schedules, but through a recognition that without viewing what most people were watching, socialists were 'not able to talk to them on equal terms'.[49]

Wilfred Pickles' *Have a Go* on the Light Programme and *Ask Pickles* on television were begrudged their popular appeal by commentators like Richard Hoggart. They were based around the down-to-earth, northern warmth and common touch with audience and participants of 'yer old friend, Wilfred Pickles'. Hoggart (himself from Leeds) found this to 'indulge the northern working-class', prone to condescension and altogether 'too evidently "all pals together"' ... for my taste'. The sentimental or trivial, whatever its popular appeal, was given short shrift by socialists. *Dixon of Dock Green* was savaged in *New Left Review* as nothing more than 'a piece of jetsam salvaged from *The Blue Lamp*' and found wanting on the rather spurious grounds that 'the programme fails as documentary'. Worse still, in the eyes of Tom Driberg's television column in the *New Statesman*, was a '*faux bonhomme*' like Michael Miles, the presenter of the popular ITV quiz *Take Your Pick*.[50] Even *That Was The Week That Was*, the toast of most anti-Conservatives in 1963, received a tetchy review from Francis Hope, the *New Statesman*'s assistant literary editor.[51]

Dennis Potter served as television critic on the *Daily Herald* for two years from July 1962. Symptomatically, he was given less copy than the theatre reviews. Potter's biographer supposes his 'quality of thought and expression must have been far beyond the expectations of all but his most optimistic readers.'[52] Yet while Potter was altogether more amenable to the creative potential of television, he could also damn 'the little grey-faced monster squatting in our living rooms'.[53] Potter demurred little from the tone set by his predecessors. Phil Diack, for instance, denounced the four plays on both BBC and commercial channels on an April Sunday in 1960 as 'junk' and 'execrable'. A week later, his fury patently unabated, Diack considered that had you wanted 'something with a minimum of thought and a maximum of mental stagnation, then last night was your night'.[54]

Political scientist and mid-1950s adviser to Labour on broadcasting, William (not to be confused with Wilfred) Pickles, contended that in the partaking of the 'daily drug' of television there was 'a connection between social conservatism and political Conservatism'. And television's influence was all the more sinister and 'all the more effective because it [was] unintentional and in part unavoidable'. In particular, it was the 'social conservatism' of the BBC that Pickles targeted. *Woman's Hour* he lambasted for assuming that women's 'interests are almost entirely limited to housework, clothes, marriage and children'. His stiffest tone was reserved for *Mrs Dale's Diary*. 'Everybody in the Dale family does and thinks what is traditionally done and thought by his class at the done time in the done way', he railed. No wonder, then, that such programmes attracted 'vast, faithful and partly moronic audiences'. 'The evidence for the low IQ of much of these audiences', Pickles vouched, was 'well known'.[55]

It was not only the commercial or other imperatives of the programme makers that were to blame for disappointing television standards then – it was the audience itself. Even the culturally tuned-in New Left argued in its submission to the Pilkington Committee (1960–2) that 'in the end, the quality of the service provided will depend upon the critical awareness of the audience'. The committee, which was considering both present and future broadcasting, had an opportunity to make providers more responsible and accountable, but also, the New Left suggested, 'to help raise the quality of response and critical appreciation of the audiences themselves; to help them become more discriminating over the whole field of television output'.[56]

Alma Birk on a 'Visit to Hollywood' in 1956 reached similar conclusions with regard to films. An excited report both of the discrimination that the industry suffered in the McCarthy era and of its vapid, synthetic atmosphere ended with the thought that the place and its product were 'ghastly' and in need of wholesale change. But, she concluded, 'probably the film-going public will have to become even more discriminating before this happens'.[57] Frank Allaun, reviewing British war films like *The*

Battle of the River Plate in the Independent Labour Party paper *Forward*, decided they were aimed at 'conditioning our minds to tolerate the dropping of H-bombs'. And they were 'propaganda . . . all the more effective since the cinema audiences' minds are relaxed and ready to absorb whatever poison is put over'.[58]

The impact on children took prime-time in socialist concerns about television. With the ending of the 'toddler's truce' (an hour of television silence between 6 and 7 p.m.), they felt they were fighting an uphill battle. The preponderance of thrillers and westerns in ITV's children's output was, Mayhew argued in 1959, 'financially shrewd, but otherwise execrable'. In 1958 the ITA Children's Advisory Committee reported 'too high a proportion of drama in which the solutions were found only by physical conflict'.[59] Adult and BBC programmes were similarly criticized. There was 'still too much violence on TV', the *Daily Herald* adjudged with regard to the BBC's popular western *Laramie*.[60] But commercial drives made the output of ITV companies all the worse in Mayhew's eyes. Advertising that played upon children's 'suggestibility' he deemed 'the lowest form of activity open to a British citizen, short of actual crime'.[61] The Council for Children's Welfare, of which *Daily Herald* and *Labour Woman* columnist Alma Birk was vice-chair, turned its attention from 1957 towards the social attitudes portrayed in children's fare.[62] The link between these and wider social attitudes was unquestionable to socialists.

Indeed, New Left reviewers could see 'in almost every programme . . . *some* view of life, some implicit or explicit social or moral attitudes'. Nor was it just violence that troubled socialists. ITV quiz shows, notably *Dotto* and *Double Your Money*, were held to 'encourage an attitude of total passivity, relieved only by positive appeals to mercenary greed'. The materialist message crept on to the BBC too – the purpose of the jury on *Juke Box Jury* was 'not to criticise the music, but rather to determine whether the records are likely to be a hit or not'. Worse still were the values of advertising itself. There was surely 'something fraudulent about the way in which the genial bonhomie of Wilfred Pickles' was 'used, and specifically relied upon, to sell a patent medicine in the commercials', the New Left's Pilkington deposition declared. And it was disturbed too by the idea that 'direct appeals to status – the invitation to compete with one's neighbour for social prestige' were 'a sound way to sell goods', involving as they did the proposition 'that emotional problems may be resolved by the acquisition of material goods'. These were precisely the values that socialists felt an aversion to in the affluent society.[63]

Socialist thought and the Pilkington Committee

After 1955, when the ITV companies started broadcasting, socialist hostility and suspicion remained unabated. Commercial television might not have been averted, but the 1954 Television Act had introduced a number of restraints, notably on advertising and in the form of the regulatory ITA, that represented a compromise well short of American-style sponsored television. The rapid expansion of television was recognized as an influential social change. Between 1951 and 1964, ownership of TV sets grew from 1 million to 13 million, the average radio audience fell by more than half between 1954 and 1957, around 800 cinemas closed in five years after 1954, and expenditure on television advertising picked up sharply from £13 million in 1956 to £48 million by 1958.[64]

As a Labour Party research department memo penned by Wedgwood Benn early in 1955 made clear, the popularity of television (and particularly ITV) not only made it a more pressing issue, but problematic for the left. Labour's 'long campaign with its warnings and threats against the commercial lobby may', Benn predicted, put it 'at a tactical disadvantage'. Yet while he urged a policy that 'would reassure viewers about their new programmes', Benn also required it to 'scare the advertisers about their new investment . . . divide the Tory party into two and precipitate the collapse of commercial television from lack of confidence'.[65]

Benn reaffirmed Labour's belief 'that all sound and television programmes must be in fact, as well as in theory, controlled, produced and broadcast by a public service system'.[66] For Benn this was an article of faith, which he carried forward into the Wilson governments as a proposal for a National Broadcasting Corporation and, with Edward Short (his successor as Postmaster-General in 1966) and Hugh Jenkins (Labour's Communications Committee chair), took into battle with 'pirate' radio.[67]

Mayhew renewed his attack in a 1959 Fabian Tract that asked (like Lenin), *Commercial Television – What is to be Done?* This accused the regional ITV companies of breaking the spirit of the 1954 Television Act by concentrating adverts in prime-time slots and inserting unnatural breaks into programmes. One programme contractor was reported as saying 'any break that brings me in £1000 is a natural break'. The ITA was charged with having 'never really challenged the power of the programme companies'. Standards, as Mayhew had anticipated, were low: a 1958 BBC survey found that one-third of its own peak-time output was 'serious' programming, compared to a mere tenth of ITV's.[68]

Entering the debate on a third television channel, Mayhew detected hopeful signs. Opinion surveys found a popular dislike for adverts: 81 per cent claimed to be annoyed by breaks in, rather than between, programmes, and 69 per cent supported Mayhew's bill to prohibit these. There was also popular support for the BBC to run the new channel, despite the fact that ITV attracted more viewers than the BBC. This confirmed Mayhew's belief in a negative correlation between 'size of audience' and 'appreciation index'. Thus, he contended there was 'no possible argument – political, technical or ethical – for letting "admass" loose on new TV channels'.[69]

This allayed Labour's fear that, as the most popular broadcaster, ITV could lay the strongest claim to run the third channel.[70] Rather, Mayhew and Labour came to advocate the formation of an Independent Public Corporation, modelled along BBC lines, to provide the new service and a strengthening of the ITA's powers over the regional companies.[71] As a Communist discussion paper observed, 'the struggle to give this channel to the BBC' was 'a rather negative way of fighting against' commercial influence, but 'the only way out at present'.[72] Funding was to come from the licence fee and either a tax on ITV's 'fabulously profitable advertising monopoly' or increasing the rates that the ITA charged to programme contractors for the use of transmitters and making these funds available.[73]

However much this involved a retreat from outright opposition – Raymond Williams denounced it as 'a shameful decision to compromise with commercial television'[74] – Labour's *dirigisme* still gave rise to the sort of political scaremongering more usually associated with its nationalization proposals. Two days prior to the 1959 election, the *Daily Sketch* reported that a Labour victory would mean the end of commercial television. While Morgan Phillips described this as a 'fantastic lie', the Tories took 100,000 copies of the *Sketch* to distribute in six London marginals.[75]

The report of the government's Pilkington Committee on Broadcasting in 1962 (chaired by nonconformist glassmaker Sir Harry Pilkington) seemed to ratify many of the left's concerns about ITV. Supportive of the public service ideals of the BBC, the report tendered that ITV had fallen woefully short of the terms of the 1954 Act, criticized its programming as vulgar and 'trivial', and called for a strengthened ITA to sell advertising time and buy in programmes, thereby separating advertisers and programme-makers. 'So long as independent television is constituted and organized as at present,' it argued, 'it should not provide any additional services of television.'[76] Critics of Pilkington vilified Richard Hoggart, a committee member, as its killjoy author and the 'bad genius' behind a 'socialistic and unrealistic report'. Under the byline 'Pilkington tells the public to go to hell', the strongly pro-commercial television *Daily Mirror* complained: 'The committee say you can't have the television programmes which . . . two-thirds . . . of you prefer. You must have a . . . set-up controlled by the government: an "Uncle" ITA, just like "Auntie" BBC.'[77]

Mayhew certainly regarded Pilkington as an opportunity to renew the attack on ITV. Opinion polls offered some support basis for this. A Gallup poll in the *Daily Telegraph* in April 1962 found only 9 per cent thought a third television station should be run by ITV, compared to 33 per cent favouring the BBC and 34 per cent some new authority; almost two-thirds wanted to leave radio provision in the BBC's hands. But Mayhew's attempts to swing Labour firmly behind Pilkington were thwarted. George Brown, whom Mayhew discovered was in the pay of Cecil King, an 'arch-enemy of public service television', argued against backing it. Nor, crucially, was the backing that Mayhew anticipated from Gaitskell forthcoming. Gaitskell was happier for Labour to discuss the report than commit to it. Whatever polling evidence Mayhew could muster and however forceful Pilkington's case might be, the two out of three constituents who preferred watching ITV to the BBC were a pressing electoral calculation. In October, Mayhew told Gaitskell, 'I feel you let me down badly over Pilkington.'[78]

But, Gaitskell pointed out to Mayhew, Pilkington did not satisfy all socialists.[79] Crosland, notably, felt that the report had come 'to broadly the right conclusions, but for largely the wrong reasons'. He made the case for state intervention, not on the grounds that there was insufficient choice, but in order to introduce 'more educational choice than we now have'. This was not just to cater for minority tastes or erase the 'inane, banal, strident, mawkish or offensive' product that it seemed 'most of the public currently wants', by 'imposing (à la Reith) a particular view or level of taste'. Rather it was to demand 'a wider range of serious programmes than would be chosen by immediate majority vote; in the hope that over the years the public, having been offered this range will more and more freely choose it'.

Crosland conceded that his thinking was premised on the BBC 'theory behind the light, home and third programmes . . . that over time, with increasing education and discrimination, listeners would graduate from the first through the second to the third'. Crosland proposed an extension of non-commercial local radio and, for a fourth television channel, 'a specialist educational channel'. As much as BBC thinking, this was redolent of the nineteenth-century liberal tradition of social and cultural thinking of Matthew Arnold – a strong presence in both Crosland's and Hoggart's writing. The left was firmly lodged in the enlightened elitism of Matthew Arnold and F. R. Leavis.[80]

For all the libertarian instincts evinced in the closing pages of Crosland's *The Future of Socialism* and its conscious shedding of Labour's puritan and Fabian reflexes, there remained an evident paternalism and urge to instruct people 'how to enjoy' their newfound affluence. 'In the field of cultural values', Crosland saw a 'deep, dividing line' and Labour resolutely on the side of 'determined government planning'. This governed Crosland's response to Pilkington in 1962. And while Labour's opposition to television had diminished (as fears of 'Americanization' faded and Labour avoided Conservative charges that it sneered at 'affluence' or threatened ITV), it remained in Labour's mind in 1964.[81] Labour's Penguin election special proposed that television advertising might be 'dispensed with altogether' to 'improve the programmes', and that alternative funding could be found in taxing TV sets or doubling the licence fee, which at £4 had doubled since 1954, but was among Europe's cheapest.[82]

Pilkington confirmed Labour's suspicion at the concentration of economic power in the regional companies. It was not only that television was 'in the hands of commercialism rather than in the hands of a democratic public authority' that stuck in the socialist throat, but the fortunes and influence accrued by its owners[83] – figures like Roy Thomson, Canadian proprietor of the *Sunday Times* and *Scotsman* and the major shareholder in Scottish Television (an acquisition he considered 'a licence to print money'), or Val Parnell, Managing Director of ATV and (according to Mayhew) an 'admirably clear exponent of the ideals and standards of "Admass"'.[84] Labour found the government indifferent to this, as to its opinion that 'an organic change was required in the structure of commercial television'.[85]

Even Robert Fraser's appointment as Director-General of the ITA choked, for he was an ex-Labour candidate, socialist journalist and friend of Harold Laski and Evan Durbin.[86] The power of these 'new tycoons' and 'their sudden emergence', as Anthony Sampson comments, 'defied the managerial revolution'. The concentration rather than diffusion of power and control was something of 'a throwback to the days of the early press barons'.[87] And this seemed to weigh against the left. The *Daily Worker*, along with undertakers, marriage bureaux and moneylenders, was barred from advertising on ITV.[88] The ITA rejected a bid from a consortium including *Reynolds News* and fifteen East Anglian co-operative societies. This, it was claimed, would have involved for the first time 'a large element of local finance, control and popular participation in the running of a commercial television station'.[89]

The stake that the newspaper industry took in the new television stations was substantial – around one-quarter of the issued share capital. The *Daily Mirror*, for instance, had a large holding in ATV, one of the most profitable companies, broadcasting to London and the Midlands; the *News of the World* similarly in Television Wales and West. Both Pilkington and the 1962 Royal Commission on the Press condemned such dominance. Indeed, Pilkington proposed that unless Roy Thomson's interest in Scottish Television was reduced their contract should not be renewed in 1964.[90]

Despite the founding of ITV being premised on ending the BBC's monopoly, it was not the concentration of power that disturbed socialists, but the increasing standardization of taste and the lack of real alternatives. Socialism's objection to the uniform, commercial edifice of mass culture (not only television, but the media as a whole and lifestyles associated with the 'affluent society') was that it seemed to be strangling alternative, more edifying cultures, leisure activities and values. It was feared that workers were increasingly in thrall to the mass media. 'We are surrounded by a press, radio and television and cinema', the Communist Party of Great Britain warned in a dread vision in 1961, which were 'for the most part feeding us a continuous diet of false values and phoney moral standards'. 'Day after day a false picture of the world', Priestley argued, was 'flashed onto millions of innocent minds'.[91] Yet, as is one of the chief refrains of this chapter, socialists were prone to find a good deal of popular complicity in this abuse of literacy. Like the ITA official who told the Pilkington Committee, 'people get the television they deserve', Priestley advanced, 'if our papers are trivial', it was 'because our people are trivial'.[92]

Socialist fears about the popularity of televiewing had a more transparent political agenda. *Leisure for Living* displeasingly noted how when there was 'an international football match on television, seeing it takes precedence over most other engagements (including, of course, voting in a local election).'[93] Labour was annoyed by ITV's evening schedule for the evening of election day 1959, featuring the western *Rawhide* at 7 p.m. and *Dotto* at 8 p.m. Not only were these programmes disliked by socialists, but they attracted large audiences, 'the ITV audience was known to be predominantly Labour' and they occupied time slots when working-class people normally voted. Labour argued, then, that to include these programmes in the schedule 'was to be responsible for a situation that was likely to interfere with the democratic process and damage the Labour Party's chances'.[94]

Equally, such concerns as socialists had about television meant that they entertained similar concerns about its political uses. It was not only cost that contrived to give the Conservatives an advantage as techniques of political communication developed in the later 1950s. Just as Gordon Walker raised the spectre of the Queen being juxtaposed between adverts for beer and deodorant as part of Labour's case against the 1954 Television Act, so he saw a debasement of British political standards in the Conservatives' use of public relations firms to sell itself and the way Macmillan was promoted as a brand like 'Chocolate penguins . . . Payne's Poppets and Amplex'. In another instance, Labour was decidedly more reluctant than the Conservatives to allow television cameras into its conference.[95] Party leaders, Bevan and Gaitskell alike, were cranky performers in the television studio – 'frightened' and 'quarrelsome'. All told, such attitudes led the young Anthony Wedgwood Benn, a fervent modernizer in this respect, to despair in 1958: 'none of our party leaders have television sets . . . how can one lead a great party unless one keeps in touch with the people?'[96]

Conclusions

In an *Observer* article after Labour's defeat in 1959, Richard Hoggart mused on the left's angst. Socialists were at present, he argued, a species of two kinds: first, 'shocked Puritans, whose knowledge of people is by now so generalised and distanced that they are convinced that masses of us have been ruined beyond recognition in a decade – all glued to the telly every week-night'; and secondly, 'cheer-leaders . . . who are uncritically in love with the gloss of the new society and only want more of it – but with the Left in the lead.'

Hoggart proceeded to diagnose a left afflicted by 'its own fears, bred from its own blurred image of people'.[97] While, as has been shown, Hoggart was not himself immune, there was much in this. The Labour Party, and socialism more generally, was rather less *The Voice of the People* than it imagined.[98] Indeed, in their present condition, as many on the left saw it, Labour contrived to change as much as represent the people. Its dilemma – an enduring one for progressive politics – was to maintain support from people whose habits and taste it also sought to improve, without seeming to criticize them. More than their unconditional support for ITV, it was the fact that Conservatives were less torn by concern for the moral condition of the people that enabled them to pose as the champions of popular pastimes – not so much beer and skittles as TV and *Take Your Pick*.

In suggesting the left's uneasy relationship with 'affluence', the newly affluent and the people more generally, this chapter recognizes that social change did not proceed as most on the left anticipated after 1945, and thus presented it with real difficulties. But it is also abundantly evident that the left's difficulties related to the specific ways in which it comprehended and articulated social change and defined the people, and to its ideas of 'culture' and improvement. Labour, *pace* McKibbin, had some interest (admittedly more so when out of office) in reforming civic society. It did not so much reflect its constituency in this respect as find itself up against their tolerance of change and moderate tastes. This chapter, then, makes a case for regarding formal politics not only in terms of its social foundations, but crucially in terms of what it said about these and how this was received.[99]

The left's disappointment that the people had not resisted the introduction of commercial television was compounded by evidence that they preferred to watch what socialists saw as its culturally inferior output. In fact, such fears were longstanding. A Labour memorandum during the Beveridge Broadcasting Committee stated that ending the BBC monopoly would mean most of the audience, who 'prefer to be entertained rather than educated, would no longer receive the talks, features, discussions, news'.[100] Labour's desire to 'make people better' and fears that they were falling short of their potential and could not be trusted to make such improvement voluntarily, were accentuated by 'affluence' in the 1950s.[101] For the British left, the state – already understood to be a potential force for cultural improvement – offered recourse from what it increasingly saw as the people's limitations as a force for progress towards a socialist Britain.

This raised the question – which Conservative Selwyn Lloyd posed of Labour on the Beveridge Broadcasting Committee – of whether the suspicion that the public would make the 'wrong' viewing choices was a valid reason for denying them such a choice. Here the ideological discourse of the Cold War meshed with that of 'affluence'. In a 'free' or 'affluent' society, should cultural standards be the responsibility of the state ('compulsory uplift', in Lloyd's phrase) or of more voluntary popular choice? Besides commercial influences, 'affluence' meant a diversification of lifestyles and an expansion of choice, and that the state was no longer the sole authority or arbiter in such matters. The left's blend of moralism, notions of bringing 'proper', 'high' culture to all and of modelling ideal-type citizens, seemed out of place and time. Labour's cultural *dirigisme* was increasingly at odds with the popular attitudes and culture emerging as post-war social and cultural change began to undermine the traditional authority of the state. As John Corner comments, vocabulary such as 'moral' and 'trivial', that Labour and the Pilkington Report deployed, struggled in the post-war cultural climate because it was 'too easily reducible . . . to the sort of explicit paternalism that could no longer find support or deference quite so available as might have been the case a decade earlier'.[102]

In its pre-Pilkington years, ITV did not only 'behave . . . like an Oxford Street barrow boy', as Hoggart later depicted it. It might at one stage have been showing a give-away quiz show every evening (and two on Saturday), but the left had less to say about efforts like ATV's *Armchair Theatre* or attempts to promote 'high' culture through Shakespeare or the Hallé Orchestra, and even less to say about the smaller audiences these attracted.[103] Undiscriminating criticism and tone – at times sounding contemptuous of television *per se* – undermined more valid criticisms that the left might have had of financial structures, programme quality and even viewers. When more discerning, the left found (like Mayhew's research in the late 1950s and 1960s) that ITV's audience was neither as uncritical nor as undiscriminating as the left was apt to suspect.

3

Functionalists, Federalists and Fundamentalists: Labour and Europe, 1945–50

Mark Minion

The British Labour Party has had a somewhat troubled relationship with Europe during the post-war period. Labour's election victory in May 1997 brought this history back into focus. The party's election manifesto of that year strongly attacked the failures of the previous Conservative administrations in the European arena. Labour was to reverse Tory 'Europhobia' and ensure that Britain played a key role from within Europe, moulding the European Union to Labour's own social democratic project.

Part of this enthusiasm for Europe arose from Labour's desire to reverse the party's own 'European history', which equated to periods of antipathy to the European Economic Community (EEC) and European Community (EC). Kevin Featherstone has remarked that 'few political parties have been troubled by questions concerned with European integration as much as the British Labour Party'.[1] Labour, and in particular the Labour left, took an increasingly anti-EEC position from the 1950s onwards, due in part to the economic interests that the EEC was seen as defending. As Michael Newman has shown, it was the revisionist right and a handful of ex-members of the Independent Labour Party (ILP) who favoured Britain's entry into the EEC.[2] Throughout the 1960s and 1970s, Labour was increasingly split on the question of membership of the EEC between, crudely speaking, a left that was against joining and a right that campaigned for British membership. The culmination of this difficulty came at Labour's annual conference of 1980, which voted by a majority of more than 2½ to 1, for withdrawal from the European Community (as the EEC had been renamed). However, this hostile position eventually weakened. Consequently, as Donald Sassoon has noted, 'the party which had campaigned for withdrawal in 1983, then wavered in 1987, finally adopted a pro-EC position for the 1989 election to the European Parliament'.[3]

Labour and Europe, 1945–50: an overview

The roots of Labour's post-war anti-European position, especially that of the party's left, are usually located within the term of office of the Labour governments of 1945–51, led by Clement Attlee. The election of July 1945 was the first time that Labour had achieved an overall majority, and it therefore occupies a unique place within the party's annals. As Andrew Thorpe's recent history of the party has shown, the Attlee government is the model by which all other administrations formed by Labour are judged.[4]

On the question of European unity, ministers of the Attlee governments resisted all calls for closer integration with western Europe. Kenneth Morgan has noted that intransigence arose from 'the close relation with the Commonwealth countries in the sterling area and in terms of trade and the need for Britain to maintain its special links with the United States'.[5] Also key were Labour's attachment to the perceived post-war British grandeur that arose from the sense of being 'unbowed' during the Second World War, and the perception of being one of the three major global powers.

Subsequently, this position developed into what became termed the Atlanticist approach. The 'special' Anglo-American relationship, and thus global considerations, were given primacy over a 'limited' Anglo-Continental association. Central to this process were the policies introduced by the Foreign Secretary, Ernest Bevin. His pursuance of military structures to resist the growing 'Soviet threat', coupled with the post-war economic weakness of Britain (and Europe), and subsequent reliance on the USA for precious dollars, cemented Labour's Atlantic view.[6]

In relation to Anglo-Continental relations, competing convictions were evident, indicating an ideological vitality operating within Labour's ranks which is more often ignored, or downplayed within the historiography of the Attlee period.[7] This diversity was in part generated by the defeat of fascism, and the sense of hope gained from the election of the Attlee government. Ministers of the government expressed their support for Britain retaining a great world power status as one of the victorious Big Three wartime allies. International relations were to be governed through the emerging structures of the United Nations Organization, which was deemed a successor to the League of Nations, indicating continuity in Labour's policy. Britain's ties with Europe were to be limited to intergovernmental relations and treaties. For the Government, Britain's European association was to have a dual focus: first, functional economic intercourse aimed at Continental reconstruction; and secondly, military structures that would safeguard western Europe against the growing Soviet threat. The Marshall Plan, announced in June 1947, provided vital American dollars to aid the economic future of western Europe and, therefore, helped fulfil the first part of the government's European vision. The emergence of the North Atlantic Treaty Organization (NATO), which was formally constituted in April 1949, completed Labour's Continental structures. Both NATO and the Marshall Plan did, of course, enhance Labour's Atlanticism.

In general, the left shared with a sizeable minority of the party's local activists an expectation that *their* government, and Bevin as Foreign Secretary, should, and would, introduce measures that reflected Labour's 'socialist foreign policy'.[8] Central to this position, as both Peter Weiler and John Saville have noted, was continued friendship and goodwill with the existing socialism of the Soviet Union. Additionally, as Jonathan Schneer recognized, Labour Party members expected their government to support the 'revolutions' that broke out in southern and eastern Europe from 1944 onwards.[9]

Cold War politics set limits upon all international relations in the late 1940s. Europe's economic and military weakness offered a choice between one or other of the superpowers, or attempting to chart a separate or neutral course as a 'third force' focused upon Europe, or a section of it. The vast majority of the party opted for the 'lesser evil' of the USA. Correspondingly, the anti-Americanism of the Labour left decreased in intensity. Growing cross-party concerns in relation to the Soviet threat were the other side of this ideological coin. The pro-European tendencies exhibited by some within the Labour Party became subsumed within global political tensions.

In June 1950 the French Foreign Minister, Robert Schuman, made a call for a European Coal and Steel Community (ECSC). His proposals were strongly resisted by the overwhelming majority of the Labour Party – ministers, backbench MPs, the left and local activists – due in part to the perceived supranational nature of the Schuman Plan. The threat to the socialist measures that Labour had enacted, such as the highly symbolic recently nationalized coal industry, governed this 'fateful decision'.[10] For the Labour government, rejection was necessary to protect socialism in Britain. Britain's and Labour's antithetical stand towards an integrated Europe was thus cemented.

However, acceptance of the government's programme did not occur smoothly and it is this journey that the rest of this chapter will focus upon. Essentially the period 1945–50 can be divided into three distinct parts, each reflecting a different part of the Labour left's search for, and eventual abandonment of, a new European orientation.[11] In turn, the effect of Europe upon the ideas of 'Britishness' – defined as a distinct national identity – held by Labour members will be investigated.[12]

Of course, to examine the issue of Europe in such a manner centres upon the political debates of the elite. What 'the people' desired in relation to Europe is more difficult to ascertain. Opinion polling at this juncture was at a formative stage, save Mass Observation and a few other instances. Moreover, as Steven Fielding *et al.* have shown, most citizens of Britain desired a return to pre-war conditions, but without the insecurity of high unemployment and inadequate public welfare: foreign affairs were of little or no concern, despite many ex-service personnel having fought in the war in Europe.[13] Similarly, many local Labour parties did not venture further than the shores of Britain when considering policy. However, those activists and backbench MPs who did voice European concerns indicate an ideological vitality during the late 1940s that requires serious consideration.

May 1945–May 1947

The first period opens with the Labour Party's annual conference (LPAC) of May 1945. So soon after VE day, a great feeling of euphoria swept the party's gathering. A number of the contributions from delegates were imbued with a sense of a bright new future for Britain and for Europe. For example, Michael Stewart, prospective parliamentary candidate for East Fulham, argued that the old balance of power politics was obsolete and should be replaced by democracy in the political arena and socialist planning in the economic sphere. Stewart further suggested that greater contact was required between Labour and its Continental comrades: Britain's future was clearly in Europe.[14]

Even at this early stage, there was a hidden tension between the idealism of many of the delegates and the pragmatism of the leadership, a number of whom had been key members of the wartime coalition.[15] H. M. Drucker stresses that the idealism (ethos) of Labour was often an unwritten understanding of the party's spirit, as opposed to the elaborated set of programmatic ideas (pragmatism). Herbert Morrison and Attlee both gave a strong defence of *international* peace based upon co-operation between Britain, the USA and the USSR. The most telling contribution came from Bevin, who eventually became Foreign Secretary in the Attlee administration. In his lengthy speech, Bevin stressed a most pragmatic view of foreign policy, emphasizing Anglo-Commonwealth relations – over and above any potential Anglo-Continental formulation – as being the touchstone of Britain's foreign policy.[16]

After Labour's somewhat unexpected election victory of July 1945, many of the party's new intake of MPs took the opportunity to voice the hopes they had for the post-war European settlement. For example, Michael Foot in his maiden Commons speech urged the government to act as an ideological beacon – a 'subtle magnet' – for its European socialist comrades. Labour Britain should provide an example of what practical democratic socialism could achieve.[17]

During the early months of the Attlee government, the left's expressions on Europe and Britain's centrality to the future of the Continent remained relatively unfocused. However, three interrelated events took place during the eight months of October 1946 to May 1947, which drew together the left's European ideas into an identifiable programme. First, 21 Labour MPs drew up an open letter to the Prime Minister which somewhat tentatively detailed a new European route for Britain. The signatories made five basic points, which in total equated to a distinct framework for a social democratic middle way that could mediate between the superpowers. Moreover, this third force, as it became known, was to be limited to 'countries suitable by tradition and by structure' for social democratic policies. This in turn narrowed the focus to western Europe, rather than geographical Europe.[18] The importance of this document should be not underestimated; Schneer has gone as far as to classify it as 'a crucial document in the history of the post-war Labour left'.[19]

The following month an amendment to the King's Speech was organized by Richard Crossman with the assistance of Michael Foot, Benn Levy, Mark Hewitson, Sydney Silverman and Joe Reeves. Within the amendment, the 'third force' of democratic socialist countries was clearly spelt out, with Britain's future clearly placed as a cornerstone of an independent Europe.[20] The wider support of Crossman's action was shown during the subsequent Commons debate. Although 'the rebels', as they were termed by the national press, agreed not to move the amendment to a vote, the two surviving ILP MPs – John McGovern and Campbell Stephen – called for a division. In total 154 Labour MPs failed to support the government's position either by abstaining or through absence due to illness or overseas travel. This figure represented nearly 40 per cent of the Parliamentary Labour Party (PLP). Interestingly, a sizeable number of Labour's activists countrywide assented to the amendment, indicating the wider support for a differing approach to Anglo-European relations and potentially the germination of a wider questioning of the adherence to 'Britain' within the party.[21]

Following the amendment, a small group of MPs set about defining their policy ideas, both domestic and foreign, more clearly with the aim of presenting their thoughts to the party's conference of May 1947. The result of this action was what is probably the Labour left's most famous document in the post-war era: *Keep Left*. Although it carried the names of 15 MPs, Crossman, Foot and Ian Mikardo took charge of writing the pamphlet.[22] The former took responsibility for the foreign policy section in which he strongly favoured a European third force, eventually organized within a federal structure. The cornerstone of this development was 'an Anglo-French alliance' that would form 'the keystone of the arch of world peace'. Furthermore, under the title 'The Unity of Europe', Crossman noted that

> A Socialist Britain cannot prosper so long as Europe is divided. The goal we should work for is a federation which binds together the nations now under Eastern domination with the peoples of Western Europe . . . For the present it would be wise to concentrate on less spectacular forms of European collaboration.[23]

As was intended, the big test for *Keep Left* came at the party's annual conference held at Margate. However, Labour's National Executive Committee (NEC) responded by publishing a counter-statement, written by Denis Healey, the party's International Secretary. *Cards on the Table* stressed the need for a 'mature understanding' of the government's direction. On the rebels' call for an independent 'European bloc', Healey stated that such a 'policy [was] both undesirable and impractical', partly because of the Soviet dominance of eastern Europe and partly because Germany remained prostrate and divided. In essence, *Cards on the Table* reiterated the government's view of Britain as a world power with global interests.[24]

Both *Keep Left* and Healey's counter-blast formed the backdrop of the foreign affairs debates at conference. The government could call on the support of the majority of the big trade unions and was therefore never in any serious danger of a defeat when it came to voting on a particular motion. Critical resolutions in relation to European unity were easily defeated.[25] However, the importance of *Keep Left* and other pro-European statements and actions – within Parliament and from activists – of the first two years of the Attlee administration is essentially threefold: first, questioning the government's search for a consensual foreign policy; secondly, indicating the existence of a vibrant ideological heterogeneity within the party's ranks; and lastly, suggesting that a federation was the ultimate solution for Europe, which also questions the adherence to Britain, its state and a common sense of citizenship. Where was legitimacy to reside, at the national or the continental level?

June 1947–June 1948

The key event of the second period occurred at its very genesis. The US Secretary of State, George Marshall, gave a historic speech at Harvard University on 5 June which totally recast the relationship between his country and Europe and as a consequence Britain's position in Europe. Marshall's speech recognized the leading role for the USA in European economic reconstruction, provided that the programme for action was initiated by the European nations themselves.[26]

During the subsequent negotiations, Soviet and east European delegates withdrew, leaving Bevin and his French counterpart, Georges Bidault, at the forefront of discussions and the organizations that evolved from the intergovernmental deliberations: in particular, the *functional* Organization for European Economic Co-operation, which was charged with distributing the subsequent funds provided by the Americans. Anglo-French bipartisanship also signified the increasing division between East and West in Europe.[27] In turn, this cemented Anglo-French relations that had been signified by the Dunkirk Treaty of March 1947.[28]

In essence, the European Recovery Programme (ERP), as the Marshall Plan was officially known, forced the Labour Party and the left into opting for one or other of the superpowers. At first the response, as shown by the left's main journals, was generally positive towards the ERP with some division over the position to be taken towards the Soviet Union. *Tribune*, for example, welcomed the 'dollars from heaven' while decrying Soviet intransigence. Kingsley Martin, editor of *New Statesman and Nation*, was no less positive in his response to Marshall's announcement, but stressed the need to avoid an 'anti-Russian economic strategy' at all costs.[29]

At this same juncture the MP R. W. G. Mackay was increasingly publicizing his long-standing support for a federal settlement within Europe, while also stressing that Britain should recognize a new non-global role: suggesting a real challenge to the British state and the post-war foreign policy consensus. He was in fact one of the few contemporaries to tackle seriously the issue of 'Britishness' within a Continental settlement, calling for a federal European settlement based on 'the abrogation . . . of national sovereignty', while also positively engaging with various European federalists who emphasized the common European culture, inclusive of Britain.[30]

Mackay used the fora of the Commons and *Keep Left* to advocate a political and economic federal European construct.[31] However, his most constructive action was the formation of an unofficial parliamentary campaign. The PLP Europe Group held an initial meeting on 13 November 1947, attended by thirteen Labour members. A foundation meeting followed on 2 December, at which it was resolved to form 'a group of members . . . who are interested in promoting the political and economic integration of Europe': a significant step further than the government's functional approach, as witnessed during the Marshall Plan discussions. At its height, the group had the support of a total of 81 MPs, which equated to 20.6 per cent of the PLP, or 25 per cent if one discounts persons ineligible to join due to ministerial position.[32]

However, it was evident from the outset that the group's defining element was the wide heterogeneity of members' attitudes towards the most viable European settlement. Subsequently, the December (foundation) meeting decided that its first task was to 'study and prepare papers on the various aspects of the problem of creating unity in Europe' with the object of finding 'whether a . . . British Socialist foreign policy [could] be constructed in the principle of European Unity'.[33]

Initially, the Europe Group envisaged two position papers. The first would 'consider the practicality of *functional* methods which might immediately be adopted with a view to promoting the integration of Europe'. Meanwhile, a second document was to be prepared 'examining the *political* developments and agreements which would be required to produce European Unity'. Agreement on completed papers proved immensely difficult to achieve, and at a meeting of 10 February 1948 the two papers became three. Aiden Crawley and Crossman were charged with tackling the functional approach; Mackay, Christopher Shawcross and John Hynd considered the federalist approach; and William Warbey and Leah Manning were given the task of expanding upon a third view, or fundamentalist line. They were called fundamentalists because they favoured socialist economic and political planning across all of Europe – East and West.[34]

Before papers could be drafted, however, three events occurred that radically altered the political atmosphere in which any such debate could take place. First, Bevin gave a Commons speech on 22 January 1948, in which he outlined his somewhat confused idea of a 'Western Union'. In essence, the Foreign Secretary saw his vision as a 'practical programme' for safeguarding the 'free nations' of western Europe, the Colonies and the Commonwealth, against the 'communist process'.[35] The second occurrence was of a more international significance: the Czech coup of late February. The Communist takeover caused much consternation within the British labour movement and proved a turning point for the left; more broadly, it cemented East–West divisions within the Continent.[36] For Bevin and the Labour government, the actions of the Communists only added to the urgency of creating a military organization capable of resisting any forthcoming pressure. To this end, Britain, France and the Benelux countries signed the Brussels Treaty, on 17 March 1948: the third event. The treaty engaged its participants 'in mutual collective self-defence over the next fifty years'.[37]

The Europe Group met on 2 March within this atmosphere of increased Continental and global tension and with the Foreign Secretary's concept of a Western Union now setting the agenda for European discussions within the Labour Party. Mackay, Shawcross, Silverman and Hynd presented the first paper, which argued clearly for a federal Europe that would eventually incorporate the sixteen ERP nations, Germany, Spain, Portugal and the eight other states of eastern Europe. Britain, argued Mackay and his group, should recognize its changed economic and political situation and become a key part of a 'new state of federation of Western Europe', at this formative stage. Such a federation would 'have power to legislate with respect to external affairs, defence, essential services, money, finance, customs and excise, economic and industrial matters and social services'. Hence it would be a fully blown federal (west) European state. Crucially, Mackay and his colleagues stated that to arrive at such a body required socialists to work with other political parties both in Britain and on the Continent, placing the issue of European integration uppermost in discussions: in essence, what could be termed a 'Europe first' approach. Further, such an argument clearly represented a challenge to the hegemony of the British state to control key economic, political and social aspects of British life by placing key responsibilities with European institutions. Additionally, the proto-European identity was placed above any British one.[38]

Crawley presented the functional approach within a second paper. He suggested that Mackay had seriously underestimated the urgency of the economic situation both in Britain and western Europe. Resources needed to be pooled and planned with like-minded countries. Crawley put his argument succinctly thus: 'what has been called the "functional approach" means simply that the situation is so desperate that we must try and increase the efficiency of production in western European countries as quickly as possible'. Future co-operation with eastern Europe was rejected due to the intransigence that Crawley envisaged would arise from these now communist-controlled nations. Hence, Europe was first and foremost seen as an economic construct, with economic concerns given primacy. Interestingly, Crawley's paper showed a marked absence of analysis of political questions. Such a proposition clearly left the British state relatively untouched, with little power being ceded to the European level: a 'Britain first' approach.[39]

Manning and Warbey presented the third proposal at the Europe Group meeting. The fundamentalists opened by arguing for a neutral 'third grouping of countries' not committed to either one of the superpowers, acting as a force capable of preserving peace. Further, they agreed with Crawley's analysis of the immediate economic problems that required short-term 'independent national action'. However, a longer-term solution was required, involving Continent-wide economic co-operation allied with European countries' 'associated dominions and overseas territories'. Manning and Warbey also examined political developments within the context of Bevin's support for Western Union. The fundamentalists argued that any 'Anglo-American military alliance' that followed from more detailed discussions of union would only be supported by reactionary regimes: Spain, Portugal, Greece and Turkey. Left-wing governments in, for example, Sweden, Denmark and Norway would oppose such a construct. Additionally, in a number of other countries, such as Holland, France and Italy, socialist forces were at present weak. Therefore, support for a political federation firstly required a 'revival of socialist political strength in Europe': a socialism-first approach to Europe.[40]

The lack of agreement between Europe Group members was indicated by the fact that the meeting of the 2 March was to be the last that the group held. It split into three tendencies: functionalists, federalists and fundamentalists. Crawley, Crossman and Foot along with the bulk of the group (and Labour Party) increasingly championed the survival of social democracy by a defensive military alliance to counter the Soviet threat, thus aligning themselves with Bevin. Mackay and Shawcross continued to canvass support for the federalist position, creating an all-party group of MPs in favour of European Union that in turn was part of the international European Parliamentary Union.[41] Despite the frosty attitude adopted by the Labour Party, Mackay and his federal colleagues also attended the Hague Congress (May 1948), called by a number of bodies across the political spectrum to further the cause of European co-operation.[42]

Warbey, Manning and others held to the fundamentalist position and embarked upon a new undertaking: the unofficial PLP Socialist Europe Group (SEG). The SEG in turn had developed from a successful composite motion at Labour's 1948 annual conference. Fenner Brockway, who had rejoined the Labour Party from the ILP early in 1947, raised a resolution that argued for the fundamental approach. His motion called for a full 'socialist programme of economic and political co-operation among the

European countries, leading towards the establishment of the United Socialist States of Europe' (USSE): a sentiment that was supported by a large number of delegates.[43] Hugh Dalton, replying on behalf of the NEC recognized this wide-ranging advocacy and accepted Brockway's resolution, subject to 'certain cautionary notes'.[44]

The development of these tendencies will be further developed in the next section. At this juncture it is worth briefly evaluating the influence of the Europe Group. In the four months of its existence, the group had given its members a valuable forum in which they could work out their respective positions on European issues. Operating at a time of unprecedented international events, it is not surprising that many took the 'easy' option and opted to support military-economic structures to defend the gains of social democracy. However, the debates within the group, although achieving little concrete in terms of government policy, do indicate a diversity of ideas about Europe the importance of which is often downplayed or ignored by historians.[45]

Returning to Labour's European discussions, international events once again set the agenda for European discussions within the Labour Party. On 18 and 24 July respectively, the road and rail links between the western-controlled zones of Germany and West Berlin were cut by the Soviet authorities, leading to what became known as the Berlin Airlift. The Cold War had taken on a sharper degree of confrontation.[46]

July 1948–June 1950

In July 1948, following the successful USSE motion at the previous month's LPAC, Warbey and six of his colleagues organized themselves into the SEG, with the aim of further propagandizing the fundamentalist position. Their first action was to arrange a number of local conferences to publicize their approach within the Labour Party and the wider labour movement.[47] Warbey's contribution at one such meeting indicated the construct that he envisaged for Europe:

> We must aim at a unitary European Union, rather than a federal 'United States'. Federal constitutions belong to the days when central authorities were not expected to do anything positive. In the modern world we need a central authority with full powers in the economic field, as well as in defence and external relations.[48]

To further their cause, and as a response to the immediacy of the global tension focused on Europe, and Germany in particular, created by the Berlin crisis, the SEG published a detailed statement. *Stop the Coming*

War was signed by fifteen Labour MPs but essentially drafted by Warbey and Silverman. The pamphlet argued for a neutralist position *vis-à-vis* the superpowers. A 'socialist economic plan' was suggested that in practice was to be a scheme for a western European group that had full trade agreements with a corresponding group in eastern Europe. Furthermore, to carry out such a plan required decisions to be made by a similarly centralized political authority. Hence at this juncture (late 1948) the SEG placed all their hopes – political and economic – at the Continental level rather than with the British state.[49]

During the latter part of 1948, other members of the Labour Party, such as the majority of the PLP Europe Group and constituency activists continued to stress their increasing support for the foreign policy of Bevin against the 'communist threat'. This meant upholding the functional approach that Bevin and his ministerial colleagues favoured towards Europe. The most visible arenas for this support were the main journals of the Left, *Tribune*, under the editorship of Foot, and *New Statesman*.[50] Crossman, writing in the former, spoke for many of those previously critical of Bevin's policies. When forced to defend the record of *Keep Left*, he argued that the foreign policy objectives of the pamphlet had been 'completely outdated' in the case of 'an independent third force between Russia and America' by the 'Harvard speech, the Marshall Plan, and the Russian refusal to co-operate in it'. These events, allied with the government's lead in pronouncing a Western Union, meant according to Crossman that *Keep Left* had fulfilled its purpose.[51]

On 4 April 1949 the North Atlantic Treaty was signed by the five signatories of the Brussels agreement in addition to the USA and Canada. The bulk of Bevin's 'critics' lent their support to the treaty, indicating the further abandonment of any kind of (west) European independent third force and concomitant questioning of the government's foreign policy.[52] In turn, the indirect ideological challenge to the legitimacy of the British state that this critical stance implied became even less of a concern, with the exception of individuals such as Mackay and Warbey. A Commons motion in support of the North Atlantic Treaty, proposed by the government, showed the lack of parliamentary opposition to Bevin's foreign policy. When the MPs passed through the lobbies, 333 votes were cast in support, and only 6 against. Included among the 'ayes' were many who had previously been the backbone of the third force and the PLP Europe Group: Crawley, Foot, Hynd, Levy, Mackay, Manning, Reeves and Shawcross.[53] What public criticism there was, was only minor. Warbey, for example, pointed to the expected dominance of the USA within the North Atlantic Treaty Organization (Nato); the potential inclusion of non-democratic countries, like Portugal; the possibility of allowing non-geographically congruent countries to join, such as Italy; and the strategic concerns of suggesting Norway as a future member of Nato.[54]

The proceedings of the 1949 LPAC were dominated by discussions of the party's election manifesto, *Labour Believes in Britain*.[55] Published by the NEC, the document unsurprisingly championed the government's achievements. However, what was most evident – although not a new departure – was the way in which the Labour leadership had, within the pamphlet, 'nationalized' their vision of socialism. *Labour Believes* was glowing in its tributes to the government's successes, which, it argued, had arisen as a direct result of the vibrancy of the party's social democracy. In turn, Labour's auspicious governance had given the *British people*, and Britain, rather than the working class, a bright future. The NEC was in essence attempting a cross-class approach: a people's party.[56] Furthermore, its very title suggested a focus that was only concerned with domestic events: an indication of the increasingly defensive mentality prevalent within (British) social democracy during the early phase of the Cold War.[57]

This latter condition also affected the bulk of those MPs previously critical of Bevin. *Labour Believes* argued strongly for European recovery and closer co-operation being aligned with the twin factors of military strength through Western Union, and the dollars provided by ERP. As to what form European co-operation would take, *Labour Believes* stressed that prudence was needed – that is, slow functional measures. 'Without a steady march towards closer European unity in the coming years, none of the States in Western Europe can hope to make their economies strong and prosperous.'[58] Discussions at the LPAC were overwhelmingly supportive of *Labour Believes* and Bevin.[59] At best what opposition there was had become, in Schneer's apt phraseology, a 'subterranean presence'.[60]

The next tester for the various visions of Europe held by the Labour government and the left arrived two months after the party's conference closed. Following discussions by the foreign ministers of the nations party to the Brussels Treaty, a Council of Europe (COE), comprising a Council of Foreign Ministers and a Consultative Assembly was agreed upon. At the demand of Bevin and the British negotiators, the deliberations of the former were to remain secret, whereas the latter was to be purely advisory in nature and with members chosen by governments rather than being a genuine European parliament, as had been proposed by France and Belgium. Strasbourg was chosen as the site for the COE; a highly symbolic venue on the Franco-German border.[61]

The first Strasbourg Assembly opened on 10 August. Labour's delegation, led by Herbert Morrison, contained a number of MPs who, at one time or another, had supported a 'third force' approach to Europe: Cocks, Crawley, Maurice Edelman and Mackay.[62] All were subsequently deemed 'loyal' to the government's position on Europe, especially in supporting the functional approach during assembly discussions.[63] The Labour delegates also presented their case to the COE's Committee on General Affairs. Welcoming 'the functional road towards European unity', the delegates cautioned:

> we cannot, at least in the immediate future . . . support proposals for European federation . . . this means that we cannot agree to hand over to a supranational authority for Western Europe the power to decide, by a majority vote, against our will, questions which we regard as vital to our economy and fundamental interests, and to those of the Commonwealth and Sterling Area.[64]

How Labour's chief 'federalist' – Mackay – reacted to such a statement is not known. However, a tantalizing glimpse is provided by his personal papers where, in a letter to Crossman, he exasperatedly remarked that he had to 'put up with a great deal at the hands of Dalton [Morrison's deputy at Strasbourg] & co'.[65]

The Labour left's wider reaction to the COE revealed the falling support for the third force. Once again a number of articles in *Tribune* and *New Statesman* were indicative. Moreover, Edelman, writing in his local evening newspaper, expressed the main tenet of the functional argument thus: 'we believe that European unity can be brought about not by an absolute and immediate surrender of sovereignty, but by co-operation through specific organisations for purposes of common interest'.[66]

From the fundamentalist camp, Warbey and Silverman sent a strategy paper on behalf of the SEG to the Labour delegates attending the COE. A number of key points were made. First, the authors stressed that the functional versus federal argument was an out-of-date antithesis; what was required was a dual approach incorporating both. Secondly, Warbey and Silverman deemed that progress within the economic sphere was the *sine qua non* for an effective European Union. A third, central point called for the establishment of a 'strong centralised political authority of the unitary type', based on a 'constitution for a European Political Union', as opposed to the 'loose federal' approach favoured by conservatives, liberals and some socialists within the Consultative Assembly. However, for such a programme to be effective required a 'European socialist parliamentary group' that would draw support from the differing political groupings. Hence, in total therefore, the SEG was still looking towards the Continental level, and not Britain, to solve the fundamental paradigm. This framework questioned Labour's foreign policy consensus and the governing role of the British state. Ultimately, defending 'Britain' or 'Britishness' remained an unimportant consideration for the SEG, reflecting its internationalist perspective.[67]

Keep Left had originally been organized in 1947 as an informal group of MPs who were concerned over the government's domestic and foreign policies. During the summer months of 1949 a more formal arrangement was reached which brought together a fresh group to discuss the 'major political issues of the day and the programme for 1950–5'.[68] This new faction was comprised of a number from *Keep Left*'s previous incarnation and an injection of 'new blood'.[69] A new tract was issued in January 1950, selling more than 30,000 copies in two months.[70] *Keeping Left* publicized the functional left's thinking across a broad range of issues. For the purposes of this paper, the dominance of military and defence issues indicated the shift away from the idealism of a 'subtle magnet' approach adopted by Foot *et al.*, particularly throughout 1945–7. Secondly, the weakened position in which the wider European left now found itself, in conjunction with the accompanying rise of Christian Democratic parties, severely dented any chance of a third force. The stark issue was now one of the survival of social democracy in the conflict with its two rival political ideologies – *laissez-faire* capitalism and Communism.[71]

On 9 May 1950 the French Foreign Minister, Robert Schuman, announced plans to integrate the coal and steel industries of France and the infant West German state, in the ECSC. An invitation was also given to any other nation that wished to take part in the project. The Labour government's response was one of initial hostility and ultimately, following a Cabinet meeting of 2 June, rejection. This was due partly to the measures being announced without prior consultation, and more importantly for the functionalist Bevin and his colleagues, to the supranationality that the 'Schuman Plan' proposed.[72]

The functional left, meanwhile, was generally in favour of the Schuman Plan. *Tribune*, for example, noted that the plan would secure peace, and that overall the proposals adhered to 'co-operation of specific economic commitments', which was welcome. *New Statesman* was no less positive. Under the title 'M. Schuman to the Rescue?' an editorial welcomed the proposals and especially the implied *entente* between Germany and France.[73]

One of the most famous, or infamous, aspects of the British response to the Schuman proposals was the publication by the Labour Party on 13 June of *European Unity*, a pamphlet that was highly critical of the French Foreign Minister's plan. Although the work had been written by Healey, and redrafted by Dalton, rather than the government or the NEC, the positions outlined were deeply indicative of the attitude of many within the party at this juncture.[74] In essence, the pamphlet posted the usual responses to any unity other than strictly intergovernmental functional measures: 'The Labour Party considers that it is neither possible nor desirable under existing circumstances to form a complete Union, political or economic . . . Instead national policies must be progressively harmonised or co-ordinated by consent through co-operation between governments.' Hence, the Labour government's functional position was defended. Moreover, what was envisaged was 'international planning', which could 'only operate on the basis of national planning': a statement that once again exposed the 'British dimension' within Labour's European considerations.[75]

The response to *European Unity* from the bulk of the left and Labour's activists revealed the adherence to the functional position across the party.[76] What dissent there was remained small. Mackay and Hynd upheld the federal position within subsequent Commons debates organized to discuss the Schuman proposals. The former stressed the need for 'full economic integration' and the obsolescence of the nation state as found in western Europe. 'The currency, the basic industries and the trade of Western Europe can no longer be cabined and confined within the narrow framework of 15 or 16 national States.'[77] Harold Davies and Silverman meanwhile defended the fundamentalist position, stressing the issue of co-operation between eastern and western Europe, around the concern of using Polish coal within any structures forthcoming from Schuman.[78]

But ultimately, by June 1950, federalist and fundamentalist positions were minority positions within the Labour Party. The dominance of the Labour government and the disciplining effects of the Cold War set the agenda for European discussions.

Concluding remarks

The ideas that were expounded on Europe during 1945–50 by many of Bevin's foreign policy critics, as addressed above, form a large pool of alternative 'European visions' that are more often downplayed by historians of the Attlee period. Periodically, these ideological trends coalesced into identifiable groups, such as the PLP Europe Group, the SEG or most famously *Keep Left*. The ideas relating to Europe that were held by Labour Party members in the late 1940s did not remain static, suggesting an ideological vitality. Changes in opinion occurred throughout the period, leading to convergence between, for example, the leadership and a majority of the (functional) left. The disciplining effects of the Cold War cannot be ignored.

The suggestions made by supporters of federal, fundamental and, to a lesser extent, functional positions also question the adherence to the British state during the period.[79] Questioning Britain's independence and placing economic, social and political functions with the European sphere suggests an evolving conception of the nation (Britain), at least in the short term. Furthermore, such discussions bring into focus the adherence to a common conception of 'Britishness'. However, with a few notable exceptions (Mackay and Warbey), contemporaries did not explore these issues in any great detail. This omission occurred despite Labour's frequent assertion of being part of the international socialist movement.

Complementary to this basic questioning by Mackay and others of Britishness, a national identity, was a rudimentary search for a (west) European identity. The suggestion of a different 'focal point' for citizenship raises the question of the processes that (may) occur when social cohesion is challenged from outside the geographic boundaries of, in this case, Britain.[80] Ultimately, such potential fissures were subsumed within the wider international issues contained within the Cold War. However, it is clear that the Labour Party's vibrant European debates raised a number of problems relating to the state and social cohesion in the early post-war years – issues that still require resolution at the opening of the twenty-first century.

4

The Pigmentocracy of Citizenship: Assimilation, Integration or Alienation?

Michael Dawswell

This chapter will examine the impact that migration of black British sub-jects[1] had on British society during the post-war period mainly from the 1950s to the end of the 1970s. It will focus on citizenship, or the lack of it, and how the reclassification of black migrants from subject to alien af-fected their sense of belonging, status and identity within British society.

It is the assertion of this chapter that 'citizenship', both in the legal and broader sense, is nothing more than a socially constructed strategy used by nation states to create a socially cohesive homogeneous national com-munity.[2] This is based on the principles of shared heritage, cultural knowledge, language and ethnicity, and excludes those who do not share these characteristics. For black migrants who entered Britain as citizens from the British West Indies during the post-war period, their status as British subjects and all the rights that this status conferred were under-mined by the racism and discrimination they experienced, to the extent that their citizenship and citizenship rights – social, political and civil – became illusionary.[3]

This chapter will demonstrate how the British state, using a succession of immigration controls and race relations legislation from 1948 to 1968, devalued the status of citizen for the black members of the Empire while attempting to assimilate and then integrate the black migrants living in Britain. It will also demonstrate that the efforts of successive Labour and Conservative governments to integrate black citizens, thus maintaining a socially cohesive national community, ultimately failed, and show how this failure effectively alienated black migrants within a country they re-garded as the 'motherland'.

The ideology of belonging to a community or society has become cen-tral to the maintenance of a socially cohesive community or society.

Today, belonging has a formal and legal manifestation: citizenship.[4] In post-industrial societies, citizenship has become one of the foundations of nation and nationhood.

Notions of citizenship are intimately linked to identity and belonging. The status of being a citizen, or a non-citizen, affects every aspect of an individual's life politically, socially and economically. The interplay between citizenship and nationality (a collective identity that the people of the nation acquire by identifying with the nation)[5] is used by ruling elites or the state as a barometer to determine an individual's identity, their ability to access scarce resources (services) and the nature of the relationship that the individual or community has with the state.

The concept of citizenship incorporates notions both of rights and of obligations. The first is a trade-off for the second: a person has the rights of citizenship if they carry out the duties of citizenship. Over the years and with the creation of the welfare state, British society has embodied contrasting and in many respects contending notions of citizenship that have rendered the rights and obligations of citizenship mutually exclusive. The first sees citizenship as a status where a citizen is entitled to certain rights and resources irrespective of whether they make a contribution or not. The second places less emphasis on rights and focuses instead on obligation, virtue and contribution. Citizenship is achieved through contribution; an individual does not and cannot have a right to the resources of society unless they contribute to the development of that society through work or other socially valued activities, if they are in a position to do so.[6] The first conception of citizenship played the dominant role concerning who is entitled to state resources throughout the post-war period.

In Britain, like many other modern democratic societies, one of the state's primary functions is to maintain social order and a cohesive society, which in turn legitimises the sovereignty of the state. It has been argued that the state no longer represents the interests of all the people it governs, but only the maintenance of social order and cohesion, which serves the interests of political elites. This situation causes tensions and strains within society between the state and groups or communities that have been excluded. Throughout the post-war period in Britain, the regular influx of people of different ethnicities, religions and languages extenuated these tensions, resulting in tears in the social fabric that manifested themselves in open conflict between the state and its people: for example, in the Notting Hill and Brixton riots of 1958 and 1981 respectively.

The fundamental principle of citizenship is to create an equality of status with respect to the rights and duties that are attached to full membership of a community. Citizenship promotes this equality by creating a sense of an imagined horizontal comradeship[7] and social cohesion. This type of egalitarianism occurs despite the actual inequality and exploitation that may prevail within a community on the basis of class and gender, which accentuates the differences between communities and individuals. Once people within a community can exercise their civil, political and social rights on an equal footing, economic exploitation, gender differences and class inequalities become less oppressive and naturalized.

After the Second World War, the migration of black peoples from the Commonwealth and colonies to Britain brought an influx of many different socio-political and religious groups. Their differences were further exacerbated by new integers of race and culture. These new integers would not easily be absorbed by the British nation. West Indian migration to Britain challenged the notion of a socially cohesive, homogeneous national community, and later radically changed ideas of Britishness and subjecthood.

The experience of many black migrants in Britain over the past 50 years has been described as of one of endless economic exploitation, political racism, disenfranchisement and exile.[8] Notions of citizenship have profoundly influenced their relationship to British society. Black migrants have been denied full citizenship rights, equal access to services, equal treatment in the eyes of the law and in some cases a right to a minimum standard of living. This has been effected through a system of both institutionalized racism and overt discrimination. Black migrants are not viewed as full citizens because of their physical and cultural differences from the general British population.

For black migrants, the effect of exclusion and second-class status was effectively to marginalize and socially exclude them from mainstream British society. As a result of this disenfranchisement, the self-identity formed by many black people is one born out of social exclusion.

The 'black invasion'

Before 1948 and the arrival of the *Empire Windrush*, carrying several hundred people from the West Indies seeking employment, there already existed small settlements of black migrants in cities such as Liverpool and Cardiff. These settlements had been established mainly by colonial seamen during the First World War. Even though small pockets of non-white migrant communities had been present in Britain since the beginning of the twentieth century, including Asian settlements in

Manchester and London's East End, British citizenship was still based on the myth of a racially homogeneous national community with a shared heritage and cultural knowledge. Immigration from eastern and western Europe was also prevalent during the years before the Second World War. These European migrant workers were not citizens and did not enjoy the rights of citizenship. They were labelled as aliens and were therefore subject to strict immigration controls under the Aliens Act (1905) and later under the Nationality and Status of Aliens Act (1914).[9]

The policy of successive Labour and Conservative governments towards foreign labour, especially European labour, before the Second World War was directed by the forces of demand and supply. When labour was required, immigration controls were relaxed to increase the supply of foreign workers. Through a period of naturalization, these foreign nationals could obtain the rights of citizenship and permanent settlement. It was assumed that in order for assimilation to be successful, European immigrants would only have to show a willingness to identify themselves with the British state and the idea of a British nation. When the demand for labour decreased, the state tightened controls and put in place a work permit system. This allowed migrants a fixed duration of work and residence, usually a year, after which they were sent back to their county of origin, thus signifying that they were not permanent members of the British national community.[10]

Immediately after the war, the immigration of European migrants into Britain was encouraged. European migrant labour was used to help rebuild and 'kick start' the British economy. By 1947, a scheme to recruit European volunteer workers (EVWs), 'Operation Westward Ho', was in operation. This scheme recruited labour from two sources: 'displaced persons' in Germany, Austria and Italy who were seeking refuge – there were 720,000 of these, the vast majority being Poles, Balts and Yugoslavs; and secondly, some of the unemployed from European countries.[11] The Polish Resettlement Act (1947) assisted in the settlement of 142,000 ex-Polish servicemen and their families, and ensured their smooth integration into the housing and labour markets.[12]

The post-war Labour government favoured European labour and resisted the introduction of a black workforce to resolve Britain's labour shortage because it was assumed that white European labour would be more skilled and valuable to British society than black labour. The government also preferred EVWs because they were subject to very strict labour controls and could be prosecuted or deported if they broke their conditions of recruitment.[13]

The Labour government used various strategies to discourage the immigration of British citizens from the West Indies, while going to great lengths and expense to recruit European workers. Such a resistance to black labour went far beyond the defensive struggles of white workers to retain their hard-won, more secure position in the labour process. Within the post-war state – indeed, within the pre-war state – there was tremendous opposition to the use of black labour.[14]

However, 1947 saw the arrival of SS *Ormonde* to British shores, carrying 110 Jamaican workers. Immediately, the Ministry of Labour visited the Caribbean in an attempt to discourage further migration by explaining that the 'paper vacancies' that people had seen advertised in England were not real jobs at all, but merely temporary vacancies for individuals changing jobs.[15]

The arrival of the *Empire Windrush* in June 1948, with 492 Jamaicans on board, further brought into question the notions of subjecthood and Britishness. Their distinctive cultural and racial nature was such a cause for concern that, on 22 June, Labour MPs sent a letter to the Prime Minister, Clement Attlee, voicing their fears at the impending black invasion:

> This country [Britain] may become an open reception centre for immigrants not selected in respect to health, education, training, character, customs and above all, whether assimilation is possible or not. The British people fortunately enjoy a profound unity without uniformity in their way of life, and are blest by the absence of a colour racial problem. An influx of coloured people domiciled here is likely to impair the harmony, strength and cohesion of our social life and to cause discord and unhappiness among all concerned.[16]

The resistance to black labour in Britain was motivated not only by economic concerns, but also by the 'otherness' of black labour and the imperial legacy of British history, which involved the conquest and enslavement of African, Indian and Caribbean people. The attitudes of the British political elite towards black migrants were structured by notions of Empire and the fact that these migrants were, until the late 1960s, still subject peoples of the crown.

The fears of the post-war Labour government ranged from notions of a 'black invasion' and an eventual 'colour' problem within British society to concerns about the possibility of assimilation and integration of black migrants. Biologically deterministic arguments were also used in an attempt to exclude black migrants from becoming a part of the British workforce. Notions that black people were biologically inferior and not of the right stock echoed around the halls of Westminster. Nevertheless, in 1948 the Nationality Act was passed, which did not impose any colour bar restrictions and allowed the free movement of citizens within the British Empire and Commonwealth.

Although Britain needed a large supply of labour to help rebuild the economy after the war, the Labour government hoped that many West Indian citizens would not want to come to Britain because of the expense of migrating and differences in climate and culture. It appears to have overlooked the fact that migration to find employment has been a feature of the Caribbean since the abolition of slavery. Moreover, imposing a colour restriction would have been visibly racist and might have alienated well over half of the British Empire, especially at a time when there was a rise in colonial nationalism.

In the years immediately after 1948, government hopes that there would be no large-scale black immigration were fulfilled and there was what can be described as only a trickle of migration from the Caribbean. It was indeed expensive to travel to Britain – people needed time to save the required funds to pay for the trip. Even though the migration to Britain has been described by some as the adventure of a lifetime, there was also an element of fear. Many potential Caribbean migrants would wait for reports from those who had already gone to Britain before they made their decision.

It was not until the post-war reconstruction and the expansion of the British economy during the 1950s and 1960s that black labour was recruited to work in Britain by British industry. At that time, labour shortages were so acute that they could not be filled by the preferred sources of labour, British, Irish or other white European workers. Even at this stage, however, the recruitment of black migrants was driven by industry, which required black labour to fill vacancies in unattractive industries,[17] and not by government policy. The recruitment of black labour also coincided with developments in the USA and the Caribbean. Until 1952 the USA was a more logical destination for West Indian migrants than Britain. But in that year the McCarran–Walter Act imposed tighter immigration controls, effectively stopping the flow of migration from the Caribbean to the USA. The closure of the USA, coupled with the worsening employment situation in the Caribbean, made Britain an attractive destination.

In 1956, about 30,000 West Indians entered Britain, and in the same year arrangements were made by London Transport and the British Hotels and Restaurants Association with the authorities in Barbados to recruit labour to Britain.[18] Far from being welcomed as a necessary and valuable addition to the British labour force, however, West Indian migrants were regarded by the British government and populace as lazy, intellectually and academically inferior, not civilized and even criminal.[19]

Although black labour was necessary for maintaining economic growth in Britain, the Conservative governments of 1951–64, like the previous

Labour governments of 1945–51, resisted black immigration. Hitherto a large proportion of the immigrants coming to Britain from the West Indies consisted of friends, neighbours and even fellow church members who had been told by black migrants already living Britain about the employment prospects in Britain. However, as Caribbean migrants were British subjects, they were not entitled to receive government assistance to find employment or housing, as EVWs did. The government assumed that because of the racism, discrimination and hardship that Caribbean migrants who were already in Britain faced, they would write to their friends and family in the Caribbean persuading them not to migrate to Britain.[20]

Another informal method used by the government to stem the tide of black migrants was to control immigration at source. Officials tried to persuade the Jamaican and Barbadian governments to issue an ever-decreasing number of British passports to black migrants.[21] However, this idea was rejected by the Jamaican Prime Minister, Norman Manly, and the Barbadian Prime Minister, Carl Lacorbiniere, who argued that immigration control was a matter for the British government.[22]

By 1955 there was a private consensus between a number of Labour MPs and the Conservative government that black immigration to Britain had reached unsustainable levels and immigration controls had to be considered. Publicly, however, the Prime Minister, Sir Anthony Eden, stated that there was no question of any action being taken to control immigration and that in any case the largest immigration was from Ireland, at the rate of approximately 60,000 per year.[23]

By 1958, with migration from the West Indies to Britain at its peak, tensions between black migrants and the general population were at their height. In the summer of 1958 there were days of violent attacks on West Indians in the west London area of Notting Hill and in Nottingham.[24] Government officials, who had held secret meetings throughout the late 1940s and early 1950s about the impending 'coloured' problem, were now publicly vocal about the threat of black immigration to the harmony and the homogeneity of the British way of life. Black immigration was viewed as a major threat to the purity of white Britain.[25] The measures proposed by the government in an attempt to keep Britain white ranged from greater immigration controls (the method favoured by state officials and the Conservative government elected in 1959) to forced repatriation of all non-British people (the main, and probably the only, policy of the British neo-fascist party).[26]

In response to public outcry and Conservative backbench demands for greater immigration controls, the Conservative government passed into law the Commonwealth Immigrants Act (1962). This Act sought to control the immigration of all Commonwealth citizens except those born in Britain, those holding passports issued by the British government and those included on the passport of a person exempt from controls under the previous measures. In reality, this meant that immigration controls provided by the Commonwealth Immigrants Act did not apply to Commonwealth citizens from the older Dominions, such as Canada, Australia and New Zealand. These territories were excluded from control because many of the migrants were of white British origin or descent, and the idea of controlling the immigration of white British subjects was, and still is, inconceivable for many.[27]

The Commonwealth Immigrants Act was not well received by the Labour and Liberal Parties. It was strongly opposed by Hugh Gaitskell, the leader of the Labour Party, by the Liberals and by some traditionalist Conservative MPs because it was visibly racist.[28] In differentiating between citizens of the older Dominions and those of the New Commonwealth, the 1962 Act transformed the status of subsequent West Indian migrants from that of migrant settlers to migrant contract workers.[29] By 1962 the term 'Commonwealth citizen' had become an accepted phrase to describe immigrants from the Commonwealth who were not white. The terms 'migrant', 'immigrant' and 'immigration' had also become synonymous with black migrants and black immigration.[30]

Policies of social cohesion

The mandate provided by the Commonwealth Immigrants Act also attempted to solve another problem. For the Conservative government, the threat to social cohesion from the immigration of a black workforce came from their perceived inability to assimilate into British society. Like European migrants, the assimilation of black immigrants was dependent on them accepting British culture. However, for their assimilation to be successful, black migrants were also reliant on white British citizens, accepting their presence as legitimate and inevitable.[31]

The Conservative government assumed that it was the regular influx of ever-increasing numbers of black settlers into Britain that created the main bulk of the problems associated with their assimilation, especially the growing friction between these migrants and the white British population. The government decided that limiting the numbers of black migrants would make the task of assimilating them into British society easier. Introducing smaller numbers of black settlers into the country would make them far more acceptable and less threatening to the host population.

Limiting the number of black immigrants would also solve the problem of their growing militancy and resistance to British culture. It was believed that lower numbers settling in Britain would make it easier to control and police the black migrants already in the country. Without the regular influx of new black settlers, who had not gone through the assimilation process and who might promote subversive ideas, it was thought that the seeds of militancy would soon disappear.[32]

In an effort to assist the assimilation of black migrants, the government created a series of advisory councils, committees and boards in an attempt to promote race relations and greater racial harmony.[33] However, like the Commonwealth Immigrants Act, the advisory councils, committees and boards were guided by the notion that black labourers were not of the 'right' stock and that their presence in Britain was a threat to the social and cultural character of Britain.[34] Black workers were seen as being unsuitable for outdoor work during the winter, owing to their susceptibility to colds and the more serious chest and lung ailments. They were believed to be unreliable and lazy, with a poor attitude to work.[35] Black men, in particular, were regarded as a real threat. They were portrayed as sexually promiscuous, violent and aggressive, and therefore a danger to British society. These stereotypes were constructed not only on cultural differences, but also on physical differences.

The purported physical differences were products of the enlightenment period and the nineteenth-century eugenics movement, which characterized black people as a different and inferior racial group according to colour and physiognomy.[36] The idea that this biologically and culturally inferior and barbaric race needed to be civilized by way of direct rule was one of the founding principles of the British Empire. However, British society felt secure in the knowledge that the 'other' was over there and not on 'our' shores.

Even though these supposed differences between black migrants and the British population appeared very real to state officials and to large sections of the British population after the Second World War, the migration of culturally distinct people to Britain was not a new or recent phenomenon. Many of the immigrants involved with the EVW schemes were considered culturally distinct, since they did not speak English as a first language and they maintained customs and practices that were considered alien to the British way of life. However, the migration and permanent settlement of people from European countries including Germany, Italy, Hungary and Cyprus was not considered a cultural or racial threat even though their culture, religion and language were very different from those of British people.[37] They were initially viewed as outsiders or even intruders, but they were of the right racial characteristics to be eventually assimilated into British society.

The policy of assimilation was directed at all migrants, but meant in particular that black migrants, especially Asian migrants who were regarded as the most culturally distinct, had to conform completely to British cultural norms and practices, even at the risk of losing their individual identity.[38] This is contrary to the notion of citizenship, which states that those who have full formal rights of citizenship are entitled to express their cultural differences.[39] For many black migrants, their identity, culture and practices were the only element of their lives that they controlled and could use to unite and combat racism and discrimination.[40]

Assimilation did nothing to promote race relations or racial harmony because, while black migrants were told by the state that they were British and not a society apart, racism and discrimination kept them on the margins of British society and excluded them from utilizing their citizenship rights. The process of assimilation imposed a set of values that many black migrants openly reacted against by asserting their own culture, traditions, history and lifestyle. For example, West Indian children could not or would not speak the Queen's English, but spoke a hybrid form of English that was incomprehensible to outsiders.[41] Their actions further alienated them from Britain's mainstream.

Using a Marxist critique, the nature of a capitalist society is such that the working class are discriminated against and denied the full opportunity to exploit their labour. On this account, black migrants were doubly discriminated against as being part of the British working class and also non-white.[42] Racism affected all aspects of black people's lives, particularly employment and housing, but also education and relations with the police and other branches of the criminal justice system. Racism and discrimination polarized black migrants from the British working class and proved to be the major obstacle to their assimilation. The divisions and hostilities between black migrants and the white working class increased the need for race relations legislation. However, removing racial discrimination and banishing colour prejudice would necessitate changing the British people's attitude towards black people. This was something that legislation could not easily achieve.

The white working classes were fearful of the competition for jobs and the economic insecurity that black migrants represented. The myth of the affluent society in the 1950s had inculcated the white working class with middle-class aspirations for a good standard of living, but they were denied the chance of achieving these aspirations because of their lack of economic and political power. The disillusionment of their class position and their frustrations and aggression became directed at black labourers, whom they regarded as illegitimate competitors for jobs, houses and the social benefits of the welfare state.[43]

Assimilation was seen as the great leveller: the British state assumed that, if black migrants were culturally assimilated, the British people would accept them into British society. However, the opposition to the assimilation of black migrants was based not on cultural differences but on racial ones; it was their blackness that was the problem. The attempt to assimilate black migrants created more problems than it solved; in its ignorance of colour and cultural diversity, assimilation maintained social injustice and allowed institutional racism to flourish. By 1965 it was clear to the British state and its people that black migrants were unassimilable into British society.[44]

In 1964 a new Labour government was elected under Harold Wilson. Its members believed that leaving the inclusion of black migrants to the process of naturalization was ineffective. A speech by the Labour MP Roy Hattersley signalled a different approach to the inclusion of black migrants. He stated that West Indians were a part of British culture, an aspect of it, a sub-culture. They spoke the same language, wore the same clothes, followed the same religions. They were not a society apart; only their colour was different. They could be integrated into the mainstream of British society.[45]

The mid-1960s saw a movement away from the process of assimilation towards a policy of integration that emphasized equality of opportunity, cultural diversity and an atmosphere of mutual tolerance.[46] Integration stated that a minority group, while retaining its own culture and religion, would adapt itself to and be accepted as a permanent member of the majority society in all the external aspects of association. The minority would enjoy full political, social and civil rights while performing all the obligations required by their citizenship status as equal citizens, but would remain a separate community with its own language, identity and social structure.[47] The policy of integration and equal opportunity was not exclusive to 'ethnic minorities';[48] it was for everybody, including women and the disabled.

Two pieces of legislation were passed by the Labour government in an effort to promote racial integration. The Race Relations Act (1965) was designed to confront discrimination in public places. It was followed in 1968 by a second Race Relations Act, which outlawed discrimination in employment, housing, credit and insurance facilities. Although the 1965 and 1968 Acts were seen as a step in the right direction by migrant groups, they nevertheless proved weak and were almost impossible to enforce because most of the legislation was oriented towards forms of behaviour.

The Race Relations Board, operating in conjunction with the 1968 Act, had to rely almost entirely on conciliation to obtain redress. It had no powers of enforcement, but could resort to the courts, in extreme cases, to obtain an injunction restraining a defendant from further discriminatory practices.[49] However, without structural change at the grass roots and the enforcement of these provisions by law – for example, making racial discrimination a criminal offence – the Race Relations Act of 1968 proved ineffectual and the Race Relations Board, far from becoming an enforcer, became an educator, educating white British society about race relations.[50]

Following a period of Conservative government, in June 1976 the Labour government passed its third Race Relations Act, which introduced the concepts of institutional discrimination and positive action. The Race Relations Act of 1976 was designed to redress the balance in some areas by discriminating in favour of disadvantaged blacks. The Act combined the Race Relations Board and the Community Relations Council into the Commission for Racial Equality, which had responsibility to combat racial discrimination and promote racial harmony. However, policies of positive discrimination created more problems than they solved. Positive action in favour of ethnic minorities further exacerbated the tensions between them and the white majority.[51]

Policies of integration and, to a lesser extent, equal opportunity were also colour-blind and did nothing to reduce the levels of direct and indirect discrimination.[52] Resources like health, education and employment are finite and exhaustible, and therefore individuals and communities have to compete in order to obtain them. Equality of opportunity does not allow equal access to the resources themselves, only to the information necessary in order to have the opportunity to obtain them. The consumption of services is achieved by those who are successful in competing for them, usually those who are in most need or those who possess the right 'tools'.[53] For black migrants, however, their ability to gain access to scarce resources was also influenced by racism, discrimination and prejudice.

Attempts to achieve equality and therefore integration in housing, education and employment were only partially successful. Black migrants had greater access to council housing, but they were usually housed in the most rundown areas where the council housing was poorly maintained.[54] Similarly, black migrants had equal access to education, but many black children were accepted by schools where the standard of education was very low, and they consequently left school with very few, if any, qualifications.[55] In employment, black migrants were still over-represented in low-skilled, low-paid jobs.

By 1988, ethnic minorities, comprising mainly Indian, West Indian and Pakistani migrants, made up only 4.5 per cent of the total population in Britain. Numbering some 2.5 million, the vast majority were concentrated in the urban areas of the south-east and the Midlands. As a result, many black migrants lived, worked and were educated alongside the host population. However, the areas where black migrants lived were the most deprived and disadvantaged neighbourhoods, such as Brixton, Hackney and Peckham in London, St Paul's in Bristol, Handsworth in Birmingham, Moss Side in Manchester and Toxteth in Liverpool.[56] These migrants lived in very small areas within districts where the majority of the population was white. The same situation was found in the workplace and in schools. Both outside and inside of these urban centres, Britain remained a segregated society.

In a similar way to the Conservative government's policy of assimilation, the Labour government's policy of integration took for granted that the black migrants themselves desired to be fully integrated with the host population. However, black people conceptualized the problems that they faced not primarily as matters of segregation, but as matters of inequality and disparity in access to and ownership of resources and the right to self-determination.[57] Far from integration creating a socially cohesive society, it developed further divisions between black and white. While promoting the integration of black migrants by attempting to stamp out racism, the state allowed discrimination on the basis of citizenship. Therefore it did not deny black migrants access to scarce state resources and services, but discriminated in the quality of these services.

In response to their disenfranchisement, the late 1970s and early 1980s saw the emergence of ideologies of Afrocentrism and black nationalism, especially among the first generation of British-born black citizens. The creation and development of black self-help groups, churches, schools and businesses emphasized difference and self-reliance. Politically, black sections were created within the Labour Party and trade unions to represent black migrants and to campaign for specific policies. This further demonstrated the failure of integration.

In their effort to recalibrate British society and maintain an imaginary cohesive society, to move away from a racially homogenized monocultural society towards a society that embraced ethnic diversity in an atmosphere of mutual tolerance, the integration policies of the 1960s, 1970s and 1980s further displayed the pitfalls of legislating for equality and integration, and against racism, without attempting to educate the white British population and to reconstitute the structures that perpetuate racial inequalities.

Conclusions: illusions, realities and identity

For the black workers who were already settled in Britain by the mid-1960s, their experience of the country, predominantly London and the Midlands, ranged from a land of opportunity where racism and discrimination, although present, did not influence their life choices, to a place where racism and social exclusion characterized every aspect of their lives. Some migrants describe how their emigration to Britain was primarily a success because of the employment opportunities it offered,[58] but other aspects of life in Britain left them bitter and disillusioned, in some cases forcing them to return to the West Indies or to migrate to another country.

The illusion of the 'mother country' was very persuasive for most West Indians. Britain was a country that they belonged to and where they would be treated as equals. 'For me the thought of coming to England was like winning the lottery. I could not wait, but as soon as I came off the boat I knew I was not going to like England. The people, like the weather, were very cold and unfriendly.'[59] The concept of the 'mother country' proved empty of all meaning; it was an artifice.[60] As the migration to Britain increased, the British state became less and less tolerant of black migrants. The devaluation of British citizenship in 1962 formalized an already established perception of black migrants among the British population; their status had fallen from that of British citizens coming to Britain to live and work, to that of aliens who were only here to take 'our' jobs and use 'our' resources. This attitude tarred black migrants and their British-born offspring alike, ensuring that they could not fully utilize their citizenship rights to adequate housing, quality education and employment.

For many of these black migrant settlers, British citizenship only entitled them to passage to England and the right of settlement. Holding a British passport (the physical manifestation of citizenship) entitled them to very little else apart from a duty to uphold the laws of British society. 'Having a British passport meant more in Jamaica than it did here. Me and my friends back home use to talk about England as we belonged there.'[61] The entitlement to state welfare services was distributed in a hierarchical manner with white people first in line. A British citizen was not completely a British citizen if he or she was a black British citizen. 'We were treated differently everywhere like a nobody, the first time I went to a proper restaurant, which was almost 15 years after I arrived, I could not believe the looks I was getting, it was as if they have not seen black people before.'[62]

For the black community, the consequence of their non-participation in the competition for services and their inability to utilize their citizenship rights fully was that they were effectively marginalized and excluded from mainstream British society. Because of this marginalization, the self-identity formed by black people was one that emphasized their social exclusion. Identity formation is a twofold process; it is assigned as well as invented.[63] For black migrants in Britain, the identity assigned to them was one of contradictions: a citizen but not fully a citizen, British yet not fully British, someone who does not really belong.[64] In reaction to this alienation, the identity that is invented, grounded in experience and structured by the social and economic context, is one that generally rejects British society, thus further alienating and marginalizing itself. Identities that were politicized or emphasized difference became a banner under which black migrants could unite.[65]

For some black migrants, their African/West Indian origin became more pronounced; they no longer described themselves as British or English, even though the majority of them held British passports. Due to British society's non-acceptance of black migrants, they viewed their stay in Britain as a temporary one, even though in reality many of them did not possess the financial means to return home. Their descendants, especially during the late 1970s and early 1980s with the rise of Rastafarianism, effectively opted out of white society, forming counter-cultures that are characterized by non-conformity.[66]

This alienation also adversely affected their ability to compete for services. Not being given full access to services, which were seen as a right of a citizen, some members of the black community further marginalized themselves by not seeking to acquire the specific tools needed to gain access to services. Other black migrants did not enter into the competition for resources because they felt it was not their right to do so, since they were not of British origin. If they were able to access these services, they put it down to luck and saw the services they received as a privilege and not a right of their citizenship status.

The immigration of black migrants from the colonies has been the biggest threat to the social cohesion of British society during the post-war period. In an attempt to reconstitute British society in order to accommodate these migrants, the state limited the numbers entering Britain and reduced their rights of citizenship in the Commonwealth Immigrants Act of 1962. This reduced the danger of these migrants becoming a major political and economic force, and was also an attempt to minimize racial tension. However, the process of assimilation and the policy of integration, which was designed to incorporate black migrants into the national community, failed to promote equality, tolerance or consensus.

Like many ideologies, the ideology of a socially cohesive national community is an imaginary one. Even at the most basic level of social organization, a homogeneous national community is an illusion. The attempted inclusion of black migrants into British society throughout the post-war period has demonstrated how ambiguous, contradictory and pliable definitions of nation and nationhood are. The racialized reconstruction of Britishness after the Second World War is one example of how the state uses its power in a coercive way, by alienating certain groups from its national community, while promoting and maintaining the myth of a socially cohesive society.

5

From 'Colour Blind' to 'Colour Bar': Residential Separation in Brixton and Notting Hill, 1948–75

Julia Drake

> We stood with our backs to the labour exchange in Coldharbour Lane, and looked slightly to the left towards the grim tenements of Somerlyton and Geneva Roads. Those decaying edifices, the refuge of the people from the Caribbean.[1]

For many black Caribbean migrants to Britain after the Second World War, the reality of the 'mother country' was far from the expectations created by colonial imagery.[2] On arrival in Britain, the first consideration for any newcomer was accommodation, at a time when the inner city housing shortage was a prominent issue. As the above impression of Brixton reveals, this was to be no 'land of milk and honey'. The overarching theme of social cohesion will be explored in this chapter by examining how black migrants, with such high expectations of acceptance in British society, were soon disaffected as they found themselves living in distinct areas incorporating 'grim tenements'.

In considering the process of residential separation in Brixton and Notting Hill, this chapter will argue that stimuli, both internal and external to Britain's black population, created social cohesion. It will demonstrate that through the development of separate black enclaves in London, social cohesion with the white population was limited – but more social solidarity within the black Caribbean population was created. This is not to argue that a homogeneous 'black community' developed; rather that within certain locations in London a realization of common circumstance occurred which led to a particular self-help ethos for the black Caribbean population in these areas.

This process will be examined by considering the racialization of class relations – firstly by looking at the rhetoric and reality of state and local authority residential policies, then considering the importance of local people in the development of separated communities in Brixton and Notting Hill. The social, economic and political arenas of black and white association will be reviewed to explain the development of a more racialized understanding of social cohesion. This chapter will establish that the housing experience of black Caribbean migrants was distinct from that of their white neighbours, which is reflected in the development of a racialized form of social cohesion. Housing location and tenure affected not only the physical experience, but also the social and economic lives of the local black and white populations.

Thus a further important voice needs to be considered in this process, that of the black population. This chapter is part of a move away from considering black people simply as victims.[3] The coercive force of racism within the host society and the developing consensus of these attitudes with government action created a situation where the seeds of a 'black' identity were being sown in Britain, which were reflected in positive action by black Caribbean people living in the areas concerned. The period under discussion is from the arrival of the *Windrush* in 1948 until 1975, incorporating the development of residential and social separation from the initial period of migration through changes that occurred as concentrations developed.

Scholarly debate on the black migration to Britain has long been concerned with issues of 'race' and 'class'. In the 1960s, scholars referred to a relationship of immigrant and host, although it was complicated by colour.[4] This has changed over the years. Rex and Tomlinson, as well as Sivanandan, have referred to the black population as a sub-proletariat, suggesting that economic relations determine race politics.[5] Miles suggests that analysis should look at racism rather than race, as the sociology of race relations fails to attribute enough significance to the position of black people in class relations. Instead the process of racial categorization in class relations should be considered – racism being a part of this process.[6] In these understandings of race, class identity plays an 'overarching' role in the lives of the British black population.[7] For Gilroy, however, 'race' is a political as well as an ideological category, which provides a basis for solidarity and political action.[8]

This chapter adheres more closely to Gilroy's argument in terms of social cohesion, although Hall's argument that 'race' is how class is 'lived' also has some relevance.[9] The process of change in race relations in Britain from 1948 to 1975 has made 'race' prominent as a cause of social cohesion, but the black population cannot escape being part of the overarching class structure. Useful comparisons can be drawn with the

American literature on ghetto formation. This literature has moved on to become a discussion of the racialization of class relations, rather than weighting the importance of race over class (or vice versa) in the analysis of events.[10] This conceptual discussion of racializing class relations has recently been pushed to the foreground in scholarly debate in Britain, as exemplified in *Racializing Class, Classifying Race*, edited by Alexander and Halpern, which is concerned with Britain, the USA and South Africa.[11] It is also highly pertinent to this chapter on housing, as the black Caribbean migrants interacted daily with the urban white working class in the same neighbourhoods, and competed for the same housing.

The measure of black residential concentration

In Britain after the First World War, residential separation of black Caribbean people became evident in the dock areas of port towns.[12] After 1948 it was the industrial towns and cities that now became home to new black residents due to the location of available employment. Thus the settlements were concentrated in the West Midlands and other industrial cities, including London, Liverpool and Manchester.[13] However, these were also areas suffering from an acute housing shortage.[14]

Further analysis of London shows that the spatial location of the black population between 1948 and 1975 was concentrated within an 'inner ring'. However, there was not one large segregated black settlement.[15] The location of black households within this area was spread over a number of boroughs, but by the end of the 1950s concentrations were becoming evident. The settlement pattern of the black population formed a crescent around the central city with a gap in the east. Through studying a sample of addresses for black 'newcomers', Glass found that in the late 1950s, 50 per cent of the group lived in just four London boroughs – Lambeth, Kensington, Paddington and Islington.[16] From 1961 to 1966 there was very little change in the location of concentration. Although between 1966 and 1971 there was some evidence of a slight dispersal, the black population remained predominantly in central boroughs.[17] This was also the period when many black migrants started to move into council accommodation. Despite this change, in 1971 the black Caribbean population was still more highly separated from the majority population than any other group in London.[18] There was very little movement out of the original areas of settlement, but movement within them causing increased localization, a picture of 'shuffling in situ'.[19] In 1971 nearly one-third of London's' black Caribbean population still lived in the four boroughs with the highest concentrations of black households. Within these boroughs the areas of black settlement were further consolidated at the ward level.[20]

Brixton and Notting Hill provide examples of how the black Caribbean migrants found themselves increasingly confined to certain locations and tenure types in the early years of settlement. A number of factors led to the location and concentrations of black settlement within these two locations. These include limits created by existing residential patterns related to class affiliation. Notting Hill was an area of disparate population; the geographical boundaries are Harrow Road to the north and Holland Park Road to the south. Within this area is the prosperous Notting Hill Gate, Notting Dale, a close-knit white working-class community, and also the Ladbroke Grove and Colville areas where the migrants lived.[21] It was made difficult for the black population to spread out into the rich or solid white working-class areas, in the former due to economic considerations, but for the latter because they contained relatively stable populations that were not prepared to include 'outsiders'. In Brixton the black settlements were slightly more diffused, but limitations were placed on their movement due to the residential middle-class areas to the south, north and north-east, and the working-class districts of north Lambeth, Southwark and Bermondsey.[22] Burney estimated that by 1966 Lambeth's population was as high as 13 per cent black if children were included.[23] Whereas by 1971 the area around Brixton saw a continued concentration of black population, Notting Hill had experienced a reduction – a process that will be discussed later in this chapter.

Brixton and Notting Hill contained streets that were already black only, or majority black, by the end of the 1950s.[24] One resident of Brixton stated that it 'didn't seem strange to me that there was a black street – it was like being back home'.[25] In the early years of migration, Notting Hill was a main 'reception' area for black Caribbean migrants.[26] In 1964 this area housed about 5,000 Caribbean-born residents, approximately 6 per cent of the total population. However, in its role as a 'reception centre' it was soon overtaken by Brixton.[27] In 1955 approximately 3,500 black Caribbean people lived in Lambeth, predominantly in the Brixton area.[28] In the Ferndale Ward of Lambeth (between Stockwell and Brixton) black Caribbeans made up 13 per cent of the population in 1966.[29] By 1971, 18,320 people of 'New Commonwealth American' origin (not including black people born in Britain) lived in Lambeth.[30]

The black Caribbean population was also heavily concentrated in specific types of housing. From 1948 to 1975 a distinct pattern of tenure can be charted for the black population of England and Wales. From an original concentration in private rented accommodation (in which they were still over-concentrated in some areas in 1975) came a slow move into owner occupation from the 1950s. However, by 1971 there had been a definite shift into council housing.[31] This trend of black tenure was exemplified in London, and was distinct from that of the general population. In 1966, 40.8 per cent of London's black Caribbean population were in rented furnished accommodation, compared to 8.6 per cent of the general population. The number of black people in local authority housing was also still comparatively low: 4 per cent compared to 21.6 per cent of the general population.[32] This pattern of tenure put the black population in some of the worst housing conditions.[33]

Although the two areas of Brixton and Notting Hill show some similarities in tenure, significant differences occur over the period covered. In a Brixton-based sample, only 23.5 per cent of the black population were in furnished tenancies by 1966; 58 per cent had made the move into owner occupation.[34] However, in the borough of Kensington and Chelsea, 68 per cent of the black Caribbean population were still in furnished rented accommodation in 1966.[35] This chapter will consider how tenure type affected social relations by examining the two boroughs.

The rhetoric of the 'colour blind'

As early as 1949 the Labour government, while considering how to limit black migration into the country, established the idea of dispersal and assimilation as the best plan for those black Caribbean people already in Britain. A Colonial Office working party suggested to the Home Office that 'dispersal of these aggregations would lessen the special social problems which result from their presence', and would allow them to 'be trained in the British way of life'.[36] Social scientists in the late 1950s and early 1960s saw that dispersal of the black migrants in Britain was the best policy for social 'integration', allowing for some cultural differences compared to assimilation.[37] In 1969 the same message was being put forward in government reports. The Cullingworth Committee concluded: 'dispersal is a laudable aim of policy'. However, it tempered this with the suggestion that 'full respect for the wishes of the people concerned' should be given.[38] It was feared that if dispersal did not take place, integration would not be possible, and the development of racially segregated ghettos in towns and cities would be the result. This was considered the worst-case scenario, as 'the ghetto is the geographical expression of complete social rejection'.[39] Thus social cohesion depended upon dispersing a strictly limited number of black migrants who were to 'fit in' with social mores.

A fear of the British social commentators was the formation of black ghettos in Britain along the lines of American segregated communities, such as Harlem and the South Side of Chicago.[40] Glass starts her analysis in the late 1950s by warning that 'there are as yet no substantial "coloured quarters" in London, though there is a danger that such quarters may develop'.[41] This came to the fore with Dr Martin Luther King Jr's visit to Britain in 1964 when he warned, 'so long as housing was restricted and ghettos allowed to develop, we were permitting festering sores of bitterness and deprivation to pollute the national health'.[42] The 'ghetto' (as found in the USA) is not just a geographical location; it is an area where the black population, from working class to professionals, has been forced to live through *de facto* racial segregation.[43] The ghetto also has an internal dynamic – a class-stratified 'community' that develops within the segregated area providing for, and representing, the needs and interests of the people forced to live within its boundaries.[44]

Scholarly debate on the British situation is divided about whether the British ghetto ever became reality. The population in the 1950s and 1960s often referred to areas like Notting Hill or Brixton as the 'little Harlems of London'.[45] However, Glass and Patterson, and more recently scholars such as Gilroy, have stated that they did not exist: 'the communities remained [too] diverse, small and scattered'.[46] The extent of concentration was never as great as in American ghettos – in Chicago in 1920, two-thirds of the African-American population were in neighbourhoods that were 90 per cent black.[47] In London the highest proportion in any district in 1961 was 38 per cent.[48] Rex, however, talks about the formation of black and Asian ghettos, and Small states that 'there has always been . . . clear evidence of ghettos and housing inequality'.[49] Although a British ghetto was not a reality by 1975, despite government intentions areas of racially separated black residence did occur. A few 'all black' streets did exist, but in other locations roads included black and white residents; thus, these areas were not as strictly defined as those found in the USA, where all-black neighbourhoods were often the case.

State and local authority (LA) policy in this period did little to alleviate the situation and tended to exacerbate the problems. Successive governments gave little direction specifically with regard to housing Britain's black population. Its original argument was that, as they were British subjects with full citizenship (under the Nationality Act of 1948), no legislation was needed to help the black migrants to find accommodation.[50] Thus any policy treating the black immigrant situation specifically would be tantamount to preferential treatment. In May 1956 the Cabinet Committee observed that slum clearance programmes aggravated the housing shortage, as there were more people to re-house than there was room in the cleared area. It was noted that 'there may well be difficult and embarrassing situations if and when local authorities are faced with the obligation of giving priority for council houses to coloured tenants evicted from slum clearance areas, in preference to people who have been on the waiting lists for a good deal longer'.[51]

Nevertheless, during this period a number of measures were established to try and eliminate the more general urban problems of poor housing quality and overcrowding. One such piece of legislation, the Rent Act (1957) that ended controlled rents, indirectly caused problems for the black community.[52] Both the black and white communities suffered the consequent rise in rent. Complaints of high rent could be taken to a Rent Tribunal, which could set what was judged a reasonable level of rent for a certain period, but fear of eviction and the reality of harassment and intimidation were enough to prevent this process from working. The Milner Holland Report stated: 'we are convinced . . . that . . . the risks of victimisation of a complaining tenant are real and serious'.[53] This made it harder for people with a low income, black or white, to find accommodation. It did not create a common cause, but rather led to resentment as the belief was propagated that black people were taking '"our" houses and enjoying "our" social services'.[54] Thus not only were government actions creating further black concentration; they were also inadvertently creating further competition between black and white people with low incomes, which started to become hostile in the areas affected.

The lack of specific government direction meant that local authorities made their own policies regarding black residents. Due to the government's *laissez-faire* attitude, Lambeth devised its own policy in which it stressed 'we are all Lambethans now'; its opponents saw it as a 'Nelson's eye policy'.[55] The council refused to set up any special provisions for its black residents. However, by 1971 Lambeth Borough Council had identified ways in which local authority policies inadvertently discriminated against black migrants.[56] Firstly, the 'points' scheme for allocating housing emphasized length of residence in a borough rather than real need. Most of the black population, despite acute need, had simply not been resident long enough in that area. The 1967, a Political and Economic Planning (PEP) study showed that, while 26 per cent of the population of England and Wales lived in council housing, the corresponding figure for the black population was less than 1 per cent.[57]

By the 1970s Britain's black population was starting to gain access to council housing in greater numbers. The integration policy was still favoured, which led the Cullingworth Committee to recommend a policy of dispersal through housing allocation.[58] However, within the Greater London Council (GLC), rehousing led to the increased concentration of black people. Of the black families rehoused, by 1976, 70 per cent were located in the four London boroughs of Lambeth, Tower Hamlets, Southwark and Hackney – boroughs that were already areas of black settlement.[59] When the black migrants did qualify for council housing, they were often given inferior accommodation.[60] According to the 1971 census data, over half of GLC tenants of New Commonwealth origin lived in high-density pre-war flats, whereas only 11 per cent of other tenants were in such housing. Thus black people were concentrated in the same areas as a result of council policy.[61]

Secondly, some LAs specifically left out of the slum clearance programmes areas with a large number of immigrant families. This was mainly to avoid provoking racial hostility due to a common racist belief that black people were getting preferential treatment for council housing. In Brixton, for example, a petition was signed in 1964 by white residents of the London County Council (LCC) flats on the Loughborough Estate protesting the allocation of a flat to a black railway worker and his family. The reason for the petition was explained by the local Conservative candidate Mr Kenneth Payne, who said people 'who were born and bred in this country should have first choice'.[62] Thus a consensus occurred between the racial attitudes of some of the local population and LA policy.

Thirdly, in some cases, local authorities rigidly defined who would be rehoused from the clearance programmes. An example is the redevelopment of Powis Terrace in Notting Hill; the new houses built meant a complete change in the type of people resident in the area. The new development was aimed at the middle class. In 1960 there were 230 coloured residents in Powis Terrace; by mid-1964 there were none.[63] In the Lancaster Road redevelopment in 1968, only tenants in unfurnished tenancy agreements were deemed eligible for rehousing by the council. The black population was more likely to be in furnished accommodation due to racially motivated restrictions. Of the black population within the redevelopment area, 75 per cent were in furnished accommodation (the word 'furnished' was used in its loosest sense).[64]

Finally, LAs attacking multi-occupancy in areas nearby created black enclaves in certain zones.[65] Lambeth held back on enforcing public health provisions for overcrowding for this reason. However, while it avoided creating further concentrations, it allowed bad conditions to continue.[66] The government passed a series of Acts to try and improve a grant system for landlords to claim from their LA to improve their housing. It was originally introduced in the Housing Act of 1949, and attempts were made to make it more attractive in the Housing Acts of 1954, 1959, 1961 and 1964.[67] This last Act included a clause that the local authority in some cases had the right to require improvements to be made. However, LAs could make selective use of this. When the Act was enforced in Notting

Hill, the black population again suffered because of the type of houses they owned, which, due to discriminatory practices, were generally those in the worst conditions, or listed for slum clearance already. One black Caribbean Notting Hill resident recalled this process: 'you know the blacks and accountability . . . a lot of them got rooked. A lot of them got their houses taken away . . . stripped of all their wealth . . . by the regulations – or rehabilitated down to Shepherd's Bush . . . Notting Hill is sanitised now.'[68] Notting Hill was slowly becoming less of an area of black domicile and, as this resident sadly recognized, was being cleansed of its unwanted population to make way for more ideal, prosperous households.[69] Settlements elsewhere were thus gaining increased concentrations and further isolation was occurring from the white society. Government policies were increasing the divisions between the black and white working class as competition for council housing emerged.

De facto segregation?

The black Caribbean population was concentrated in the lower forms of tenure, which meant that it was also overrepresented in areas of overcrowding, multi-occupancy and deprivation. Thus a sense of shared experience and identity was being created among the black population, but separate to that of the host society. The accounts of black residents in Britain describe living conditions almost unimaginable today: 'I had three little children and all of us, five of us, living in one room with a kitchenette in Notting Hill.'[70] The picture painted of Notting Hill is replicated in accounts of migrants in Brixton. Isolyn Robinson's aunt found her a room in a house on Geneva Road: 'it was so small I called it the spoon room'. Again essential facilities were inadequate: 'there was no inside toilet in the house and the only running water was a tap in the back yard'.[71] This was Britain in the 1950s – the 'age of affluence'. The black experience, like that of their white working-class neighbours, was 'the paradox of squalor in the midst of progress'.[72]

Over the period discussed little changed; the 1973 PEP test showed 'no dramatic improvement in the quality of housing occupied by West Indians'.[73] This picture is reflected in the statistical analysis from the period. Overcrowding is considered to mean over 1.5 persons per room. From 1961 to 1966 over half of the black Caribbean population in London lived in these circumstances. The distinctive nature of their experience is shown when compared to the host population, of which only 8 per cent were in overcrowded conditions in 1961 and by 1966 only 5 per cent.[74]

There were aspects of the British housing situation that affected all, white or black, but which were causal to the location of black households. The Milner Holland Report highlighted the problems that the migrants were to face with other members of the working class – a shortage of homes, multiple occupancy, high rent, ageing housing stock and homelessness.[75] The black population was mainly working class and overrepresented in the low-income group. This was due to the nature of the jobs they had been hired to fill, and racism in the labour market.[76] However, their pattern of tenure did not fit that of the white working-class population, as the picture of council accommodation suggests. Brixton and Notting Hill were located in 'Zones of Transition' – deteriorating areas that the white population had been escaping from for a number of years.[77]

In the 1950s, Notting Hill contained what had originally been respectable houses, built in the 1860s, but now being sub-divided by landlords into room lettings for profit. This area was already quite cosmopolitan by the Second World War, Irish and Indian immigrants having already located there: in the 1920s it was called 'Little India'.[78] Therefore, migrants were moving into an area that had already been inhabited by other immigrant groups. The residential status of Brixton had been in decline since the 1920s. Between the two world wars, rent control, among other things, made houses in Brixton a poor investment – it became more advantageous to rent out rooms rather than flats.[79] This process resulted in a change in the type of resident found in Brixton. Before the Second World War, the population was described in the *South London Press* as the home of the 'true cockney'; however, after the war there was an influx of continental Europeans and black Caribbean migrants.[80]

The type of housing available in the two areas was the same, old and let on a room basis, rather than self-sufficient flats. However, a slightly different picture is found in Brixton – the migrants' welcome was not historically assured by previous immigrant groups located in the area. Nevertheless, the location of Dr H. W. Moody (who set up the League of Coloured Peoples) and other prominent black citizens nearby created an area where migrants felt accepted.[81] Also, on arrival in 1948 the *Windrush* passengers were temporarily housed at the Clapham underground shelter nearby. The Mayor of Lambeth held a reception for a few of them where he stated that the 'newcomers' were welcome in Brixton.[82] Thus the type of housing in an area, and its previous inhabitants, started a process of separation. This process was, however, exacerbated by the racial attitudes of local inhabitants.

Members of the local white population introduced a 'colour bar', Sam King remembered: 'In those days I wouldn't even try to get a room for myself. Some people tried to get rooms but they suffered humiliation.'[83]

One theme that runs through oral testimony of black migrants to Britain is the treatment they received when first looking for housing. For those without friends or relatives to stay with, the search for accommodation proved to be a miserable and, as Sam King realized, humiliating experience. The image of a board in the window 'no Irish, no coloured, no dogs' is often shown to represent the experience of those searching for a house. The process of obtaining a room, and the type of accommodation in which black Caribbean people ended up, represents one of the first steps towards separation imposed upon these people through white racism. Baron Baker recalled the attitude of landlords: 'usually, once you told people you were coloured, they would say their place has been let'.[84] However, the colour bar need not be blatant to have effect, since for many white people it was not the done thing to admit to racial antipathy. As A. G. Bennett noted with keen perception, 'the neighbour was always worried about the soul of the people next door'.[85] Many migrants noted that excuses were proffered that the neighbours wouldn't like it, or the other lodgers would be unhappy. When an English person says there is no room free, 'one is charmed and put completely off guard by cosy smiles and polite, mild-mannered language, as one hears the word "no", dressed up in the habit of the English gentleman'.[86]

The 'colour bar' was also apparent in newspaper advertisements and instructions given to letting agents. Through this process limits were placed on the areas where the black population was able to locate. An article in the *West Indian Gazette* in 1960 described the process of finding a house, mentioning advertisements specifically stating 'Europeans only' or 'no coloured'. In some cases, the letting agent prevented the prospective tenant from even getting as far as an interview with the landlord. The author then went to Mycrofts letting agency on the Edgware Road, where he was told that he could not be shown a flat because he was black. Here again there is a refusal to admit to racist sensibilities by passing on the blame: 'you see it is not a question of the agency discriminating at all but rather the landladies'.[87] The fact that the agency could have refused to propagate the 'colour bar' is not an issue.

The PEP report confirmed these details. In 1967 it was found that two out of three estate agents and three out of four accommodation bureaux practised racial discrimination.[88] The PEP results also revealed that racist attitudes cut across class lines. The survey included 60 requests to landlords for accommodation for a 'coloured' applicant; half represented themselves as working class, the other half as professionals.[89] Of the 38 times the 'coloured' applicant was rejected, there were no significant differences as to which class they represented.[90] Dipak Nandy, writing in the *New Statesman*, observed: 'it looks . . . as though colour discrimination is cutting across traditional class distinctions'.[91] Thus traditional class relations were becoming racialized. Rather than being placed with whichever socio-economic class they belonged to, black people were being grouped together based on perceived racial difference.

There were also economic reasons for black separation. The black population was mainly working class, and was overrepresented in the low-income group. This was due to the nature of the jobs they had been hired to fill, and racism in the labour market.[92] However, there was more than just income limiting their choice of accommodation; the small selection available was even further constrained by a 'colour tax': 'Before I started my search [for accommodation], I was aware that I had, by virtue of my pigmentation, two strikes against me. First as a person of colour and secondly, as regards the price of any accommodation I was likely to get.'[93] The black migrant was forced to pay more rent than his white counterpart for the same accommodation; Britain's black population satirically dubbed this the 'colour tax'. Donald Hinds noted that in Brixton the old dilapidated houses, home to so many of the black population in the 1950s and 1960s, were 'gold mines to their owners . . . when one's white fellow workers were paying less than twenty shillings per week, the going rate for a single room was fifty shillings'.[94] This emphasized a shared experience among the black population, rather than with white neighbours.

The problems associated with renting meant that many black migrants chose to buy their own house. However, the process of locating and buying a house once again met the barrier of white prejudice. The 1967 PEP report states that 'coloured' migrants wanting to buy a house experienced discrimination two out of three times.[95] When black Caribbean migrants went to purchase a house, it was found that a large proportion of homes were unavailable to them and it was very difficult for them to obtain a mortgage on normal terms.[96] This placed further limits on the location and type of residence available to the black population.

It was found necessary to include in the Race Relations Act (1965) a provision declaring invalid covenants in tenancy agreements and leases that prevented the tenant from declining the tenancy or lease to a person on the grounds of colour, race, ethnic or national origin.[97] However, not covered under this Act were other racist practices, such as covenants with similar restrictions on the sale of freehold property. It also failed to cover covenants in leases designed to put off black prospective buyers, or to discriminate against them once they were in residence. These included banning the resident from entertaining black guests.[98] Black migrants ended up having to buy houses with short leases or those designated for slum clearance.[99] Building societies were unlikely to agree a loan on this kind of property.[100] Thus an institutional consensus with prejudiced views was creating a separate experience for black and white home-owners.

Voluntary separation?

Residential and social separation through the agency of white people and local authorities is, however, only part of the story. The location of black settlement was also a positive reaction to the hostility found in Britain. To overcome the difficulties of the limited housing available to the black population, they relied on each other to provide a solution. For this they turned to the traditional saving schemes they had used in the Caribbean, such as the 'pardner' scheme or 'sou sou'.[101] The black population rallied together to provide housing for friends and relatives. The schemes were usually set up with people they knew from their home country, as it needed to be those whom they could trust. Money was pooled together by a group of savers and eventually each person received a lump sum. This method of saving also bypassed many of the problems that racial discrim-ination created for obtaining a mortgage. As Sam King found, 'because we couldn't get a mortgage we pooled all our money to help others. We called it a "partner" which is what we called the same pool in Jamaica.'[102] Thus savings organizations were based on a racial solidarity within family and friendship groups.

Many black people became the victims of 'finance houses' that provided short-term high-interest loans.[103] This explained the need to charge high rent and overcrowd the premises to pay off the loan. This is where the black and white working class did have some grievances in common. Connie Mark, a black Caribbean woman who lived in Notting Hill, described her experience of black landlords: 'if you lived in one room and dared even to have a radio your landlord was so terrible they would charge you extra rent ... I am ashamed to say my landlords were all black.'[104] However, black landlords also created further inter-racial tension by trying to get rid of sit-ting white tenants who were often paying a controlled low rent. The Milner Holland Report talks of the 'sensationalised stories' of actions attributed to 'coloured' landlords. In a survey carried out for the report, of 790 cases of abuses, black landlords were only mentioned in 99.[105] However, these did tend to be for illegal eviction or improper attempts to gain vacant posses-sion. Although some of these cases could be explained by ignorance of the system of security of tenure and rent control legislation, black landlords also wanted to provide homes for family and friends, due to the difficulties of gaining accommodation.[106]

Although the distinctive circumstances of the black population were not completely voluntary, it is possible to show that black Caribbean people played a part in the location and concentration of settlement. According to Peach, the 'positive' forces behind segregation, those based on black agency, were actually more important in the early years than the limitations on dispersal created by the 'host' society: 'at the moment the positive reasons for clustering are dominant and the negative forces recessive or latent'.[107] This is, perhaps, overstating the case because, as Smith points out, 'even if black people prefer segregation, it is hard to understand why they should pursue this in the more run-down segments of the housing stock'.[108]

On arrival any 'newcomer' would want to live near people they knew. As already discussed, black people located where they thought they would be assured a welcome. Pamela Stewart came to live in Notting Hill because that was where her cousin lived: 'a friend of mine told me that my relative was living there and I wrote him'.[109] Once slum clearance programmes began in Notting Hill and Brixton, the continued concentration of the black population was noted. It was assumed that the black population did not naturally want to disperse. This was reflected in the location of council housing and housing association accommodation that they were moved to: 'more black people made local moves, they travelled shorter distances from their old to their new [council] addresses'.[110] Loretta McKnight stated that when she was moving into council accommodation, others were asked about moving to Milton Keynes; however, 'I chose to stay in this area.'[111]

Nevertheless, this does not represent a general social cohesion among the black population. 'The fact that most West Indians are black and working class has, of course, affected their lives in England. Other status distinctions and inequalities among them, however, tend to be overlooked.'[112] By locating with people they actually knew, or were related to, black people built up settlements based on Caribbean Island affiliation. Loretta McKnight, who came to live near Notting Hill, stated, 'I'm a Jamaican . . . the house that I come to was part of Jamaican peoples, well they live on the top floor they rent the basement that I was living in.'[113] From the results of the 1971 census it is possible to see that these island affiliations continued throughout the period. Jamaican people made up the bulk of the Caribbean-born black population in London (51.4 per cent), and were mainly located south of the river with concentrations in Wandsworth, Lambeth, Southwark and Lewisham. North of the river there were only two concentrations of Jamaicans in Brent, and Haringey.[114] Directly north of the river Thames are concentrations from the 'other' Caribbean islands, as the Windward and Leeward Islands were classified in the 1971 census.[115] This is not to suggest that there was no mixing between the groups, but it does clearly highlight that there was a variance in location between people from different islands.

Island differences were not just geographical; they were also cultural. When Pamela Stewart, a Jamaican, was asked if she mixed with people from other islands, she stated, 'Me I don't mix with them up to today . . . "Good morning" and that's it.' When asked if she didn't mix with people from any specific island, she replied, 'Well you have Grenada you have the whole bunch from that side they are of a different category . . . Jamaica I should call that mix American . . . I would call that an American country.'[116] Another resident of Notting Hill stated, 'The Grove was explosive because they didn't like the Trinidadians . . . the Dominicans and the St Lucian and all them guys they didn't like Trinidadians.'[117] The hostility that could occur between people from different islands suggests that a homogeneous black community could never really exist, but the situation that was faced in Britain did lead to some softening of the barriers created through island loyalties.[118]

To a lesser extent, differences developed in this period within the black community through class affiliation. So far a rather bleak picture has been created of an almost impermeable barrier surrounding increasingly 'black' enclaves. However, the barrier was a little less impenetrable to those with money, who wanted to separate themselves from areas of concentrated black settlement. A small black middle class developed in Britain. Evidence suggests that some of this group physically distanced themselves from other members of the community by moving away from the main centres of black concentration. In the late 1950s, an advert appeared representing the attitude of the middle-class or professional migrant: 'room wanted, but not in Notting Hill'.[119] One Notting Hill resident 'moved out to Finchley . . . and I suppose I got lost in its middle class safety for a while'.[120] The boundaries were not as constricting in Brixton as in Notting Hill. Although the concentration of black households increased over the period 1948–75, a wider area of settlement was created as those who had been there longer, or were more financially secure, were able to move out of the original 'reception areas', such as Geneva and Somerlyton Roads.[121] This movement was further enabled by the Race Relations Act (1968), which prevented owners from discriminating in who purchased their house.[122]

Some of the differences within the black community were overcome between 1948 and 1975. As stated, black agency was involved in creating and perpetuating black separation, and part of this process was the creation of a black Caribbean identity. To start with this may have just involved greeting a fellow 'newcomer': 'few looking on understood the crushing loneliness, which could prompt a man to cross a busy street to talk to another man for no other reason than the man was also black'.[123] The development of black identity also occurred as migrants created their own social life, wanting to experience a bit of familiar culture. Shops that catered for black Caribbean needs were set up as areas of concentrated demand increased. Frequently advertised in the *West Indian Gazette* was the barbers and cosmetics shop 'Martyns', owned and run by black Caribbeans, and restaurants such as the Mangrove.[124] In Notting Hill and Brixton, Saturday night parties, blues and gambling clubs were set up in people's basements: 'we used to go out every Saturday night searching for reggae and dances and blues. They were always in little houses and we used to go from hall to hall.'[125] Notting Hill became infamous for its black social life: 'they had gambling houses in St Stephen's Gardens and they had another gamble house/club in Lancaster Road'.[126]

However, although some of the social life may have been for both genders, there was a difference between the activities of men and women, as in white society. Women from the same island often visited each other's homes, Connie Mark remembered: 'it was the thing to visit each other at weekends'.[127] According to Pearl Jephcott's rather judgemental study of Notting Hill, 'the coloured mother's social life as far as visitors go may be more lively than that of the Notting Dale young mothers. But their visitors are always other migrants . . . [and] very often from the host's own island.'[128] Men were apparently more likely to be found gambling on dominoes, for example, at each other's houses or in pubs.[129] The home was an important part of social life for men and women, but within them the reasons for and area of association differed. Men and women had different 'communities' of people with whom they shared experiences, and related to each other differently, according to gender roles. Thus difference and cohesion were occurring among women and men separately in the social sphere. However, racism created a link for black men and women that, to an extent, counterbalanced the effects of gender difference.

Further social aspects that separated the black and white communities, and increased the links within the black population, were related to religion. The black population was in no way assured a welcome by the local congregations, and the religious practices that they were used to in the Caribbean were more flamboyant than those found in the Church of England. The British population was not a nation of churchgoers, especially when compared to the religious life that the migrants had been used to in the Caribbean.[130] Many of those arriving in Britain followed the British pattern and no longer attended church. However, there were still a large number, especially women, to whom the church remained an important part of their lives. The Baptist, Pentecostal and less orthodox sects started to appear in areas where the black population settled. Basement rooms and front parlours were used as places of worship.[131] Miss Marcella White set up Brixton's first Pentecostal church in the Gospel Hall on Sussex Road.[132] The church was important in establishing a black identity in Britain; religious life created an outlet particularly for women, affected by the joint problems of gender, race and class.[133]

Concentration and social separation?

Changing racial attitudes caused black residential concentrations; however, these concentrations exacerbated racial antipathy. Complaints were made that black tenants were noisy and continually having late-night parties.[134] The 'colour bar' went beyond housing to include social activities, with many pubs refusing to serve black people.[135] One Notting Hill resident lamented, 'there was nothing really for black people so you had to create your own social environment'.[136] A lack of understanding of the different cultures that were evident in Caribbean life led to further hostility due to proximity. Donald Hinds remembered, 'we were an outdoor people! We hailed each other from a distance and stood around in groups chatting and waving our arms around in the excitement of it all.'[137] White neighbours were not used to this kind of flamboyant behaviour, finding it (ironically) anti-social.

The threat of diminishing house prices as black families moved into a neighbourhood caused the white exodus to become a reality. The creation of racial stereotypes helped to persuade many white neighbours to leave increasingly black areas. Thus black concentration was increased by white outward migration: 'The "law of the escaping white man" . . . the drain of white people from places increases in proportion to the number of coloured people moving in.'[138] By 1961, 80 per cent of black Caribbean people were located in London boroughs or wards that showed a population decrease.[139] The concentration of the black population was being caused not only by a continuing decrease in the white population, but also by natural increase. Many migrants were young and starting a family, and others, after settling in Britain, brought their children over from the Caribbean to live with them.[140] Areas like Lambeth and Notting Hill had been losing their white population before the arrival of the *Windrush*. In Kensington the rise in population by 1961 was actually attributable to the black population.[141]

The limited location of black settlement into the poorer areas of certain London boroughs through the 'colour bar' created concern that black 'ghettos' were developing. However, the causes of this concentration of black settlement were not analysed by contemporaries in this light, as Hinds observes: 'West Indians did not create the ghetto. They were caught, as in the statutory scene in films, where if you are discovered standing over the corpse, you must be the murderer.'[142] The white man, however, did not just vote with his feet; some were prepared to express their racial opinions violently. Norman Taylor was the first black man to buy a house on Reservoir Road in Brockley; in protest at this encroachment, his van was set on fire.[143] When Adrian McKenzie moved to Nelson's Row, Clapham Common, his house was stoned and KKK (for Ku Klux Klan) written on his front door.[144] The black population was being created as the scapegoat for many of the problems of the urban housing experience and this led to a further, and in some cases violent, separation of the two communities.

The activities of landlords like Perec Rachman also helped to provoke further hostility and create black concentrations of settlement. After the 1957 Rent Act, when rents were decontrolled, Rachman and others were able to charge high rents, backed up with the threat of violence should a resident consider getting help from a Rent Tribunal. The first period of notoriety for Michael DeFreitas (later known as the Black Power activist Michael X) was as a henchman for Rachman. This 'fortuitous' association gained him a better flat in Powis Square.[145] One reason why it was hard to prosecute Rachman was that the mortgages were in another person's name, or those of his numerous small businesses. Michael DeFreitas obtained a house for Rachman in Colville Terrace.[146] Rachman was also able to get the most from his properties by getting rid of white tenants who were still in controlled tenancies.[147] To remove people, to whom the threat of violence was not enough, Rachman moved black residents in, relying on prejudices against black people to hasten the white tenants' departure. The *West Indian Gazette* reported that 'Rachman refined the exploitation of racial tension to the point of making it literally pay.'[148] The work of Rachman led to a greater concentration of black people in houses that, through lack of repair and overcrowding, were becoming increasingly uninhabitable. In doing so, it also furthered the stereotypes of the black community that causally linked them with urban decay.

To put an interesting spin on racial and ethnic divisions, Barry Carmen, an Australian, interviewed an Irish barman in Notting Hill. The barman spoke of a further stereotype of the black man in this area: 'I never get a night's sleep . . . last night a row going on between white girls, prostitutes . . . keeping coloured men . . . nearly every second house is a brothel all run by darkies.'[149] Although the stereotype may have had some basis, perhaps more pertinent was the fact that white women who associated with black men were labelled prostitutes. The fear of miscegenation was an emotive force in the dislike of black people. Carmen also interviewed three white men in Shepherd's Bush in 1958. One of the men, described as a 'teddy boy', stated that it was 'just that there are a lot of ponces live round there. I mean, it's not very nice to see a coloured bloke with a white girl out in the streets is it?' When asked why he felt this way, he replied, 'Well it's not them it's the children . . . well we don't want a lot of half-castes running around.'[150] This kind of racial hostility led to further estrangement between the black and white communities.

The lack of cohesion between the black and white populations was violently represented in north Kensington. Racial antipathy came to a head in Notting Hill with the riots in 1958. The developing stereotype of the black person as a noisy neighbour, the increasingly bad image of the black landlords, and links between the black population and poor housing conditions were all starting points for the riots. However, the development of racialized stereotypes was also intensified in Notting Hill by the increased activities of organized racist groups in the area. One resident recalled that just before the riots 'we had marches and stuff like that . . . The National Front people. It wasn't Mosley it was Colin Jordan.'[151] The riots saw horrific scenes of violence towards the black population and their property. Sivanandan, who was still living in Notting Hill when the riots started, described it as a 'double baptism of fire', having just left the problems in his country of birth, Sri Lanka, to find himself in the middle of the riots in Notting Hill.[152] Many of those involved in the riots were not local people, but the silence of many locals while hostile actions took place showed the widening gap between white and black.[153] Some local people were willing to help. When an African student came out of Ladbroke Grove tube station, unaware of the riots, and was chased by an angry mob it was a white shopkeeper who was prepared to harbour him until the police arrived.[154] The riots were the most violent expression of brewing racial hostility that occurred during this period.

Carter has argued that government policy shaped racial attitudes.[155] From the 1950s, the government created an ideal 'character' for migrants to continue the homogenous racial characteristics of British society. Debate on immigration restrictions in the 1950s attempted to impose a 'colour filter'; the black community was seen as a threat to the continuation of a 'white' Britain.[156] The understanding of race was based on colour distinctions; 'belonging' was associated with white skin colour. Thus government activity was concentrated on the problem of restricting migration, rather than acting on problems that the black population faced, such as bad housing conditions and racial abuse. The government also sought to blame the black population for the housing conditions in which they were forced to live. In May 1956 the Cabinet Committee on Colonial Immigrants laid all London's housing problems at the feet of the black population, mentioning 'fresh arrivals, who lend themselves to exploitation particularly by others of their own race, gravitate to existing communities resulting in gross overcrowding in insanitary conditions'.[157] No mention was made of white hostility playing a causal role in this process. The Notting Hill riots did not create a situation where Fenner Brockway's Anti-Discrimination Bill was finally passed; rather it created further debate on how to limit black immigration.[158] The Immigration Act of 1962, by imposing a voucher system that limited migration from the New Commonwealth countries, institutionalized racist views and helped create the hostile attitude that had developed towards black migrants.[159]

It is true that government actions and opinions did and do hold some sway in shaping public opinion. However, this chapter argues that these views developed through the agency of the people as well as the state. The Notting Hill riots were not caused solely by government policies. Overcrowded conditions, a lack of cultural understanding and fear of competition, as well as the activities of racist grassroots organizations, created hostility that was aimed against a visible minority who were easy to use as scapegoats.

As time went on, the hardening of racial attitudes was reflected and caused by government action. If the removal of citizenship status for black people had been against public opinion, surely a more prominent outcry would have been heard against the 1965 White Paper, the Commonwealth Immigrants Acts of 1962 and 1968 and the Immigration Act of 1971. By 1968 black people arriving in Britain were accorded the rights equivalent to those of a German *gastarbeiter*.[160] This is not to say that there was no protest: a number of groups were set up to try and change the course of British race relations, such as the inter-racial Campaign Against Racial Discrimination. Yet to many, the rhetoric of people like Enoch Powell was not the ranting of a lunatic; he was someone actually brave enough to put British racial fears into a public speech.[161] However, reflecting the duality in British society on the race issue, Race Relations Acts were passed which protected the black population from certain forms of discrimination. Housing was not really dealt with until the second Act, passed in 1968, the first, in 1965, was mainly concerned with places of public resort.[162] These Acts were passed almost concurrently with restrictive immigration legislation, suggesting to many black people that they were 'sweeteners' to pacify the black population already resident. Thus they could be viewed as a coercive attempt to create social cohesion in Britain, albeit one that met with little real success.[163]

'Black' as a political colour

Although there were attempts by local people to create an inter-racial class consciousness, racial attitudes prevented overall class solidarity. In Brixton and Notting Hill, there were members of the community who tried to alter the course of black concentration through social rejection. These were groups of people trying to create social cohesion based on the shared problems and interests of the working class in London. In Brixton in September 1957, St John's Reverend D. Shewing and Father Campbell, a chaplain for black Caribbeans, established an Inter-racial Council. The group intended to look after the welfare of the local community and bring the congregation together, running lectures and conferences.[164] However, not all members of the clergy were sympathetic to this ideal. A vicar in the Colville area of Notting Hill told Ivan Weekes that he would rather not see him the next Sunday. His reasoning again shows the refusal to admit personal racism: 'I don't mind, but my congregation might.'[165] Inter-racial organizations tended either to be short-lived in nature or to collapse altogether as racial antagonism evolved.

The 1958 riots broadcast the horrendous living conditions of both black and white residents, and highlighted the lack of facilities within these areas. The Golbourne Neighbourhood Council (GNC) was set up in Notting Hill after the riots to improve facilities. However, racial antipathies still caused problems within the local population as arguments ensued over the correct solution. In the end there was only one black person left on the council, Granville Pryce, who was 'constantly at war with the racist elements'.[166] The Coloured People's Progressive Association (CPPA) was set up by Mrs Frances Ezzrecco to work for a wide-ranging goal of inter-racial understanding.[167] However, although the group was still active in 1961, this was exceptional.[168] This is explained in part by the fact that many of the black population still believed that they were only in Britain for a short period, and were going to be returning to the Caribbean eventually. The impetus to organize was hard to come by, as people had little time available due to work and family commitments.[169] Not surprisingly, many were also suspicious of white organizations.[170] Thus local attempts to create cohesion on the basis of class affiliation were made, but it was hard to overcome suspicions and racial antipathy.

As inter-racial organizations faltered, black groups emerged. Although internal differences were present within the black population in Britain, racial discrimination and black organization sidelined these disagreements. During our period, organizational activity became more concerned with 'black' issues, rather than with those of disparate islands and backgrounds. The process of the creation of a 'Caribbean' identity, or rather a 'black' identity, was causally linked to the racial hostility that was found in Britain. The colour bar started to create an alternative 'community' socially and politically within the black neighbourhoods of areas like Brixton and Notting Hill.

The black organization surrounding the Notting Hill riots illustrates this point: 'Notting Hill, though shameful to Britain, unconsciously served as a stimulant to mould togetherness among West Indians in Britain.'[171] While the riots were taking place, the black community organized to protect itself. This ranged from making sure that black people walked around in groups for security, to a more forceful reaction. Renee Webb remembered that at a black headquarters in Blenheim Crescent, defences were installed to fend off Teddy Boys: 'the teddy boys knew the location, sent a message they were coming to do damage'. When the defence mechanisms were let off, 'I never knew those Teddy boys could run so fast.'[172] Michael DeFreitas spoke of a more aggressive form of organization that attacked racist group headquarters after they were taught how to make petrol bombs by some American soldiers.[173] The death of Kelso Cochrane in 1959 near the area of the riots also brought home the need to unite to survive in the increasingly hostile British society.[174] For many of the black population, this event highlighted a growing distrust of the police, who refused to accept the view that Cochrane was killed in a racist attack.[175]

However, it was not really until the mid-1960s that a distinct, black identity emerged from within the black population. As the 1960s continued with little sign of improvement in race relations, some elements of the black community decided to take matters into their own hands – 'black' became a political colour. Following the visit of Malcolm X in 1965, Michael X set up the Racial Action Adjustment Society (RAAS), an organization that promoted black nationalism. Its policy included 'black only' membership, and it represented a form of militancy that promoted a parallel black society.[176] This was one of a number of groups that were created, loosely forming a Black Power movement in Britain. However, other organizations under the Black Power mantle were also concerned with class: for example, the Universal Coloured People's Association (UCPA) regarded the struggle as that of an international working class based on racial solidarity.[177] The black press, such as the Black People's News Service, produced by these groups, discussed the problem of poor housing conditions and the allocation of the worst council flats.[178] However, housing problems were only one issue in a list of grievances. The black population was addressing other concerns that united them, such as racism in education and employment, and the problems related to homeless black youths.[179] They had also developed a more global view of the 'black' problem, illustrated by the first Black Power march in January 1969, concerned with racism in Britain and Rhodesia.[180] Although these groups were small and short-lived their influence was significant, as they instilled in the next generation a new sense of identity.[181]

Conclusions

Throughout this period, the understanding of 'race' underwent a change from a distant sense of colonial responsibility to a new relationship where black and white people were competing for accommodation and employment. The black Caribbean attitude to race also saw a hasty revision from a view based on colonial imagery of the British as welcoming and middle class, as found in the colonies. This led to a fundamental change in the concept of 'race' on both sides. The 'host' society and the black Caribbean population in Britain were agents in this change and the resulting understanding of 'race'. This new understanding, evident by the mid-1960s, included the formation of a new 'black' social, cultural and political identity through white racism, as well as through black self-identification. Although the working-class status of most of the black population was a material reality, this new understanding of 'race' and its evolution complicated class consciousness (also a social, cultural and political understanding of place in society).

Through using the examples of Brixton and Notting Hill, this chapter has sought to show how residential separation reflects social division. This occurred through a process that can be traced over the years 1948 to 1975. The original residential separation during the 1950s was brought about by a colour-blind state, including local authorities, and by the development of a 'colour bar' in British society. This prevented the black migrants from competing on equal terms for the scarce resource of housing. Racial discrimination forced the 'newcomers' into certain areas that contained cheap and rundown housing. It was made difficult for the black migrants to rent or purchase property through numerous methods of discrimination by the local white population and local authorities, from discriminatory adverts to outright rejection. The black population also chose to locate together, as a reaction to a new environment, the necessity of finding cheap housing, and racism. Overcrowding, which created further racial tension, was partly caused by discriminatory lending policies, council housing allocation and the development of racist stereotypes.

Unscrupulous landlords, both black and white, also affected the pattern of black residence.

Social tension resulted in the riots of 1958, where the white population showed their resentment to the build-up of 'coloured enclaves'. Through the 1960s and early 1970s an increased concentration of black settlement was accompanied by an increase in social separation as racial stereotypes were being created, and the black population became a scapegoat for the problems of urban decay. The increased concentration within neighbourhoods, and an accompanying increase in racial hostility, also led to changes within the black community. After the riots of 1958 the black population looked to itself for help, which blurred the distinctions within the black population. This was the impetus for developing a more inclusive black Caribbean identity. These changes were reflected in the organizations that were created. The attempts to develop inter-racial organizations were soon defeated and efforts were made by the black population to organize protest on the basis of an emerging black identity. While these black organizations were small and short-lived, they had a significant influence on later grassroots activity.[182]

Within these neighbourhoods, as concentrations increased, the black population was able to establish its own social life, as well as some businesses catering for specific needs. They relied on each other rather than the white community to obtain rented accommodation and purchase homes. Although the black enclaves that developed were scattered around central London, they did not represent one mass settlement. The concentration of the black population within these areas was high, but although there were all-black streets the majority still contained white and black residents. In Brixton the black population spread out as more established residents, or those who had managed to improve their economic conditions, were able to disperse. Acts preventing discrimination, although hard to enforce, did improve this situation, enabling those who could afford it to leave the area. Dispersal was evident from Notting Hill by the end of the 1960s through council policy, but this caused further concentration in other areas of black residence, including Brixton. Thus although there are similarities between the British situation and the American ghetto, it is not possible to conclude that a British ghetto was a reality. Class was still of some significance, as interaction was taking place between black and white residents, encouraged through proximity. Class already delineated society; the black population on arrival took their place in the areas that were designated by the 'host' society as related to their socio-economic status.

Therefore, it is possible to conclude that social cohesion was based on a racialized understanding of life in Britain. It took place through the creation of a new black identity that developed out of social division, which was physically represented in black residential separation. Cohesion with members of the white working class was limited as class consciousness was complicated by race.

6

Local Government, Rates and Rents: The Policies of the London County Council and Three Borough Councils

Zoë Doye

The debate concerning how far rates should subsidize council house rents in the 1950s was an emotive one, and is a valuable tapestry from which to examine the issue of social cohesion. This chapter examines the dilemma faced by four Labour Party-run councils, St Pancras, Lambeth, Islington and the London County Council (LCC), when deciding their rent policies in the 1950s. It argues that, despite local political priorities, the concerns of the national Labour Party drove the agenda, often to the detriment of the locally elected councillors and in opposition to locally decided policies.

It is clear that both the main political parties, due to the problems surrounding rate valuation and assessment during the 1950s, were particularly sensitive to the needs of the ratepayer. Consequently, if a locally decided rents policy threatened to raise the rates more than was deemed necessary, the national Labour Party rapidly squashed either the policy or, in the most extreme cases, the 'ringleaders' of the policy. This chapter, therefore, argues that local authorities were important tools of the state, both by allowing a level of local choice – apparent by the obvious differences in local priorities – and by ensuring that local decisions did not threaten or dilute centrally driven priorities.

The Labour Party and the role of local government

It is worth briefly giving some thought to the Labour Party's perception of the relationship between local and national government. The views of the Labour Party on this relationship can be loosely divided into two. First, the Labour Party has seen the relationship as the long arm of central government reaching out to the localities, ensuring that decisions and policies taken from above were implemented below. In contrast to this, local government has been seen as a proactive, democratic tier of government, determinedly autonomous and separated from the tendrils of Parliament.[1]

The view that a major function of local government was to provide credibility to national ideology or policy can be found in the ideology of the Independent Labour Party (ILP) at the end of the nineteenth century. As Cole points out, the Fabians encouraged the ILP 'to capture municipal government with the aim of using it as an instrument for the achievement of some measure of constructive Socialism'.[2] Between the two world wars, as John Gyford argues, the Labour Party's views on local government changed somewhat: 'Parliamentary socialism came to be the dominant strategy with its notion that the road to socialism lay through the electoral capture of central government.'[3] This strategy, Gyford continued, placed local government in compliance with centrally driven initiatives. Gyford reinforces this argument, noting that Attlee stated that a socialist government might need to employ commissioners who would be 'sent down into a locality to see that the will of the central government is obeyed and its plans implemented'.[4] Gyford argues that 'the view of local government as . . . the handmaiden of central government persisted in the decades after 1945'.[5] Goss reaffirms this view of the role of local government after 1945:

> The role of local government changed slowly under Labour . . . to that of a secondary structure involved in the implementation of nationally determined programmes. Labour's task locally, therefore, was no longer to demonstrate 'municipal socialism' in action but to fulfil its share of national progress. The local Labour 'project' was diminished by its transfer to the national stage.[6]

In contrast to the view of local government as the handmaiden of central government, advocates of local government proclaimed its democratic credentials and fought hotly for its autonomy from the state.[7] The LCC in particular was clear that the local government should not act as an arm of the national party. As an institution caught between national and local government, the LCC was in many respects in a stronger position than the borough or district councils with regard to local autonomy. As John Mason states, the problem for the LCC members was their role was often closer to that of Members of Parliament than to that of borough councillors.[8] The autonomy of the LCC was strongly advocated by Herbert Morrison,[9] who felt that the Labour Party outside the Council should not instruct Labour councillors how to act, and argued in the 1930 party conference that local government could not be operated 'on the basis of Councils being marionettes whose actions ought to be decided in detail from outside'.[10]

This chapter argues that both functions of local government – relaying centrally driven initiatives and providing an avenue for choice – have played a role in maintaining cohesion. Furthermore, contrary to their opposing positions, both functions can work in tandem. However, as seen below, local government as a mechanism for local choice can place it, at times, in juxtaposition to the state. When this occurs, a situation of conflict can arise, with quite dramatic consequences.

Rates – 'This is the mess, the muddle and the tangle'[11]

Concerns over the plight of the ratepayer during the 1950s derived from three areas: the strained relationship between the financing of local government and the post-war growth of local services;[12] the public perception of rate poundage; and lastly, battles over industrial and agricultural derating.

Although the Labour Party was out of office nationally, in areas like London, where the Labour Party held office in several borough councils as well as the LCC, contraction in local services or expansion in local rating had very real implications for politicians. Therefore, the Labour Party had to inform and implement an agenda locally that would, on the one hand, ward off the worst excesses of Conservative Party policy and, on the other hand, create an environment favourable to re-election, both locally and nationally.

Under the Local Government Act (1948), control over rate valuation moved from the local to central government.[13] Local authorities thereafter were not able to establish their own rateable base (how much a borough was worth), although they could still determine the poundage borne by the ratepayer (how much was paid per pound of the value of a property). However, rate valuations only occurred in 1956 and 1963, as opposed to the statutory five-yearly period set out in the Act of 1948.[14] This resulted in prolonged periods of time between valuations, meaning that the rateable values of the authorities were kept superficially low with resultant rises in the levels of rate poundage.

This situation had no direct financial consequences for local government. The problem was purely a political one. Using decimalization for example's sake, local authorities could levy 10p on each pound of a property worth £100 in order to raise £10 towards local revenue. Equally, the

Inland Revenue could decide that the same property was worth £200, after which the local authority could levy 5p in the pound to arrive at the same income. In both instances, the ratepayer pays £10. However, although the cost to the ratepayer may remain the same (e.g. the 5p or 10p in the pound), poundage, as realized by central and local government, had a specific importance to the public. As Young and Rao explain, the wide unpopularity of rates 'fed the supposition that local rateable capacity was subject to some kind of natural limit'.[15] The rateable capacity evidently reached its 'natural limit' just before the 1956 revaluation, when many rate poundages approached 20 shillings in the pound. As Young and Rao continue to expand: 'This figure had great symbolic significance, there being a public perception of a "sound barrier" . . . occurring at that level of poundage.'[16] Without periodic and timely revaluation, there was no tool to raise the valuation of a hereditament up and to push the poundage down.

The concern that the government felt over the rate poundage was emphasized during the passing of the Rating and Valuation (Misc. Provisions) Act (1955), introduced by Duncan Sandys.[17] This was, simply, an Act dealing with the miscellaneous parts left unfulfilled by the 1948 Act. *The Economist* reminded its readers that it was 'a purely tidying-up measure', and 'a temporary step in the direction of making an unworkable and indefensible system of rating work'.[18] *The Economist*, however, was more on target when it stated that the Act was

> designed to foil a howl of protest and a flood of appeals from ratepayers when, about a year from now [in the 1956 re-valuation], they find that the rateable values of their properties has been assessed substantially higher . . . One of the objects of the new Bill is to make sure that the new and higher valuations and the new and lower poundage rates will go through the ratepayers' letter boxes together.[19]

However, despite concern over public perception that rates were increasing, it was also true that as a proportion of local revenue, rates were decreasing. Rates actually fell after the war and, as a proportion of local authority finance, continued to fall throughout the 1950s. At the outbreak of war, rates exceeded 52 per cent of local revenue. In 1946/7, despite the growth in local authority services, rates had fallen to represent only 40 per cent of local revenue. Indeed, paradoxically, it was because the remit of local authorities was growing that rates decreased. As Young and Rao explain:

> grants soon came to provide a larger proportion of local revenue than rates, as a result of a national requirement to develop new services, and the need felt by the successive central governments to persuade and aid

the poorer authorities to keep to a higher standard of provision through grants-in-aid.[20]

When the review of local government finance was undertaken in 1955 by the Home Affairs Committee of the Cabinet, under the chairmanship of R. A. Butler, it was noted that local rates were growing more slowly than income or taxes, resulting in a dependence on the centre and central finance.[21]

A further cause for concern was that, following the war, different hereditaments were subject to different levels of assessment. In 1955, Sandys, in a move to modernize rates, drafted the Rating and Valuation Bill. This bill proposed that domestic properties should continue to be assessed at 1939 levels, with shops assessed at contemporary values. The government based this decision on the argument that there had been a free market in such property, as opposed to, for example, rents under rent control. However, the government soon realized that to punish the shopkeeper in such a way, when the domestic, industrial and agricultural ratepayer were in one way or another being aided, would not be acceptable. Subsequently, Clause One of the Rating and Valuation Act (1957) reduced the rates of shops, commercial and miscellaneous properties by one-fifth. The government passed this clause as a temporary measure and on the basis that it would cease at the next revaluation, when the Inland Revenue was expected to assess domestic properties at their current value.[22] Agriculture and industry remained untouched by the Rating and Valuation Act, with agricultural properties 100 per cent derated and industrial properties rated on current values with 75 per cent derating.

Unlike the devaluation of industry and agriculture in the 1920s, local authorities did not receive a block grant to recoup their losses arising from commercial rate relief. As various Conservative and Labour backbenchers pointed out, this did not bode well for the domestic ratepayer, who had to pick up the tab for rate loss for local government. It was further stressed that, unlike the industrial and commercial sector, domestic ratepayers did not have the same means as their industrial counterparts of writing rates off against taxes: the burden of rates would forever remain a burden. *The Economist* pointed out in January 1956 that a gross increase in rate payments for commercial properties would rank as a deduction for income tax. Commercial proprietors could therefore discount it by about half.[23] Indeed, the articulate rates vigilante, Mr Mitchison, MP,[24] was swift to point out that one of the beneficiaries of the rate reduction for shops was the Treasury: the less that industry could recoup on rates via tax, the more tax would line the Treasury's pockets. Furthermore – and Mr Mitchison was not alone in stressing this point – commercial relief did not just concern the small shopkeeper, the local corner shop or retailer. Clause One embraced all 'shops', including breweries, bank premises and those financial giants such as – again, Mr Mitchison was keen to point out – Unilever.[25]

Equally as contentious as commercial rate relief was industrial and agricultural derating. The Conservative government soon realized that one way of reducing the problem of local finance would be to place more of a burden on industry, thereby 'reducing the financial dependence of local authorities on the Exchequer and enlarging the scope for local initiative and enterprise in local government'.[26] The Cabinet, however, was by no means unified over this, with those such as Peter Thorneycroft, President of the Board of Trade, arguing that

> British industry is already today perhaps the most highly taxed in all the world . . . to tell it, on top of all this, that it is to bear another £25 millions in rates . . . will appear an odd sort of Christmas present . . . To court such unpopularity with industry for such minimal advantages to local authorities is surely a policy of doubtful wisdom.[27]

A year later, Thorneycroft, along with Enoch Powell and Nigel Birth, was to resign from the government in protest over the Cabinet's refusal to make cuts in public expenditure. The government finally compromised by reducing industrial derating, as an interim measure, to 50 per cent. This eventually came into effect with the Local Government Act (1958).

The Labour Party's views on the rating system were mixed. Tony Travers notes that the Labour Party was not impressed by the government's lukewarm proposals to rerate industry and cites Arthur Bottomley, speaking for the Labour Party, who argued that the bill failed to meet the financial difficulties of local authorities because it neither fully rerated industry nor gave local authorities the full benefit of the additional income from such rerating.[28] Equally, the Labour Party was quick to ridicule both the Rating and Valuation Acts, alongside the government's own backbenchers. The Labour Party's argument focused mainly on disparities in the rating system, and claimed that ad hoc Acts were being passed in lieu of a thorough review of local finance. The negative effect on the domestic ratepayer due to the delayed publication of the draft lists (the Rating and Valuation (Misc. Provisions) Act, 1955) and commercial rate relief (Rating and Valuation Act, 1957) was argued angrily by the likes of Mitchison and Jegar. However, opposition to the government's rating proposals was conspicuous by the avoidance of the generic plight of local authorities, as rating authorities and as a provider of services elected by the ratepayer, although individual examples were mentioned by the more discerning MPs.[29] Equally, the Labour Party seemed to be confused over how the rating system should be structured. Indeed, as *The Economist* pointed out, the Labour Party was as reticent as the Conservative Party, if not more so, to tackle the issue of agriculture rerating.[30] After all, the Labour govern-ments of 1945–51 had done little to tackle this issue, specifically during the passage of the Local Government Act (1948). Consequently, it could be argued that the Labour Party was keen to keep both agriculture and indus-trial interests complacent before the 1951 election defeat and wished them attentive in anticipation of subsequent elections.[31]

Local authorities and rent

Rates, therefore, were a problematic issue and, as will be seen below, only succeeded in confusing the equally problematic issue of rents for the Labour Party-run local authorities. To subsidize public housing from the rates was both politically and economically precarious. It would have been a brave politician who deliberately asked their electorate to pay more money (think of that 'sound barrier'), and, moreover, to pay more money for a service from which not all benefited. On the other hand, to place the burden of housing on to tenants – supposedly people in financial need – was also politically troublesome. The debate also had very real consequences for the local administration in office. If a council did not find a compromise that was deemed reasonable by either the government or local constituents, the residing administration could face numerous pit-falls ranging from individual surcharges to the loss of a majority at the next local election.

Nonetheless, the Labour Party lacked a thorough-going policy on rents during the 1950s. At the 1956 Labour Party Conference, the National Ex-ecutive Committee (NEC) encouraged the use of rent rebates.[32] Equally, at a conference of local councillors in London, January 1956, Gaitskell called for a system of differential rents and means testing.[33] As Gaitskell argued: 'the party is not, and never has been, opposed to means tests', but only to unfair and oppressive examples of them. The NEC therefore 'ac-cepted' the principle that for some Labour councils it 'might be wise to introduce differential rents, and to vary subsidies according to individual need'.[34] However, the NEC also emphasized that local authority response to rents was a question of local discretion.[35] Consequently, Labour coun-cils' policy on rents – at least initially – varied dramatically according to both local finance and politics. However, as shown below, the one local authority that deliberately lowered the rents – St Pancras – soon came up against insurmountable opposition from the leaders of their own party, with devastating results.

St Pancras Borough Council

The Labour Party in Holborn and St Pancras had a long radical tradition. As D. Mathieson expounds, the Constituency Labour Party (CLP) supported the Bevanites and took a radical position on most national and local issues, frequently offering advice to the NEC over party policy.[36]

The policy direction of the St Pancras Labour Group was led in the mid-1950s by John Lawrence. Without placing too much emphasis on one personality, it is worth giving some background to Lawrence. He joined the Labour Party in 1948 and was the editor of *Socialist Outlook*, a weekly paper published between December 1948 and October 1954.[37] Lawrence believed that socialism could only be achieved by overt pursuit of fundamental goals. In order to develop these ideas, the Socialist Fellowship was conceived in 1949, as part of the Labour Party, with John Lawrence on the Executive Committee.[38] Come April 1951, however, the Socialist Fellowship was disbanded by the NEC, which decided that it was following its own policies and not those of the Labour Party.[39] This was a severe setback for the *Socialist Outlook*, which split, accused Lawrence of becoming a Stalinist and then, by 287 votes to 213, sacked him as editor, in May 1954.[40] Throughout this turmoil, Lawrence's career in local government progressed. In 1953 he was elected as a councillor for St Pancras and, in the same year, as Chairman of the CLP. The scene was thus set for the battle over rents.

In St Pancras, various differential rent schemes were in existence in the post-war period. During 1949–53 when there was a Conservative majority at the Town Hall, different levels of rent were set according to the type of property, with pre-war property receiving the lowest rents. The incoming Labour administration disliked this system, since it introduced a system whereby the better-off lived in the newest estates – social segregation. Instead, the authority promoted a policy whereby rent went up by 2 shillings per floor. Thus, the tenant of a fourth-floor flat would pay considerably more than a tenant living on the basement level. The Housing Committee, however, found this scheme unsatisfactory. As Peggy Duff, Chairman of the Housing Committee, said: 'when we came to housing people from the waiting list, we found there still weren't enough families who could pay the high rent . . . We don't believe in segregating the poor from the rich. We believe that the rich and the poor have to learn to live together.'[41]

When John Lawrence became Labour leader of the council in May 1956, one of the first moves of that administration was to change to a system of equalized rents. As Peggy Duff states: 'The first thing I did was to get rid of the differentials, so tenants on the top floor had a rent reduction of eighteen shillings, and so on, arithmetically. This was a momentous occasion. It was probably the last time a council in Britain actually *lowered* rents.'[42] The council stressed that a reduction in rents would mean only a slight rise in rates, which John Lawrence justified: 'by that half penny, we can carry on with the good work of rehousing the people who really need rehousing, at rent they can afford. I don't think that is too much to ask of the average ratepayer.'[43] In fact, fortuitously, the penny rate was not raised, but, due to the new valuation list, lowered quite considerably.[44] For the financial year 1955/6, the penny rate was 21 shillings in the pound; in 1956/7 it was 14s 6d, a reduction of almost a third.[45] The change in rate calculation therefore aided the housing agenda of St Pancras considerably: a halfpenny increase for housing would mean little when hidden in a decrease in the rate poundage.

The decision to lower rents was taken at a time when the contribution from the Housing Revenue Account (HRA) towards the cost of housing was growing rapidly and other sources of income were decreasing. In 1952, the council would have expected to receive £83 per flat from the Exchequer and £14 from the LCC, with £46 contributed from the HRA. By 1956 this balance had vacillated, with the Exchequer paying £20 only for expensive sites and one-bedroom dwellings, the LCC £3 and the council finding £120: a significant decrease over four years of £74 per flat in external contributions.[46]

Despite this, in June 1957 the council decided to reduce the rents on a further 182 flats by half. This meant a loss of revenue of £4,575 for the part year and £6,000 for the full year, and therefore an extra £6,000 per annum needed from the HRA.[47] By July 1958, the council had a deficit of £250,000 in its Housing Account.[48] None the less, Peggy Duff assured the electorate that 'We want to try and keep the rents scheme going as it is . . . Our intention is to try and keep the rents at this level for as long as possible.'[49] The council simultaneously passed the following motion: 'we would like to reiterate the fact that we disagree in principle to a differential rent scheme, as we are opposed to any form of means test'. It continued by assuring the electorate that: 'despite the deficiency on the Housing Accounts attributable to the rents charged at the present time, there is no necessity for the Council to raise the general rate to offset deficiency'.[50]

In 1957 St Pancras had just seen the value of the borough drop because of the Rating and Valuation Act of that year. Due to the London equalisation scheme, the amount it had to find from rates did not change dramatically. Nonetheless, in 1957/8, rates were adjusted to 2s 10d above their previous level, bringing the total amount to 17s 4d.[51] Most of the rate rise was due to increased precept rates: police rates rose by 2d and the LCC rates went up by 2s 4d. St Pancras Council collected only 4d of the increase for itself.[52] Simultaneously, the banks raised interest rates by 2 per cent, which lost the council £12,000, necessitating the borrowing of loans on a weekly or short-term basis.[53] The need to create extra income from rates was not only due to the rent policy.

Up to this stage, changes in rates and valuations had aided St Pancras. The increase in the valuation lists in 1956 allowed it to hide any increases in rates that were due to the rents policy in the general decrease in the rates poundage. Equally, the loss of commercial and/or charitable income in 1957, which could have been extremely detrimental, brought in additional funds from the London equalization scheme. To all intents and purposes, St Pancras was making no waves as rents equalized and rent income decreased. Even a visit from the District Auditor, Mr Munrow, reaffirmed the council's housing policy: 'The Council have a very wide discretion and I should be loathed to interfere provided I was convinced that in reducing these rents, they were being reasonable.'[54]

The trouble started in 1957, when St Pancras embarked on two highly controversial campaigns. In March 1957, the council decided to cut the annual mayoral allowance from £1,795 to £300. As John Lawrence said:

> I disapprove of spending ratepayers' money on purely social functions which are absolutely useless, especially at a time when the cost of living is going up and up and people are having to go on strike to get a decent standard of living ... In future our Mayor will have to go about the Borough on public transport. Anyway, what's wrong with the Mayor going to a schoolchildren's party on a number 68 bus?[55]

From that time on, the Mayor was irreversibly linked to the 68 bus, gaining a certain notoriety for them both.

At this stage, the Labour Group of St Pancras Council came under fire from the Conservative councillors. Conservative councillor P. A. Prior accused the 'socialist council' of sacrificing great sums of money at the 'alter of the housing policy', announcing that 'housing is only one of the very many items which the borough council is called upon to supervise. It is a service which affects a comparatively small proportion of the ratepayers, so it is quite unjustified to sacrifice everything else for it.' Lawrence retorted by saying: 'local government is in crisis, but it is not due to our rents policy but the Government's strangulation of the local authority'.[56]

The council also attempted to cut its costs by cutting civil defence, which was a statutory duty. This created much publicity nationally, although Coventry had recently done the same. However, the council held strong. On 4 June 1957, in the middle of a small demonstration outside the

Civil Defence Headquarters, John Lawrence chained himself to the gates, declaring: 'We want these premises for housing, not for useless Civil Defence purposes . . . There is no Civil Defence against the H-bomb. There are 6,000 on our housing list and we want to provide homes for our families here.'[57] Unlike cutting the mayoral fund, this action had major financial ramifications for the council: as civil defence was a statutory service, part of the cost of running it was match funded by government grants. As the service was now being removed, the government no longer provided a grant and the full cost was still liable to the council. Therefore, despite the dramatic gesture staged by St Pancras, it only placed further financial burdens on the council. Subsequently, and unlike its housing policy to date, these schemes heralded the end for Lawrence's Labour administration.

St Pancras Council refused, 'in spite of pressure from the Tories and the Labour right, to increase rents'.[58] Indeed, it refused to consider any scheme that would segregate the poorer tenants from the more wealthy ones. The administration's housing principles remained firmly wedded to the ideal of welfare, and to equitable welfare. Until 1958, the council, perhaps helped by the idiosyncrasies of the rates, managed to implement its housing policy without any strife from the Labour Party executive. However, when the Labour Group began to show signs of increased activism and dissent, and an increasing disregard for the ratepayer's money, it was their housing policies that eventually brought their downfall.

As Peggy Duff explained: 'the real problem arose on something that seemed a minor issue: this question of the rents of tenants in de-requisitioned houses'.[59] The Requisitioned Houses and Housing (Amendment) Act (1955) repealed the existing requisitioning powers available to local government that allowed local governments to take over housing stock formally abandoned by their owners. Under the provisions of the Act, local governments were now obliged to hand back these properties to their original owners by April 1960. The Act gave no security of tenure to existing tenants: if the original owners were not prepared to allow them to stay as statutory tenants (licensees), they had no facility to contend this and could only hope that the council would find them alternative accommodation. By the end of 1958, there were still 28,000 requisitioned properties left, 90 per cent of which were in London.[60]

In keeping with its equitable rent policy, St Pancras decided to pay the difference in the rent for the tenants of properties that had been derequisitioned but were then subject to rent increases under the Rent Act (1957).[61] Section 4 of the Requisitioned Houses and Housing (Amendment) Act stated that councils might subsidize a tenant's rent until 31 March 1965, as long as the council could justify every individual case. In March 1958,

St Pancras 'considered the circumstances relating to over 100 cases' and considered 'that it is impossible to give consideration to individual cases without investigating the question of the tenants' income', and this the council was not prepared to do (the spectre of means testing looming).[62] Therefore, the Housing Committee decided to tackle the problem as a matter of principle. Although the council did not have any power to lower the rents, it was decided that the licensees should be treated as council tenants, and since council tenants were not liable for rent increases, neither should these tenants be. Importantly, under the Rent Act, 75 per cent of the cost would be met by the Exchequer, and thus the cost would not be borne totally by the rates. The motion was carried by 26 votes to 20.[63]

The problem was created by the fact that the council decided to deal with the situation 'en bloc'. As Duff explains, 'this is what caused the trouble, the totality of it. If we had exempted only half a dozen, we might have avoided a surcharge.'[64] However, further strife only added to the existing problems. In February 1958, a 'riot' broke out in Holborn Hall when Henry Brooke, the Conservative Housing Minister, came to talk about the Rent Act.[65] Duff described the scene:

> The hall was fairly full of the oddest collection of people. There were the Tory faithful, come to hear the word. There were John and his friends, well to the front and ready for action. There were also the fascists . . . After a while the Tory hierarchy moved out of the back room and took their places at the platform table. Trouble started almost immediately. Before long there was uproar. John Lawrence had taken over the meeting and the platform had withdrawn to the back room.[66]

Lawrence held an open-air meeting afterwards along with Jock Nicholson, Communist candidate for North St Pancras, which, Duff believed, 'was one of the sins that finished him'.[67] As an indication of the divisions between the local and national party, Lena Jeger, MP for Holborn and St Pancras, apologized for the meeting in the Commons, claiming, 'I feel that the arguments against this vicious piece of legislation do not need balloons and bicycle chains to underline them.'[68] She was later criticized by the CLP General Management Committee, to which she replied that she was already overdue for a three-line whip.[69]

The battle was lost: any ideals that the Labour Group attempted to implement were being prevented not only by governmental fiscal policies, but by their own party. In May 1958, the NEC suspended the whole of the Holborn and St Pancras South Labour Party, including John Lawrence, whom the NEC ousted as Group Leader. John Lawrence was finally expelled,[70] although the Holborn and St Pancras South Constituency Labour Party voted against throwing him out of the party.

In July, the District Auditor returned, somewhat ominously, to listen to the ratepayers. That month the Housing Committee decided to retain the present rent scheme. The meeting, however, came to a somewhat unfortunate and premature end when Councillor Humberstone collapsed and died.[71] In August, the auditor admitted that the situation in Islington was influencing his thoughts concerning St Pancras. Although the two boroughs had previously similar levels of rent, Islington had since adjusted its rents to the accepted level, which was the equivalent of twice the gross value of the properties involved.

For the year ending March 1958, the District Auditor placed a surcharge of £200 on each of the 23 Labour members of St Pancras, including the Mayor, who had voted for the rent subsidies.[72] In addition, in November of that year, J. W. Cooke, the Borough Treasurer, produced a report that detailed the full effect of the council's rent policy. The report ended by warning: 'even were a rent of 22 times gross value charged there would still be a deficiency of about £80 000 per annum to be met by the additional rate contribution'.[73]

On 12 November 1958, the Conservatives put down two motions for discussion at the council meeting, including the reinstallation of civil defence and a review of rents of all requisitioned and derequisitioned houses. The majority of the Labour Group (now headed by C. J. Ratchford) abstained during this motion and it carried with only the Lawrence faction voting against it as independents. By February 1959, the Housing Committee had exchanged the policy of equalized rents for a differential system of six rent scales. Evidently, local people were not impressed with the recent political arguments within the Labour Party, or the resultant policies, for come May that year the Conservatives were a majority in the council.

Bernie Holland believed that the Holborn and St Pancras South Constituency Labour Party was suspended from the Labour Party due to its condemnation of the 'anti-working class' activities of Woodrow Wyatt, who sought to 'vilify and bring into disrupt the Electrical Trades Union by an unscrupulous use of TV'.[74] Bernie Holland related that

> there had been so many complaints about Woodrow Wyatt. There was a meeting in Doughty St where the question arose about his fitness to be a member of the Labour Party, or certainly our Labour Party . . . and we carried the day, which was that he should be suspended or expelled from the local Labour Party, but we had to get the OK from further up . . . but this was just thrown out of the window. Next thing we knew was

this overnight suspension of the entire Holborn and St Pancras Labour Party.[75]

The Labour Party Annual Conference Report says little by way of enlightenment about the suspension of the CLP. However, the report does comment that

> the activities of Mr John Lawrence have been a matter of concern to the National Executive Committee for some time. Strong representations have been received . . . to the effect that the situation had become intolerable and that action was necessary . . . Also the National Executive Committee decided that the Holborn and St Pancras South Constituency Labour Party should be reorganised.[76]

The NEC particularly condemned the development of the 'Lawrence faction' on the council that voted against the reinstallation of civil defence and a review of rents of all requisitioned and derequisitioned houses.[77]

It is clear that the fate of the Holborn and St Pancras South Constituency Labour Party and of John Lawrence was tied not only to the fiscal and rent policies of St Pancras, but to the Labour Group's general dissent. However, it is interesting to note the financial implications of the dissent. Clearly, St Pancras could afford, up to a point, to introduce fair and equitable rents without raising the rates too much. However, when St Pancras removed services paid for by the ratepayer that 'benefited' all constituents of the borough (the mayoral account and civil defence), the state, including the Labour Group's own party, really became concerned. Therefore, arguably, it was not so much the amount of rates levied that concerned the Labour Party, but for what services St Pancras deployed this income.

Islington Council, indeed, had pursued a quite different strategy concerning its rent policy. Unlike St Pancras, Islington was reluctant to retain rents at a certain level. However, also unlike St Pancras, the Rating and Valuation Act (1957) proved to be costly to the borough. According to Lambeth's estimations, Islington received a fall of 7.3 per cent in its rateable value following the Rating and Valuation Act, which resulted in the council having to find approximately £83,000 from the rates.[78] Islington simply could not afford to be as strident as St Pancras over equitable welfare. However, it is clear that the rent payer verses the ratepayer led to divided opinion within the council chamber, with a number of casualties.

It was estimated that by the end of 1957, the outgoings of all the housing estates in Islington would be £561,127. The Finance Committee estimated that the composite contributions towards this would be £162,609 from the Exchequer, £46,132 from the LCC, £29,192 from rates and £5,287 from the rent of shops. This would leave £317,907 met from rents. Current rent contributions were £196,363. Thus, either rents or rates had to rise. It was estimated that raising rates would mean a 62 per cent increase to 10¼d in the pound. In November 1957, the full council agreed a report from the Estates Committee and from April 1958 the council increased rents to twice the gross value of the properties, leaving the excess income to be utilized for those in hardship.[79] A month later, 'rent rebels' Councillors Raymond Morley and Alexander MacDonald were expelled from Islington Borough Council's Labour Group.[80] North Islington Labour Party likewise expelled Councillor E. J. Simmons in May 1958.[81] Islington's rent policy also did not go down well with the local population. On 21 February 1958, police had to clear more than 200 protesters from Islington's public gallery during a debate over rent rises.[82]

However, the rent rebels' disgust with the Labour Party did not last for long. In February 1958 Councillor Morley asked the NEC to investigate his expulsion by the management committee of North Islington Labour Group and in August 1958 Morley made a second appeal against his expulsion from the Labour Party, following on from the announcement that Councillor Simmons was successful in his appeal for reinstatement.[83] It seems that Morley was not successful in his plea, since the *North London Press* reported that Morley lost the St Mary by-election to Labour at the end of October 1958.[84]

Lambeth was perhaps the only borough council out of those surveyed here that survived the fallout between rents and rates. Lambeth, in contrast to Islington and St Pancras, had in place since July 1948 a rent rebate scheme that reduced the need deliberately and publicly to raise the rents. Unlike St Pancras and Islington, Lambeth found a scheme of this nature, with its foray into their tenants income, a satisfactory solution: '[it has] ensured that accommodation, provided with the aid of public funds, shall not be denied to any section of the community in need of accommodation on account of the low level of their income'.[85] Lambeth seemingly by-passed the problems facing the other boroughs in question by establishing a scheme whereby rent was, at least superficially, divorced from the finance of the borough. Lambeth, via the rent rebate scheme, firmly connected rent to earnings, with only those on low earnings receiving the benefit of subsidies. In such a way, Lambeth avoided the pitfalls that besieged St Pancras and Islington.[86]

The LCC is perhaps the most interesting of the four councils mentioned here, since it both raised the rents of council houses and, although adamantly against means testing, it managed to dodge the political quagmire of rents and rates by creating a tier of 'economic' rents.

Like Islington, the LCC steadily raised its rents throughout the latter half of the 1950s. In October 1955 it raised the rents by 1 shilling to 5 shillings[87] and also placed charges on individuals lodging with tenants under the expectation that it would increase income in the HRA by £1,833,200 a year. By 1958, it had become apparent that this was a gross underestimate of the amounts needed. Interest rates and debt charges were increasing, the cost of materials and labour continued to rise and the Housing Subsidies Act (1956) reduced in total the amount of subsidies returned from central government. Estimates predicted that rate contributions could actually rise so much in forthcoming years as to overtake Exchequer contributions. However, the Housing Subsidies Act had stipulated that local authorities were no longer obliged to contribute a statutory set amount from rates to the Housing Revenue Account. Thus in October 1958, LCC rents were raised again within four bands of sliding scales according to size of dwelling, nature of the accommodation and estate, reducing the HRA contribution to the equivalent of the former statutory rate contribution. The overall rent contribution would now be 70 per cent of all outgoings for occupied dwellings. Rates would still subsidize other outgoings, such as debt charges on undeveloped sites and contributions to new and expanding towns and the borough councils, which the LCC did not think should be borne by the tenant alone.[88]

It was at this stage that the so-called 'Crown Prince Affair' occurred, in which Tom Braddock, a new LCC member from the infamous Holborn and St Pancras South, raised the subject of rents.[89] The background to this is worth outlining since it exemplifies the political tensions within the LCC.[90] In the 1950s, a small number of left-wingers became prominent within the LCC. One of these was Hugh Jenkins, who felt that there was too much discipline at County Hall. Since councillors were obliged to obtain the permission of the Chief Whip prior to asking questions at full council or open meetings, and to table motions prior to group meetings, this criticism was not unfounded.

Holborn and St Pancras South elected Tom Braddock to the LCC in 1958. Predictably, given the rent battles fought at his doorstep, he argued adamantly against LCC rent increases and urged tenants not to pay. He drew on the Labour promises before the 1958 election and decreed that it was outrageous to rush through rent rises after previously making such a stand against them.[91] In response, the Policy Committee of the LCC promptly threatened to expel all councillors who made use of the press or the council chamber to voice their disapproval of LCC decisions. The environment of intolerance within the LCC brought the Labour administration unfavourable publicity in the *Tribune*.[92] Subsequently, in March 1959, Isaac Hayward, the current leader of the LCC, declared that he was to resign.[93] The 'groups of would-be king-makers got busy at once',[94] with the Chairman of the Housing Committee, Alderman William Friske, suggesting to 30-odd colleagues the possible appointment of a deputy leader for the remaining months of Hayward's leadership. The incident finally concluded with Friske stepping into the new post of deputy leader and all attempts to oust Hayward forgotten. During this process, London's administration effectively silenced dissent against rent rises.

Conclusion

Central government in the 1950s was growing increasingly concerned and confused over the financing of local government services, as the extent of local services themselves grew. Subsequently, local authorities found the sources of finance available for services, and for housing specifically, increasingly problematic and often limited. If the means to finance housing was restricted, i.e. if governmental subsidies were restricted, rents or rates (or both) had to increase somehow. Local authorities had little leeway to manoeuvre around this issue, insofar as domestic rates were a particularly sensitive issue to the public. At the end of the day, it was the local councillors who had to make very real choices between raising rents and raising rate poundages. However, these choices cannot be seen as a locally isolated decision.

In the main (Islington, Lambeth and the LCC), the views of the national Labour Party translated themselves to the local Labour Groups, with the domestic ratepayer cushioned from paying any more towards public housing. Indeed, more than the national party, the Labour Groups were immediately aware of the detriment of antagonizing the local ratepayers – a constituent group far larger than the rent payers. St Pancras, as a wealthier borough that benefited from the changing valuations throughout the 1950s, had, out of all the councils mentioned, the greatest flexibility with regard to rates. Islington and Lambeth did not have the same luxury, and clearly felt the pressure of the rate-paying constituency when planning their rent policies. As Hepworth explains:

> an important factor to recognise is that the extent of discretion available to individual local authorities is different and can change differently. This affects the extent to which a local authority can or will respond to any pressure which may be exerted upon local government generally to contain or increase the growth in its expenditure.[95]

For each of the housing authorities mentioned, the rent solution varied, not only due to the politics and political groupings of members, but also due to the character of the borough and their specific problems, areas of concern and finance. The response of St Pancras Council therefore differed greatly from Islington and so on. Members of the Labour Party acknowledged this diversity of response: 'when it comes to local councils which are controlled by Labour majorities, you cannot get that unity. You have some introducing differential rents and some . . . which are not very much in favour of that.'[96] This diversity shows that local authorities did thrive on local choice, thus demonstrating an important function of social cohesion. However, local choice was only allowed up to a certain point. Once that point was found in juxtaposition to nationally ordained policies, as was seen with St Pancras, local constituency parties were given little choice but to toe the line.

7

Planned Communities: The Social Objectives of the British New Towns, 1946–65

Andrew Homer

The maintenance of the policy of 'social balance' was one of the key social objectives of the 'mark one' new towns. The 'mark one' new towns were those communities developed following the passing of the New Towns Act in 1946. The policy of social balance sought to bridge class cleavages within British society by encouraging members of the different classes to live close together. It was anticipated that this proximity of habitation would encourage social interaction, reduce class differences and result in a more socially cohesive society. However, it was not intended to create a society that was classless. The differing preferences of the classes, particularly with regard to housing, were acknowledged and planned for.

This chapter investigates the implementation of social balance within the first British new towns. It traces support for the policy among those responsible for framing the new towns legislation and key members of the post-war Labour government, and the sociological and popular reaction to it. There is also discussion of the role of the neighbourhood unit concept as a device to encourage interaction between the classes. The chapter evaluates the results of the policy with particular reference to one of the first new towns, Hemel Hempstead. It argues that the encouragement of social balance and its subsequent rejection by both the middle and working classes raises important questions about attempts to encourage social cohesion and class consensus within British society.

The British new towns

The establishment of new towns was very much a priority for a Labour government haunted by the unfulfilled 'homes for heroes' policy after the

First World War. To this end the government established the New Towns Committee almost immediately following its election in 1945. Lord Reith, who had previously served as Minister for Works and Buildings in the wartime coalition government, headed the Committee. The terms of reference for the committee charged it with considering:

> the general questions of the establishment, development, organisation and administration that will arise in the promotion of New Towns in furtherance of a policy of planned decentralisation from congested urban areas; and in accordance therewith to suggest guiding principles on which such Towns should be established and developed as self-contained and balanced communities for working and living.[1]

The Reith Committee worked at a frenetic pace, being appointed in October 1945 and completing its final report by July 1946. The committee also produced two interim reports dealing with matters requiring urgent attention. The first was published in March 1946 and dealt mainly with the question of deciding what type of agency should administer the new towns.[2] The second, published the following month, was not planned but was forced upon the committee by the government's attempts to push through the new town legislation ahead of schedule. The report dealt with all matters that needed to be considered before the legislation could finally be framed. These questions included: the acquisition of land; finance; land policy; and the local government status of the future communities. Despite the apparent speed at which the committee was working, the report was anxious to emphasize that all of the issues had been considered thoroughly. It argued that most of the matters raised had 'already reached an advanced stage of discussion' and that it had been a simple matter to pull all the strands together.[3] The *Final Report* of the New Towns Committee was intended to lay down the principles of planning and social life within the new towns. These included discussion of the factors to be taken account of during the preparation of the new town plans and the execution of the plans themselves.

The policy of 'social balance'

In its *Final Report* the New Towns Committee attempted to deal with the 'complex problem of founding the social structure of a new town and fostering its corporate life'.[4] The committee returned to its original terms of reference, stating that while the meaning of 'self-contained' was evident, the concept of a 'balanced community' was in need of greater definition.

The report saw the question of 'balance' in terms of social class, arguing that 'if the community is to be truly balanced, so long as social classes exist, all must be represented in it'. It continued:

> In all existing communities there is a tendency towards segregation by income group . . . If a socially homogeneous community is to be created, a conscious and sustained policy to that end will be needed on the part of the agency itself, and of the leaders of local industry and commerce and of social activity. It will not be enough merely to attract a representative cross-section of the population, to locate skilfully the sites for houses of all classes in the various neighbourhoods, and to provide at the earliest stage suitable buildings for various amenities.[5]

However, while it was committed to the concept of the socially balanced new towns, the Reith Committee was rather hazy as to how it could be attained: 'We believe this issue is vital to the success of these new communities; that what is achieved here may have an effect far beyond the field of its immediate application, and that there is need for much more thought and study on this subject.'[6]

The New Towns Committee was not the first to discuss the concept of social balance. It had also been examined in the Ministry of Health report *Design of Dwellings*, an addendum to an investigation chaired by the Earl of Dudley in 1944.[7] The Dudley Report pinpointed the major failing of housing during the inter-war period as the growth of single-class housing estates, such as Dagenham and Becontree, and exceeded its terms of reference in order to 'suggest means for the erection of complete communities rather than the development of purely residential estates for a single social class'.[8] It was hoped that once the different social classes had intermingled, any tensions between them would disappear.

The policy of creating socially balanced communities was supported by senior figures within the Labour government. The Minister of Health, Aneurin Bevan, declared: 'We have to have communities where all the various income groups of the population are mixed.'[9] This view was echoed by Lewis Silkin, the Minister of Town and Country Planning, who proclaimed: 'The first thing that we want is a variety of sections of the community.' Silkin wanted this variety 'in types of persons, in social and economic position, so that each person, each member of the community, may be able to make a contribution to the life of the community, and so that each may enrich by his experience the experience of others'.[10] However, it was not regarded as sufficient for the different social classes to be living within the same town. If the policy was to be successful, there would have to be 'social balance' within the streets and neighbourhoods of the new towns.

The role of the neighbourhood unit

The main tool used to aid the creation of these socially cohesive communities was the neighbourhood unit concept. The neighbourhood unit was based upon the ideas of the American town planner Clarence Perry, who published *The Neighbourhood Unit, a Scheme of Arrangement for the Family-life Community* in 1929.[11] Perry attempted to create a residential area possessing distinct local characteristics to meet the needs of family life. This was to be achieved by providing localized services such as schools, shopping facilities and community centres without supplanting the town centre, which the neighbourhoods would surround. He regarded the neighbourhood unit as a means of reinvigorating community feeling at local level within American cities. Instead of unplanned development leading to impersonal, overpopulated, high-density areas, it was intended that the more spacious, lower-density neighbourhood unit would rejuvenate community life. James Dahir, the compiler of a 1947 bibliography examining the neighbourhood unit, argued that 'modern life, based on an impersonal system of prices and mass production of goods, has created a way of life hostile to neighbourliness'. Dahir feared that the existence of 'mass men in a mass culture' could be 'the raw material for a totalitarian society'.[12] He believed that this depersonalized society could provide a fertile ground for communism.

According to Dahir, the neighbourhood unit consisted of four distinctive local factors.[13] Firstly, there was to be a centrally located elementary school within easy walking distance of all the houses (it was anticipated as being no more than half a mile from the furthest dwelling). The school was intended to be a focal point of the neighbourhood community. It was expected that parents walking their children to the school would begin to associate with each other, thus adding to the community's strength. Secondly, 10 per cent of the neighbourhood unit area was to consist of parks and playgrounds. This was an attempt to challenge the urbanism of American cities and produce a greener environment that had greater opportunities for leisure activities. The third aspect of the neighbourhood unit was to be the existence of local shops situated together at accessible points round the periphery. While the main shops were to remain situated within the town centre, smaller outlets were intended to provide for daily needs. The fourth aspect of neighbourhood units was that they would be residential environments. There would not be any industry contained within the units; it would be zoned in separate areas. The units would be self-contained: there would be no main roads cutting through them to disturb the peace or endanger children. It was anticipated that a community spirit could be stimulated by the careful situation of institutions such as churches and community centres within the neighbourhood units. While it was not expected that the use of the neighbourhood unit concept alone would create cohesive communities, it was intended to create greater opportunities for association among the residents and to stimulate community growth.[14]

While the neighbourhood unit was to become an accepted planning concept in Britain, there was to be a dramatic departure from its American counterpart. Along with reinvigorating community spirit by stimulating community interaction, the innovation was also expected to spark a greater understanding and interaction between members of different social classes. It was intended that residents with different income levels should live together within the same neighbourhoods. This went against the evidence and accepted planning practice, as summarized in Dahir's *The Neighbourhood Unit Plan: Its Spread and Acceptance*.[15] Significantly, Dahir made no claims that the neighbourhood unit created socially homogeneous communities. However, it is certain that this was firmly intended by the Labour government. Lewis Silkin was to declare, at the time of the passing of the New Towns Bill, 'the different income groups living in the new towns will not be separated'.[16]

Much of the original impetus for the notion of neighbourhood units containing representatives of all social classes came from the Dudley Report. It argued that various types of dwelling should be located within the units, suggesting that the neighbourhood should be '"socially balanced", inhabited by families belonging to different ranges of income groups, or at least not so unbalanced as to be restricted to dwellings and families of one type or income level only'.[17] The report claimed that this could be achieved by 'the grouping of the various types of dwellings in such a way that they satisfy the desires of the various social groups . . . and yet at the same time are part of the neighbourhood'.[18] The New Towns Committee firmly enshrined the concept of the neighbourhood unit within new town planning:

> The principal roads within the town . . . as well as other topographical features, tend to group the residential areas of the town into more or less clearly defined parts or neighbourhoods. Convenient placing of primary schools, minor groups of shops, churches, refreshment houses, meeting places, and other public buildings, may also, as nuclei, have the same effect. The neighbourhood is therefore a natural and useful conception.[19]

An 'urban village'?

The advent of the socially balanced neighbourhood unit was regarded as reminiscent of a more genteel and civilized age. Many compared the urban neighbourhood units with small rural communities. This idyllic view of village life was promoted by at least one member of the Labour government. Aneurin Bevan observed: 'We have to try to recapture the glory of some of the old English villages, where the small cottages of the labourers were cheek by jowl with the butcher's shop, and where the doctor could reside benignly with his patients in the same street.'[20] This view was reinforced by a Ministry of Town and Country Planning technical report examining the role of the neighbourhood unit in the planning of residential areas.[21] The ministry also regarded the neighbourhood unit as a means of recreating village life within the new towns. The report noted that in the 'village or small town where personal contacts are continuous and close, the community spirit is still lively and perceptible'. The neighbourhood unit was intended to recreate this spirit within the new communities by providing them with 'physical backgrounds which will encourage their growth, and to preserve in peacetime the spirit of neighbourliness and mutual reliance which flourished so strongly in civil defence and other activities of war'.[22]

However, the suggestion that 'village-style' life could be recreated within the new towns did not meet with universal approval. The sociologist Gordon Campleman challenged the assumption that the greater interaction between the classes within village life was solely due to their spatial proximity:

> Community life may have been highly developed in the villages, but this can, in large part, be ascribed to comparative remoteness and hindered mobility, which, together with a more common pattern of work in various aspects of agriculture, compels activity to turn inwards, as it were, and manifest itself in an increased community consciousness.[23]

A further attack upon the notion that the neighbourhood units could recreate an 'urban village' came from the sociologist, Peter Mann. He believed that the concept was based upon a romantic and idealized vision of village life. While he admitted that villages 'did have a mixture of social classes, with the squire, parson and teacher having important social positions', he did not regard this as evidence of a society that was socially cohesive. 'Interaction was surely never on a basis of equality: one would suggest that the social structure had many aspects of a caste, rather than a class, system.'[24] Mann concluded that the attempts to use socially balanced neighbourhood units to recreate a form of village life could reveal an underlying concern about life in post-war Britain. He claimed that the idea was '"anti-urban," and its adoption and support may well be taken as an instance of our society refusing to face up to the social structure of urban life'.[25]

Contemporary views of social balance

J. E. MacColl discussed the social implications of the new towns programme.[26] MacColl was a member of the Hemel Hempstead Development Corporation and Mayor of Paddington. He argued 'the ideal is a wholly admirable one for any new town corporation to set before it'. He continued: 'That the Colonel's Lady and Judy O'Grady should join together in the joyous adventure of building up a new community would be a social demonstration of first rate significance.'[27] However, this would be a difficult task to achieve. MacColl warned that 'Poplar and Cheltenham will not easily lie down together.'[28] The main obstacle to overcome would be the differences in class culture.

> Class distinctions are obstinate things and the middle classes have peculiar social customs which are not likely to make their normal representatives relish mixed development. To the Colonel's Lady a garden wall exists to enable her to read in peace in the open without interruption. To Judy O'Grady it is something to be talked over. There are differences of language, of social behaviour, indeed of ethics, which will not easily be reconciled.[29]

Gordon Campleman argued that the division between the social classes was a natural phenomenon. He felt that any attempts to encourage them to interact could result in class conflict rather than cohesion. He claimed: 'Social stratification has led to geographic separation, and this in turn has accentuated social stratification, and perpetuated class divisions and it is unrealistic to assume that these class divisions can be overcome merely by reducing the physical distance between classes.'[30]

The suggestion that class differences could be overcome by the increasing spatial proximity was further undermined by sociological research. The policy of the different classes intermingling went against popular opinion. A survey carried out by Bertram Hutchinson in Willesden assessing popular attitudes towards the new town programme emphasized a preference for living in single-class areas. The higher up the social scale Hutchinson surveyed, the stronger the preference was emphasized. Hutchinson concluded that it was 'contrary to the wishes of the majority of the Willesden people that the planning of a new town should result in the close intermixture of classes in the same street'. Hutchinson did suggest an alternative: 'the planning of mixed neighbourhoods, however, is another matter, and might be acceptable'.[31]

The campaign against the idea of socially balanced neighbourhood units was growing. A vitriolic attack upon the concept came from Peter Mann. He argued that the idea was 'based upon an erroneous analysis of the social structure of urban society'. It was 'an ideal that is unlikely to be attained without a complete change in the structure of our society'. Mann implored, 'let us bury it quietly, and begin to think again from a sociological rather than an ideological basis'.[32]

Ruth Glass's study of Middlesbrough also introduced qualifications. She acknowledged that the units had practical advantages, but attacked the romantic notions of resuscitating a village-type life within a town as being of dubious validity.[33] Indeed, Glass was to be at the forefront of an attack by the left against the concept of social balance. She argued that it was a strategy to keep the working classes in their place and prevent political action. Glass denounced 'the dispersal of working men to model villages under the aegis of their "masters" as a means of dispelling the danger of working class combination'.[34]

Socially balanced communities?

One of the first British new towns designated was Hemel Hempstead in Hertfordshire. The master plan for the new town steadfastly followed the New Towns Committee's commitment to ensure that a social balance was maintained within the town. However, the Hemel Hempstead Development Corporation acknowledged that 'to achieve this in practice and without compulsion it would seem that some compromise should be made in the distribution of the classes of houses'. To this end, each of the town's neighbourhoods was to be given different class characteristics depending upon whether it contained subsidized (i.e. primarily working-class) or unsubsidized (middle-class) housing. 'Middle-class' housing would be built at a much lower density. For example, the 'primarily subsidized' neighbourhood of Adeyfield would contain 19.3 persons per acre while the unsubsidized area of Warner's End would contain only 11.4 persons per acre. In Hemel Hempstead, there were to be three neighbourhoods containing primarily subsidized housing, with two neighbourhoods containing a majority of unsubsidized housing. However, Hemel Hempstead Development Corporation did not shy away altogether from the prospect of socially balanced neighbourhoods, since two areas, Grovehill and Aspley, were allocated to 'equally subsidised and unsubsidised housing'.[35]

In its final annual report before dissolution, published in 1962, Hemel Hempstead Development Corporation claimed that 'the desired balance has been achieved so far as types of occupation and income groups are concerned'. The corporation attempted to justify this argument by comparing types of housing contained within the five neighbourhoods completed by 1960. It replaced the terms 'subsidized' and 'unsubsidized' with 'grade one' (houses and flats with inclusive rents up to about 55 shillings) and 'grade two' (houses and flats renting at £150 per year, houses sold and private enterprise housing). Overall the town had an average of 76.6 per cent 'grade one' housing and 23.4 per cent 'grade two' housing.[36] In 1961 the population of England and Wales was 19.2 per cent middle class and 80.8 per cent working class.[37] Within the neighbourhoods themselves, Adeyfield (primarily unsubsidized) had 75.3 per cent 'grade one' and 24.7 per cent 'grade two'. Examining these figures, it appears that the neighbourhood had achieved the social balance intended in the master plan. However, in Warner's End, an area intended to be wholly unsubsidized, the figures matched those of Adeyfield with 78.2 per cent 'grade one' and 21.8 per cent 'grade two'. Bennett's End (the eventual name for the Aspley neighbourhood), which had been allocated to equally subsidized and unsubsidized housing, showed the greatest amount of social balance, containing 69.7 per cent 'grade one' and 30.3 per cent 'grade two'.[38] This suggests a serious failing in at least one of the first new towns: its predominantly working-class population and its failure to attract the middle classes in sufficient numbers.

Many members of the middle classes did not find living in a new town an attractive proposition. In 1953, the rector of Crawley new town was moved to write to *The Times* that 'higher income groups are not being attracted . . . in a sufficient proportion'. The rector feared that this would have a negative impact upon the development of the new town, as there would be 'deficiency of local leadership to which English people are accustomed'.[39] The former Deputy Social Relations Officer of Stevenage Development Corporation recalled: 'senior management tended to look for a house outside the new town . . . if they didn't want to live in a village then, by and large, their wives did'.[40] He explained that the managers 'tended not to want to live in what they regarded were . . . council estates. They preferred to pay a lot more for inferior housing, sometimes outside the town.'[41] One of the biggest obstacles to the middle classes moving into the new towns was that, initially, all housing was for rent rather than private ownership. The Ministry of Town and Country Planning was aware of this problem and urged the new towns to increase the number of privately owned houses.[42]

Hemel Hempstead Development Corporation was so concerned with its failure to attract members of the middle classes in sufficient numbers that it was prepared to undermine the key policy of self-containment, which required that the householder should work as well as live in the new town in order to discourage commuting. A memorandum from the corporation's General Manager admitted that self-containment had for the middle classes 'been reduced in status from a principle to a mere preference'. The memorandum also declared that the 'rules governing eligibility for the middle classes are considerably more generous than ... for the working classes'.[43] The development of this policy was ac-knowledged by the ministry, which declared that Hemel Hempstead should be 'prepared to sell or let a middle class house to any Londoner, wherever he works'.[44] The memorandum admitted that the dream of the Labour government and the Reith Committee, that the middle and work-ing classes would live side by side, was not practicable. The middle classes demanded housing that was planned at a lower density and was available freehold rather than leasehold. It added: 'it would be undesir-able ... to get too much intermingling of freehold and leasehold plots'.[45] Writing in 1961, the former General Manager of Stevenage Develop-ment Corporation admitted that not one in ten of the managing directors and senior executives of the new town industries had moved into the town. The General Manager believed that an executive would not wish to live 'cheek by jowl with his own work-people, nor they with him'.[46]

The myth that the neighbourhood unit had social properties for bring-ing the classes together was finally laid to rest in 1968. The sociologist Brian Heraud carried out a study of the different neighbourhoods con-tained within Crawley new town. He discovered that the different neighbourhoods had 'taken on distinctive class characteristics', rather than becoming class-balanced areas.[47] There were two main reasons for this. Firstly, there were the personal preferences of those who moved between the neighbourhoods: middle-class families who had initially moved into one neighbourhood often moved out to those areas which they felt better represented their aspirations.[48] The second reason was a change in policy by the development corporations: desperate to ensure that sufficient members of the middle class moved into their towns, the corporations had begun to sponsor the construction of more select neigh-bourhoods.[49]

Conclusion

The sociologist Norman Dennis has claimed that 'housing estates represent that exaggerated result of processes that are common to our society'.[50] This view was echoed by the geographer James H. Johnson, who believed that the 'various forms of urban development being built on "green field" sites are likely to give a direct expression of the behaviour of contemporary urban society'.[51] These views are particularly pertinent when examining the attempts to encourage social cohesion and class consensus within the first British new towns. The failure to create socially balanced communities and stimulate social interaction was not a problem peculiar to the new towns. Rather, it outlines more acutely the resilience of the different class solidarities within post-war British society.

The attempt to use the first new towns to create class cohesion delineates both the desire of the post-war Labour government to break down class barriers and its outright rejection by both the middle and, to a lesser extent, working classes, who preferred to remain with the people they regarded as their own. The major reason for the failure of the socially balanced neighbourhood unit was that, while it was an honourable intention, it failed to take account of class prejudice and culture. Very few of the new town migrants wished to live in areas that contained a mixture of classes. Indeed, the continuation of this policy severely hampered the abilities of the new town development corporations to attract members of the middle classes. A more realistic and less idealistic policy might have met with greater success.

8

Reconstituting the Family: Education for Parenthood and Maternity and Child Welfare, 1945–60

Louise Tracey

The welfare state was based on an idea of the family. This family contained a male breadwinner with a dependent wife and children, and was viewed as a unit to be supported from the outside. Consequently, welfare policy can be used to explain the post-war reinforcement of the ideology of women's role as a full-time wife and mother.[1] However, such an analysis does not assess the beliefs surrounding the dynamics within the family beyond this external gender division of labour: for example, it does not explain how women were to mother once they were in the home.[2] While much important work on the welfare state and the maternity and child welfare (M&CW) services in the post-war period has focused on the increased medicalization of these services, the role of education for parenting has largely been ignored.[3] The history of the infant welfare movement demonstrates the great importance placed on maternal education in the early part of the twentieth century. This arose out of high infant mortality rates and concern for the health of future generations. However, despite improved medical knowledge and health, and declining infant and maternal mortality rates by the end of the Second World War, education for mothering remained an important aspect of maternity and child welfare provision.

At the end of the Second World War there were fears surrounding the breakdown of the family, arising primarily among politicians and professionals. Consequently, two committees were established:[4] firstly, an Advisory Committee on Mothers and Young Children, 1943–4, 'To consider and report upon the existing arrangements for the teaching of parentcraft and how this might be extended and developed', which

136

reported directly to the Ministry of Health; and secondly, an Interdepartmental Parentcraft Committee in 1944, organized jointly between the Ministries of Health and Education, with the aim of co-ordinating such education. Implicit within these two committees was a desire to 'rebuild the family', and education for parentcraft was seen as the key to this. Yet there was an inherent contradiction implicit within this: between the idea of establishing a stable and viable family unit and the belief that the family is a natural institution that should, and can, function effectively without outside interference.

This chapter will question why education for parentcraft was considered important, what particular form of family it was seen as desirable to reconstruct or 'recreate', and what the implementation of the maternity and child welfare services tells us about the constructions of the household and the family over the period 1945–60. In particular, the ideas of these committees will be used to illustrate state ideals surrounding the post-war family. In addition, it is important to remember that such policies towards education were implemented by welfare workers on a professional and individual level. The welfare state and the National Health Service (NHS), under whose umbrella the maternity and child welfare services sheltered, were heralded to uphold the principle of universality, and were to be provided free at point of contact. How far was there a consensus on parenting roles? Finally, the interactions of gender and class in competing notions of the family will be examined together with the contradictions contained therein.

Concerns surrounding the family

Expressions of concern about the family are 'episodic responses to perceptions of actual or incipient family failure'.[5] In the early decades of the twentieth century, wartime encouraged attempts to improve the physical welfare of children. The infant welfare movement can be seen to have arisen out of the Boer War, and the Maternity and Child Welfare Act was introduced at the end of the First World War.[6] Similarly, the Second World War 'had the effect, in Britain at least, of turning thoughts towards children and their mothers'.[7] Certainly war does focus society on its own future and the reason for fighting. That future is no better exemplified than through children. Mothers, as those believed most crucial to a child's development and those with the primary responsibility for child care, are generally incorporated into this spirit of concern. However, the concerns surrounding mothers and children in wartime can also be linked to notions of masculinity. In a time when men are being urged to die for king and country, a further image of patriarchy is used. If the nation-state is the protector, then it is women and children who are used to arouse the desire to protect.

The need to support the family as it was constructed during this period was due to the fact that, as an institution, the family was considered to be the foundation of society.[8] In particular, children were important for democracy and the future of the nation. The family, as the location of the socialization of citizens, was seen as vital because 'The home is, of course, the place in which the child's future is most shaped.'[9] Yet this does not explain the desire to intervene within the home. This was caused by the concern that there were changes occurring within the family itself. Consequently, it was believed that 'a change of heart is needed if family life is to be rebuilt'.[10]

Although in hindsight the 1950s is seen as a highpoint of domesticity and there is little indication that family and gender relationships had changed, the fear that family bonds were being substantially destroyed was very real. The war was perceived to have caused change and insecurity, and in particular to have damaged family bonds. Families were separated, women were increasingly in employment, and children were evacuated and in war nurseries. There was anxiety that there had been a loss of family discipline and that a change in gender relationships was occurring. Such factors and the inherent social dislocation caused by war and wartime measures were seen to have made 'the task of keeping the home together almost impossible'.[11] A fall in the birth rate, a rise in juvenile delinquency and increased illegitimacy and divorce rates appeared to support such concerns.

War may seem an important catalyst, but longer-term trends were also significant. The Parentcraft Committees believed that the trend of modern life was to 'replace the home rather than to reinforce family life'.[12] Several factors contributed to this. Firstly, women's roles outside the family were of particular concern. Women, including mothers, were increasingly taking up paid employment (albeit part-time employment) in the post-war period, following the pre-war trend. They were therefore believed to be losing the domestic skills and valuable time thought necessary for a successful family life. For example, the Women's Institute was concerned that women were losing their mothering skills, not only through involvement in the armed forces but also by their involvement in industry.[13] The impact on household management of wartime conditions, such as rationing and the undertaking by women of the dual roles of domestic and paid employment, was entirely ignored.

Secondly, the falling birth rate, associated with pronatalism and illustrated by the Royal Commission on Population reporting in 1946, meant that mothers needed educating as 'given the dearth of large families at the present time, the majority of women are novices in the field of motherhood'.[14] Therefore it was not only existing families that were at risk but future home-makers. The busy life of working women in the war was seen to have meant that young women had missed out on the opportunity of learning how to raise a family by example within their own homes. Consequently, courses were run for women leaving the armed forces at the end of the war, covering 'all aspects of home-making', and a need to make similar provisions for young women leaving industry was also identified.[15] Similar concerns, particularly surrounding women employed in factories, continued in the 1950s.[16] This was compounded by the fact that traditional community and family ties were also seen to be diminishing and this informal method of education was declining.[17] Therefore, it was working and working-class women who were thought to need the most help. In this sense, the state could and should step in where previous generations had now 'stepped out'.

While it would appear, therefore, that it was in fact a rebuilding of the family that was desired, this does not take account of the changes that were occurring in beliefs surrounding the nature and needs of the child. During the inter-war period, scientific principles of health and hygiene had advanced with considerable success, particularly in improving the physical well-being of children. Such successes led to scientific approaches to child-rearing methods themselves and the behaviourist school of thought, dominated by John B. Watson in the USA and Frederick Truby King in Britain.[18] Behaviourism was to socialize the baby to fit the world into which she was born, and character building was classed as of primary importance. Therefore mothers should feed, sleep and play with their infant according to the clock rather than in response to their baby's demands.

However, in the post-war period psychological theories began to stress the importance of the mother–child relationship and the emotional as well as the physical care of the child. The man identified as most responsible for the change in ideas was John Bowlby. Bowlby was a psychoanalyst who in research prior to the Second World War had found a statistical correlation between a disrupted childhood and a delinquent personality.[19] In 1948 the World Health Organization (WHO) asked him to report on the long-term effects of institutionalization on children, and the results were published as *Maternal Care and Mental Health*, in 1951.[20] In this he found a connection between 'affectionlessness' and delinquency, drawing on evidence from the experience of wartime evacuation. He argued that a child's early attachments were crucial for her future mental health. Importantly, however, this affectionlessness was termed 'maternal deprivation'. It was the quality of the mother–child bond that was the crucial factor. Bowlby's report became a most influential document and was reissued by Penguin as *Child Care and the Growth of Love* in 1953.[21]

Although such ideas are generally attributed to John Bowlby, this is mainly due to the fact that by reviewing the field in 1951 he was the first person to draw the strands together into one coherent argument. He was by no means the only proponent of such views.[22] The Second World War did not give birth to these ideas, but the experiences of children in war-time, for example in war nurseries and through evacuation, did give credence to many theories already in existence. Therefore, historians of child-care literature have noted that the immediate post-war period was marked off from the pre-war period by a 'radical change in the advice the new generation of experts offered'.[23] This new advice is generally encapsulated by the term 'permissiveness'.

The flood of literature after the war shifted the focus of attention much more to the mother in the wake of the newly discovered psychological importance of the mother–child relationship. Although differing in perspectives these psychoanalytical theories had certain themes in common: firstly, the importance of the mother–child bond, a relationship based on love; secondly, the significance of both the maternal instinct and the child's will; and finally, the importance of stability in terms of a continuous relationship with the mother for a child's future emotional well-being. The socialization of children and the importance of good mothering became frequent themes.

This renewed interest in child care in the post-war period can be evidenced by the growth in the number of child-care manuals and their rising sales since 1945.[24] However, while 'completely new and up-to-date instruction manuals were necessary for mothers who were self-consciously cutting themselves off from the examples of their own mothers', there is little evidence that these reached the mass of the population.[25] The establishment of the maternity and child welfare services at the beginning of the twentieth century and their extension under the NHS, however, did provide an important source of advice. For many women, working-class women in particular, the welfare state would have been their only contact with child-care experts.[26] Therefore, while child care is perceived to have undergone a 180° change in the immediate post-war period, as evidenced by child-rearing manuals, how far did the maternity and child welfare services subscribe to these new ideals? And how far did this represent a change in the desirable family ideal?

Reconstructing the family

This emphasis on 'the family' and 'parenthood' is relatively gender neutral. The word 'parentcraft' itself was defined by the Advisory Committee on Mothers and Young Children as 'the satisfactory rearing of children and the art of good home-making'.[27] The Interdepartmental Committee certainly saw a great deal of scope in the use of the term: 'The definition of the term "parentcraft" is difficult to embrace and it is not easy to set narrow limits to our inquiry.'[28] Yet the Ministry of Health favoured involving 'a study of the mind and body of the child' as the focus of parentcraft rather than home-making, which it was feared could divert attention towards what was disparagingly termed 'table-decoration'.[29] The interest in the emotional well-being of the child was emphasized with the publication by the Ministry of Health with the support of the Parentcraft Committee of a booklet *You and Your Children*.[30] The author was Dr Doris Odlum, 'a woman medical psychologist', and the book dealt with 'the psychological handling of children'.[31]

Among welfare professionals specializing in education for parentcraft there was also a move towards psychology and psychoanalysis, the emotional as well as the physical care of the child, with emotional aspects increasing in priority over the period 1945–60. Yet, the practical elements of child care could not be ignored. For example, it was felt that parents should now 'understand something of the child's physical needs and quite a lot about his emotional needs'.[32] A child's earliest experiences were considered important in the development of her personality. In contrast to the inter-war period, the child should also be seen as an individual, allowed to develop her character or habits in her own way and at her own pace.[33] This should be facilitated by a secure and loving environment. The essential need of the under-five was for understanding.[34]

The use of the term 'parenting' in these committees was important. The increase in concern for the emotional and mental health of the child meant that fathers could be further involved in child care. The change from the term 'mothercraft' to that of 'parentcraft' is identified as occurring in the early 1940s.[35] This is interesting as it occurred during a time when men were increasingly likely to be away at war. Yet, such definitions did not preclude gender differences in 'parenting' roles. The emphasis on the emotional care of a baby has implications for the fathering role, despite the fact that it was the mother who was the traditional 'carer'. However, given the emphasis on the mother–child bond within psychology and psychoanalysis, the mother's care was considered paramount, particularly in the early years, and there were conceptual differences between parents in who provided what.

A mother was responsible for her child's intellectual growth, emotional adjustment and chances of future happiness in relationships. Constant care and security were important, as was the mother–child dyad in which this was to be provided; the mother 'represented the child's gateway into the world and [her] link with reality'.[36] Given the changed beliefs surrounding the nature of the child, mothers were to follow their baby's lead. In practical terms, this entailed some radical changes from the rules and regularity of the inter-war years, and the professional journals echo some of the suggestions provided by the new child-care manuals. For example, behaviourism and scientific principles of child-rearing had argued for breast feeding, inspired by the nutritional and immunization properties of breast milk. However, post-war this was infused with psychological advantages for both the child and mother, not least the strengthening of the mother–child bond, encapsulated by the phrase 'the nursing couple'. Recommendations were also made for feeding on demand, rather than the old three- or four-hourly feeds. Babies knew when they were hungry and how much milk they needed. Picking up a baby who cried was no longer spoiling that child, but was a necessity, ensuring security in future life.[37] Bad early mothering could result in a damaged adult personality, juvenile delinquency or, in girls, sexual promiscuity.

This new emphasis on the psychology of the child also engendered a psychology of the mother. Mothers should respond to their child's needs, and that response should be given in a particular manner. Being a good mother meant possessing a positive and loving attitude towards one's infant. A baby needed the close relationship and feeling of love to be imbibed with her nourishment. A mother needed to be 'constantly, even though subconsciously *aware* of her children'.[38] All a mother had to do to achieve this status was to act naturally. When a child could not explain what was needed, helped by her own 'maternal instinct' a mother would know what was best for her child. While a mother's pleasure was vital for her baby, this was also linked to satisfying a woman's deepest instincts in the process. In this relationship, both partners found satisfaction and enjoyment. The mother would have the knowledge that she 'herself has provided her baby with its instinctive demand for her'.[39] The responsibilities and duties of mothering were expanding and the price of failure increasing, but by couching this in a litany of pleasure for the mother, the true implications of mothering work were hidden. However, by the late 1950s some voices were being raised in concern that this had gone too far and caused increased anxiety in mothers, a theme also adopted later by many feminists.[40]

As, from the outside, the family was treated as a single entity, 'When considering the family, the father must be included.'[41] The awareness of psychology alongside the term 'parentcraft', as mentioned above, did suggest an increased role for the father. The Interdepartmental Committee on Parentcraft began by proposing to make a film that would be of interest to fathers, particularly for those men returning home after the war.[42] Although such a project was never completed by the committee, the mother–child dyad did not completely exclude the father, although it did make his role secondary. The father's role held certain key duties; primarily those providing economic and emotional support. Initially the father's role was that 'He contributes to the happiness of the mother and to her ability to found a family.'[43] The father enabled the mother to devote herself to the constant care of her child. He was needed to help the mother feel well in body and happy in mind, and to give her moral support.

Fathers were also to provide a role model to children of both sexes. The father acted as a giver of material advantages, he was the remote bearer of the authority of the outside world, and a healthy mother–father relationship would provide 'a degree of security in early life which will prevent people from seeking it in strange ways later on'.[44] In this way, the family would perpetuate itself. The father was brought into the family more in the post-war period, enabled by the psychological significance now placed on child-rearing. However, this was at no risk to his role outside of the home, as breadwinner. Instead it was predicated by this role.

This model of parenting was also influenced by changing ideas surrounding marriage. In the post-war period, equality and companionship in marriage were seen to be increasing in importance. In contrast with the inter-war period, fathers were at home more, working shorter hours and receiving paid holidays, and homes themselves were also becoming more attractive. Within this context a new sexuality within marriage was also being promoted. For Dr L. G. Housden, the Chairman of the Parentcraft Committee for the National Council for Maternity and Child Welfare and adviser to the Interdepartmental Committee on Parentcraft, marriage was the crux of a good family. The parents should spend time together to strengthen their relationship, as well as with their child; 'Marriage should be one of *man's* chief means to a full and contented life.'[45] It was only through this that healthy children could be produced.

Yet this family was not formed just through wedlock; a happy marriage was vital. Not only was a healthy childhood unable to be produced outside of marriage, but it was not possible within an unhappy marriage either. However, rather than advocating divorce, Dr Housden suggested learning to be 'happy *though* married'.[46] Therefore, in a period when the mother–child dyad was being emphasized, so was the wife–husband bond. In both relationships, though, the wife/mother is the centre and therefore located as the keystone of the family. The mother was essential to the child *and* to the husband. For example, in talks given at M&CW clinics, women were told that while a 'Mother [may have] her proper times for self-attention', this had hidden benefits as 'Father does not feel neglected and therefore shoulders more cheerfully his share of the extra work a baby makes.'[47] So, given the importance of this model family, how should they be taught parentcraft?

Education for parentcraft

Given the importance placed on the family and parenting, the Parentcraft Committees believed that, in an ideal world, everyone should be taught parentcraft and it should be gradually built up throughout life. However, the focus was actually on young and prospective parents. As was acknowledged in a circular of 1944 from the Ministry of Health to local authorities, while it was 'probably desirable' that young people be instructed, it was 'as expectant mothers and as actual parents that the welfare authorities will touch them more closely'.[48]

As stated above, these activities were primarily directed through the already established M&CW services; through ante- and post-natal care as well as through Parents', Mothers' and Fathers' Clubs. This focused attention on the child under five years of age, which, in effect, coincided with the years at which education for parenthood was considered most important. Psychoanalytical thought prescribed that there was a particular time when parents were perceived to be most receptive to advice: 'It is important to remember that parentcraft instruction given in advance of the baby's arrival is in many ways more valuable than that given afterwards', as 'You have probably had the experience of seeing a child with established problems at your first visit, as early as the first or second week of life . . . It is quite simple to undo the physical difficulty as a rule, but it is not so easy to undo the emotional disturbance that has arisen between the child and the mother.'[49]

However, in effect this principally meant education for mothers. Firstly, such education was focused within the already established M&CW services and could be combined with the medical care that was their primary focus. Secondly, the importance placed on the role of the mother over this period, as mentioned above, ensured that education for mothercraft was given priority. Therefore, although there was a desire to promote education for 'fathercraft', as seen above, this was found difficult to implement. They were rarely at home when health visitors called and Fathers' Clubs were few in number and more voluntary in nature.

In addition, over the period 1945–60, there were increased opportunities for teaching women how to mother through the M&CW services. The development of the M&CW services had been taking place throughout the twentieth century. Wartime in particular had increased this process. However, the NHS, in particular, enabled mothers to be in closer contact with health and welfare professionals and therefore increased the potential for such teaching. The welfare state made these services free at point of contact under a universalist principle. The main contacts with mothers were midwives, health visitors, hospitals and M&CW clinics. These all had specific roles within education for mothering. Health visitors were the principal educators and did so within the context of a woman's own home.[50] Midwives helped and advised during childbirth and generally the first 10–14 days of the child's life. The clinics provided advice and support for up to the first five years of the child's life.

However, perhaps most significant is the change in the place of birth which was occurring during this period. The post-war years saw an upwards trend, already established during the inter-war years and accelerated during wartime, in hospital births. In 1933, 24 per cent of births took place in hospital. By 1946 this had risen to 54 per cent.[51] The introduction of the NHS meant that health services were to be provided on the basis of need, rather than material status.[52] Consequently, while the birth rate in hospitals was by no means as high as it was from the 1960s and onwards, it was steadily rising. Rather more importantly, this targeting of need meant that it became increasingly common for women to have their first child in hospital, based on a scale of risk in childbirth. Therefore this was increasingly the first experience for most women of becoming a mother. As opposed to home births, hospitals were more likely to isolate women from their family and the domestic sphere, and also provided a greater potential for education in mothering. For example, a woman giving birth in the 1940s at home would have a midwife calling at her home for the first fortnight, initially twice a day, to check her and her baby's progress and to help care for the new-born child. However, a woman giving birth in hospital would be confined in hospital for fourteen days with only limited visiting hours. This increased isolation in relation to the place of birth reinforces the idea of a professional sphere of knowledge and contains implications for the education of mothers in the initial mothering period. While Ann Oakley argues that the medicalization of childbirth in the 1960s had significant implications for women's power over their own bodies, such developments in the 1950s have implications for the social aspects of mothering in the immediate post-war period.[53]

As indicated above, teaching in parentcraft was directed principally at women, but this education also came primarily *from* women, thus establishing this as a specifically gendered area of expertise.[54] The educators for motherhood were mainly midwives, health visitors and the nurses who worked on maternity wards in hospitals. Health visiting developed out of the nineteenth-century Public Health Movement and developed into a profession in the early twentieth century. From the beginning of the twentieth century, the professionalization of midwives began with a series of Midwives Acts between 1902 and 1939, with systems of instruction and examination designed.

Such professionalization occurred within the context of middle-class women establishing a realm of expertise and a body of knowledge out of an already acknowledged moral superiority in 'feminine occupations'. Health visitors and midwives were originally unmarried and therefore able to devote themselves to their vocations, but increasingly throughout this period the marriage bar was relaxed. This originally developed out of the initial shortage of midwives and health visitors, but it gradually came to be seen as helpful that they should be married, although those with young children were discouraged as setting a bad example to other mothers.

The increased interest in the psychology of the child which was appearing in both government and professional circles also influenced the direction that such education should take. Given the preposition of the importance of the maternal instinct, the suggestion was increasingly made that the health visitor, or educator, was to 'reinforce that mother probably knows best through what she thinks should be done',[55] as 'Often all that is necessary is reassurance.'[56] In this sense the health visitor could protect the mother from those who would deter her from her task. Consequently, to some extent, the role of the 'nurse and health visitor [was] to provide support, encouragement and understanding [which] can be of greatest value to the mother'.[57] Alternatively, the welfare professional should tell the mother the facts and allow her to make up her own mind, as she probably knew best. Yet this did not prevent the idea of where these instincts should be taking the mother and child, and it did not prevent the sharing of ideas within professional circles of what correct mothering should contain beyond care by the mother. In fact the idea of 'telling the mother the facts' and allowing her to 'make up her own mind' is not as objective as it appears to be. Although the direct giving of advice in theory would suggest that the maternal instinct was faulty, the concept was not by any means abandoned.

Such information nevertheless had to be given in a particular manner. There was value in the person-to-person contact and a need for a friendly relationship as between equals to be established, therefore negating the imbalance of power. This was enabled by the gendering of child-care education, by women for, or to, women. Therefore for welfare professionals 'It [was] a wise rule not to "talk down" to the mothers but rather to put oneself on their level and discuss a subject as between friends and equals.'[58] The health visitor and the midwife are seen as the mother's friend and there are ideas of a continuous relationship that sustains the transmission of ideas within this gendered relationship. Welfare professionals needed to know not only the psychology of the child, but also the psychology of mothers, to appeal to their better (and maternal) nature.

The emphasis on 'maternal instinct' encouraged peer education and learning through experience; as one welfare professional noted, 'Mothercraft classes are invaluable to me as a health visitor. I have gathered many household tips and much sound advice on babies, which I have "passed on" in the course of visiting. After all, who knows better than a mother about the blessings and problems of babyhood?'[59] In this context, the health visitor is merely a conduit through which the collective experiences of women as mothers can flow, yet she is a fully trained professional. A further dimension of this was not just the idea of knowledge being received from health visitors, who passed on helpful advice from one mother to another, but also that of getting women to talk to each other about how they addressed a certain problem in child care and to discuss how successful the result was. In this sense, there was an empowerment of the mother, through a sharing of experience and a recognition of common ground.

Yet the emphasis on maternal instinct also promoted the importance of instinct and experience for welfare professionals. By 1960 it was being proclaimed that the doctor, midwife and health visitor can only really teach if *she* combined the three jobs of being a 'successful wife, a successful mother and a successful home-maker'. This therefore lay emphasis on their gender and maternal qualifications rather than their professional abilities and qualifications.[60] The fact that these were women educating women was important, but not necessarily because they were professionals; their own experiences were taking precedence. This implies equality between women through their biological abilities within a gendered advice system. However, primarily the power lay with the welfare professional, who was in control of such sessions. So, ultimately, where should a woman's instincts take her, or, in other words, what information should be given?

Constructions of the family

Evidence on the emerging psychoanalytical views surrounding mothering and the needs of the child indicated the naturalness of mothering and an increasingly permissive approach to child-rearing. However, this does not detract from the potential contradiction between the need for education and educating for something perceived to be so natural. The belief in 'natural' and 'maternal' instincts calls into question how and why to teach mothercraft at all. Yet there were reasons why mothers might need advice on how to mother. Civilization was believed to have dulled the maternal instinct and welfare professionals could help women to develop it, as well as indicate which direction these instincts should take.[61] Outside influences, childhood experiences and psychological factors causing mothers uncertainties about their own womanhood could also be influential. Moreover, rather than decreasing the need for education in parentcraft, the emphasis on the individual requirements of each child can be seen to have increased the need for advice as child-rearing became more complicated and different children were perceived to need different care. So how could welfare professionals judge these needs?

Wartime and the austerity measures subsequently imposed were perceived to have reduced class barriers. This sense of a new egalitarian society was reinforced by the welfare state and, perhaps more so, by the 'affluence' of the post-war years. Consequently, it was believed that 'the spirit of the individual and his or her approach to parenthood override[s] all other influences'.[62] However, it was welfare professionals who had to judge exactly what this spirit was. While the emphasis inevitably lay on the mother, all mothers were not equal.

The welfare state was designed to provide services free at point of contact to all mothers. Yet class as well as gender was important in parentcraft teaching. E. Wilson argues that the permissive approach was 'an indictment of élitist upper-class forms of child rearing – nannies and boarding school', and a validation of 'implicitly working class warmth and spontaneity towards children'.[63] Evidence from the inter-war period of behaviourism argues that 'it is not unusual to find references to the failure of working class mothers to teach their children disciplined habits'.[64] There was an assumption of the middle-class family, with its rules and regulations, as the 'norm' and right.[65] Mother-blaming had always been working-class mother-blaming, particularly in the context of the debates surrounding maternal and infant mortality, and had been influential in the establishment of the M&CW services themselves.[66]

The post-war period and changes in ideas show certain paradoxes in the perception of the mother. Such references as those made above suggest that working-class mothers were regarded during the inter-war period as uncivilized. Yet civilization was also argued to impair the maternal instinct. However, in the context of a shortage of health visitors in the post-war period, there was felt the necessity for some selective visiting to be made for those felt most in need of help. This meant working-class rather than middle-class women. Although this necessity was exacerbated by their lower levels of clinic attendance, the fact that these women were believed to need greater attention and care is demonstrated by the books produced. For example, a publication by the National Council for Maternity and Child Welfare was described to the Interdepartmental Committee by Dr L. G. Housden as 'intended primarily for health visitors and teachers of Parentcraft and although it might be read by more intelligent mothers it certainly could not be recommended as suitable for parents generally'.[67]

Decisions were being made as to who was capable of benefiting from the 'maternal instinct' and an extra element was added to the family and the mother–welfare professional relationship. It was middle-class women who were seen as being more capable of implementing the permissive approach. This had significant implications for what was taught, but more immediately for the nature of women themselves and how best to teach them. Consequently, while the 'spirit of the individual' may have been important, welfare professionals 'wouldn't make the mistake of imposing the standards of one family on another set at a different social level. All classes [are] limited, within [these] limitations the health visitor has to work to be of maximum use.'[68] What they taught and how they taught it varied with the social and educational background of the parents involved. More specifically, this meant that

> On the one hand there is the home which mainly needed advice on cleanliness, clothing, diet, sleep, vitamins and immunisation, whilst on the other hand there is the home of the more educated parents where advice on character training and behaviour problems is more urgently needed than instruction on hygiene.[69]

In practice, therefore, many women were still provided with specific advice on how to care for their children, when and how to feed them, and how to care for them. The dichotomy revealed within the definition of 'parentcraft' between home-making and psychology is not as clear-cut as the committees on parentcraft may have wished, but rather was a dichotomy between classes. As in the inter-war period, it was still the working-class family and the working-class mother, as the keystone, that was failing. This also extended to the role of the father. For example, when fathers were originally being advocated to attend confinements, their educational status was deemed relevant in the consideration of their suitability for this, and therefore for their involvement in the family sphere.[70] If working-class children were as individual in their needs as middle-class children, their parents' ability to provide for those needs were not.

In conclusion, the family was seen as an institution to be supported by the welfare state. The importance placed on this, and in particular on the child in the post-war period, meant that some intervention was seen as necessary. After the Second World War, there was an expressed aim to 'rebuild' the family. An exploration of education for parentcraft through the maternity and child welfare services is significant as it demonstrates that this was in fact an attempt to reconstitute the family. There was also a consensus between the state and welfare professionals as to the form that this 'ideal' family should take. New psychoanalytical theories of the time emphasized a new 'emotional' form of mothering and the importance of the mother–child relationship. At the same time, fathers were increasingly being brought into the family and the child's development, although this was not at risk to their role as the primary breadwinner and provider. This new family form was one that was believed to be inherently middle class. Consequently, education for parentcraft was based on gender and class differences. While parentcraft was thought important, it was considered to come easier to some than to others. A minimum level of parenting was required, but not all families could aspire to the ideal.

9

The Organization Man: George Haynes at the National Council of Social Service

John Jenkins

Perhaps surprisingly, Margaret Thatcher shared with Karl Marx a basic insight into the condition of human society under capitalism: the fact that the economic engine of the society cannot generate an organic social whole. 'I don't believe in society,' she asserted, to the rage of liberals. 'There is no such thing, only individual people, and there are families. And no government can do anything except through people, and people must look to themselves first. It's our duty to look after ourselves and then to look after our neighbours.'[1] In *Capital* Karl Marx observed:

> the labour of the individual asserts itself as a part of the labour of society, only by means of relations which the act of exchange establishes directly between the products, and indirectly, through them, between the producers . . . the relations connecting the labour of one individual with that of the rest appear not as direct social relations between individuals at work, but as what they really are, material relations between persons and social relations between things.[2]

Mediating institutions are required to connect atomized individuals into the semblance of an organic whole.

Social groupings whose membership is entirely elective are widely promoted as the bedrock of civic life. This point of view coloured the attitudes of politicians during the 1940s when, as a result of the development of the welfare state, the future of voluntary organizations was widely discussed within the political class. Opening a parliamentary debate on the voluntary sector on 22 June 1949, the veteran Liberal peer and former Home Secretary Lord Samuel incorporated voluntary organizations within a continuum of institutions mediating between the individual and the state. Whatever specific services they provided, voluntary organizations were an essential component of the great welfare experiment. Their continued existence within the welfare state manifested an underlying social health and, according to Samuel, 'no one can understand the working of our present-day civilisation without taking account of this hidden, all-pervading network of social activity, which is silently busy all through the year, all over the land'.[3] Lord Beveridge, whose report on *Voluntary Action* had initiated the debate, regarded voluntary social services as a vital bulwark against totalitarianism, believing that 'there are certain things which should in no circumstances be left to the State alone'. Certain welfare provisions (he cited adult education as an example) should be left to voluntary organizations making use of individuals' free time. Conflating leisure and voluntary social service, he argued, 'we shall reach the last stage in totalitarianism when all our use of leisure is dictated to us by the state'.[4]

This counterposing of voluntarism to the state is a common theme. The historian Frank Prochaska elevates this fetishism of voluntary social service into a political agenda. He confers on voluntary organizations a special role in democratic politics. Through voluntary organizations, citizens are empowered as active 'producers' rather than merely passive 'consumers' of government. Voluntary organizations, he argues, have acted as a counterweight to the dominance of 'indirect, representative democracy'. Prochaska rejects what he regards as the indirect democracy involved in voting and the testing of public opinion at the ballot box in favour of the 'spontaneous, pluralistic form of democracy which was immanent in the voluntary institutions of civil society'.[5] As a result, the range of institutions that Prochaska is able to encompass within his grand democratic alliance includes the monarchy and the hereditary peerage alongside voluntary organizations.

This chapter takes a more jaundiced view of voluntary organizations than is normally encountered. It focuses on the career and thinking of one of its leading figures, George Haynes, Director of the National Council of Social Service (NCSS) between 1940 and 1967. Haynes was a professional manager of a large national voluntary organization, which combined providing voluntary social services on its own account with the functions of an umbrella body representing voluntary organizations to government. The early years of his tenure coincided with the establishment of the welfare state – a period of upheaval for the voluntary sector. The NCSS played a pre-eminent role in the discussions of the future of voluntary social service in this period and Haynes was a leading protagonist. The chapter examines the intellectual foundations of Haynes's contribution to the development of the voluntary social service in the

1940s and 1950s. Just how solid was the body of ideas that justified and promoted voluntary social service during the post-war decades?

Future prospects

Haynes, already Deputy General Secretary, was appointed Acting General Secretary of the NCSS on 20 September 1940 following the sudden retirement on health grounds of his predecessor, Leonard Shoeten Sack, in the spring of 1940. Although Sack was retained as a 'consulting officer' during his absence, and the appointment was officially temporary, later declared as being for the duration of the war plus six months, Haynes was the effective leader of the NCSS throughout the war. His confirmation in office by the Finance and General Purposes Committee on 26 March 1946 was a formality.[6] Haynes's appointment as the senior paid officer of the Council, at the comparatively young age of 38, was the natural progression of an already blossoming career in the management of voluntary organizations. It was also partly a matter of luck: Sack had been in office for barely four years when he fell ill; his predecessor, Captain Lionel Ellis, had served for eighteen.[7]

The NCSS was a complex alliance of different interests. It was an umbrella organization and it had two aspects. On the one hand, it really was a council consisting of representatives of voluntary organizations. Its precise make-up fluctuated, but in 1949 it had 176 members. In addition to 27 individual members, there were 65 representatives of major national voluntary organizations. These included the National Association of Guilds of Help, the Family Welfare Association and the Soldiers, Sailors and Airmen's Families Association, all founding members. The NCSS also included representatives of ten government departments covering health, social security and education, nine representatives of local authority associations, and representatives of professional bodies such as the National Union of Teachers and the National Association of Local Government Officers. Representatives of the major religious denominations rubbed shoulders with the delegate from the decidedly secular National Institute of Economic and Social Research. These organizations came together once a year, usually in Church House, Westminster.[8]

Between annual meetings, the NCSS existed as a large voluntary organization in its own right. It operated at a national level, employing some 150 officers in its headquarters in Bedford Square and conducting a number of social welfare programmes, promoting the principles of the NCSS and following policy directions set by annual council meeting. The NCSS also had an expanding network of regional, county and local branches. It lobbied government on behalf of voluntary organizations and, in addition to promoting co-operation between voluntary organizations working in the same field, it encouraged collaboration between voluntary organizations and national and local government.[9]

The effective leadership of this unwieldy institution required tact and patience, two attributes with which Haynes was amply endowed, according to those who knew him well. Sir John Wolfenden, who as Chairman of the National Council from 1953 to 1960 had the chance to observe at close quarters, praised Haynes for his ability to maintain an even temper, and no matter how 'tiresome other people might be – committee members, officials of central or local government, enthusiastically indiscreet voluntary workers' he displayed 'a tireless readiness to listen and then to explain, with modesty and even apparent diffidence, what the other side of the picture might be'. Margaret Brasnett, who worked under him, thought he brought 'a temperament and personality admirably fitted to the tasks' of leading the organization during the crisis of the war and the period of reconstruction that followed, praising especially 'his skill and devotion as a patient, sympathetic negotiator'. Wolfenden and Brasnett respected the breadth of Haynes's vision of voluntary social service: Brasnett admired his 'gift of being able to see both the wood and the trees'; Wolfenden admired 'the wisdom that [had] matured over the years' and his 'capacity for a synoptic breadth of view into which the details must be made to fit'. As the latter comment suggests, Haynes's contribution was not – and Wolfenden had no qualms in spelling this out – 'primarily as a theorist or a spinner of philosophical words about service'. His vision of voluntary social service was subordinate to action, for he spent 'his time living out his conviction rather than indulging in lengthy rationalisation'.[10]

Haynes appeared to demonstrate the skills and aptitudes of the diplomat more often bracketed with intellectual flexibility than with rigour. He was clearly most comfortable negotiating person to person or in the numerous commissions and committees of which he was a member. There was, as Wolfenden's comments show, a natural tendency to see Haynes as all practice, and to underestimate his social philosophy. His renowned pragmatism did not spring from an absence of principle, but flowed naturally from a set of ideas formed in the course of his experience.

Pivotal in Haynes's conception of the future of voluntary social service in the 1940s was greater co-operation between state and voluntary organizations. The general tenor of his approach may be gleaned from his encomium to George Astbury, his opposite number at the Family Welfare Association (FWA), on the latter's retirement in 1956. Reflecting on the changed intellectual climate since Astbury's appointment in 1938, Haynes noted with approval his readiness to 'think the unthinkable'. Haynes singled out Astbury's role in persuading the Charity Organisation Society (COS) to endorse 'the main recommendations of the Beveridge report', and contrasted Astbury's readiness to embrace the 'new relationships between statutory and voluntary agencies' with the Society's approach under its first Secretary Sir Charles Loch, for whom state welfare had been anathema. Haynes believed that Astbury's policy departure was justified by the 'silent revolution which had transformed many of the issues of his day'.[11] Haynes was himself deeply implicated in this 'silent revolution'. His support for co-operation between the state and voluntary organizations was not the sudden conversion implicit in his narrative of Astbury's reorientation of the FWA, nor was it a pragmatic response to changing political realities. It was fundamental to his outlook and to that of the NCSS, and it came into its own in the political conditions of the late 1940s.

Towards the end of the war, Haynes detailed his ideas on the future of voluntary social service in an internal discussion document entitled 'The Future Purposes and Organisation of the National Council of Social Service'.[12] Haynes's comments give an insight into the complex operations of mid-century voluntary organizations. In a short introduction to the Council's principles, Haynes expressed his warm approval of the organization's founders, praising especially their 'empirical approach' and the consequent breadth of mission they had set out. This had given 'the Council maximum freedom in selecting its tasks and creating its machinery'. Haynes acknowledged the importance of integrating voluntary social service with a strategic approach to social change, arguing that it was 'crucial in the whole process . . . that the attack on any social problem shall be informed by a full appreciation of its relation to general social progress'. Rejecting a common criticism of voluntary effort, he maintained that social work should not be 'regarded merely as a social palliative . . . [but as] a necessary instrument of social regeneration'. Haynes declined to elaborate any but the most general of principles for social service, however, and limited his observations on the role of the NCSS in developing a strategic synthesis to the generalized 'any contribution the Council can make towards a better appreciation of the relation between specialised activities'. Haynes adopted a subjective focus superficially similar to the philosophical Idealism that had informed the COS. He asserted that the work of the NCSS rested 'on a belief in the value of individual personality'. He also accepted the Idealist recognition of a connection between subjective and social existence, for an individual could 'only find himself an outlet for his powers in association with others'. Haynes emphasized the actuality of social relationships and deferred their theoretical elaboration.[13]

Haynes's avoidance of prescription was partly, no doubt, tactical. The character of the NCSS meant that its leadership required great political sensitivity. His reluctance to evoke a social theory also reflected what some have seen as a wider intellectual crisis of the social sciences.[14] What it produced was a focus on organization as such. Haynes concluded that 'it is with organised group life that the Council is primarily concerned', and particularly with fostering relationships between groups. 'Satisfactory relationships between groups do not', he argued, 'develop automatically but require just as careful thought and planning as the organisation of the group activities themselves'.[15] This was the level at which the NCSS could intervene 'to create out of this diversity of group interests and activities a real partnership of effort'. The role of the NCSS's leadership was to ensure that the 'conditions for efficient administration and organisation exist'.[16]

The bulk of the report was concerned with the technicalities of administering the NCSS, though here again Haynes's attitude was revealing. The partnership in diversity that Haynes advocated was to be achieved by means of decentralization. This was partly functional. Haynes argued that, at its existing size and with its variety of disparate activities, it was 'impossible for one committee of the Council to be executively responsible for all the work carried out in its name'. The attempt of the Executive Committee to oversee all aspects of the Council's activities had resulted in 'overburdened agenda and reports from groups and committees'. This had made it 'impossible for members of the Committee to concentrate their attention on important general matters of policy'. Haynes's solution to this overloading of the administrative machinery of the NCSS was to call for further devolution of authority. He acknowledged that there were 'important questions which arise from time to time on which general unanimity should be sought'. He argued that for the most part 'activities should be left free for the determination of the different groups and committees which are competent to deal with them'. Concentration of power in the hands of the Executive resulted 'in frustration and delays' and was in any case a 'sterile method of promoting the aims' of the Council.[17]

Decentralization is an attractive strategy for the managers of voluntary organizations, since it tends to augment the power of the professional managers at the expense of the voluntary management committees. The remoteness of the central management from the activities of the organization increases its dependence on the chief executive, without necessarily increasing the power of those involved in service delivery.[18] Implicit in Haynes's proposals for the dispersal of power was a drifting of power towards the professional managers of the NCSS. His plans for decentralization of authority from the Executive Committee envisaged a greater role for the Council's administrative machinery. It would provide premises, staff and secretarial services for the autonomous groups working under its aegis. The Executive's remit was to be confined to the setting of broad general policy, ensuring that 'the conditions for efficient administration and organisation exist and [giving] its main concern to the provision of the services required'.[19]

The influence of Frederic D'Aeth and the Liverpool Council of Voluntary Aid

The roots of Haynes's intellectual outlook can be found in the context of his early career in social welfare work. Born in 1902 of middle-class parents in the Cheshire village of Middlewich, Haynes's formative experiences were in the north of England during the economic depression of the 1920s and 1930s. His involvement in voluntary social service began while he was a student of physics at Liverpool University. His scientific studies had to compete with a growing interest in social problems, and he found himself 'attracted to the thought of a social science'. Years later he recalled the impact of social conditions in Liverpool, where he 'confronted, for the first time, really, with a physical and mental shock – a rampant slum of a great city'. The poverty and squalor led him to campaign 'to get one particularly fetid district removed'. Haynes's campaign followed the conventional pattern of Edwardian social reformers: an enquiry to gather information was followed by lobbying of the City Council's Director of Housing for a clearance and rehousing scheme. An unexpected result of his success had a profound influence on Haynes's future outlook. In spite of the improvement in the occupants' physical environment, Haynes learned, 'many of them could not bear the monotony, the loneliness and the emptiness of this new urban environment, and pressed back into the neighbourhood from which they had been removed'. Haynes drew a moral lesson from this experience, concluding that material improvement alone was insufficient, having 'discovered then that you can never be sure what it is that creates and makes a community live'.[20] Haynes's conclusion from this experience was not that material improvements sponsored by the state had no role to play, but that something extra was required to supplement them.

After graduating in 1923, Haynes spent a brief period as a schoolmaster before becoming Warden of the Liverpool University Settlement. He joined the NCSS as its regional organizer in the north-west in 1933, and three years later transferred to the Council's headquarters staff in

London's Bedford Square.[21] His voluntary social work in Liverpool in the early 1920s, particularly as Warden of the University Settlement, put Haynes at the centre of one of the most dynamic provincial centres of voluntary social service at a formative period in his development. As Warden, Haynes played a leading role in establishing the city's 'service clubs' for the unemployed in response to the appeal launched by the Prince of Wales in January 1932. The clubs, quickly renamed 'occupational centres', in deference to the objections of local trade unionists, provided training and occupational therapy for the unemployed. The re-naming of the service did not placate its labour movement critics, but the network of centres survived the withdrawal of trade union support and grew rapidly both locally and nationally.[22]

The dominant influence in the Liverpool social service scene in which Haynes learned his craft was the Council of Voluntary Aid (LCVA). The LCVA was launched at a meeting of representatives of the city's voluntary organizations on 25 October 1909 presided over by the Lord Mayor, H. Chaloner Dowdall. William Grisewood, Secretary of the Liverpool Central Relief Society (LCRS), which had been established in 1863 to co-ordinate voluntary effort in the city and operated on the same lines as the London Charity Organisation Society, also sponsored the new LCVA. By the time of its first annual general meeting in May 1911, 100 of the city's charitable agencies were affiliated to it, and it included 50 represen-tatives of official agencies as well a scattering of individual members representing Liverpool's great and good. The LCVA was already the powerhouse of Liverpool voluntary social services by the time Haynes ar-rived in the city. It became independent of the Relief Society in 1913 and progressively supplanted it, finally absorbing it in 1932, and changing its name to the Liverpool Council of Social Service in 1933, the same year that Haynes joined the NCSS as a full-time official.[23]

The Mayor's support was important in establishing the NCSS, but its ultimate success depended on the commitment and flair of Frederic G. D'Aeth, a lecturer in the School of Social Sciences at the university and Honorary Secretary of the LCVA. D'Aeth was an archetype of the social entrepreneur favoured by contemporary policy makers, and his approach provided the template for Haynes's career in the national leadership of voluntary social service. Social entrepreneurs have to be able to articulate a sense of 'mission coherent and clear enough to command support, but flexible enough to allow growth'. The organizations they found depend on generating 'the support and enthusiasm which keeps them going', often communicating 'their values and motives through stories and para-bles', and encouraging their supporters to think 'imaginatively rather than analytically or procedurally'. Their aims tend to be concrete, often radical, and 'if an opportunity comes along they will try to take it, even if it does not fit their original plan'. The social entrepreneur's emphasis on practical results entails a reluctance to 'be tied down to a political position as this would cut them off from potential supporters'.[24] D'Aeth fitted this profile of the 'visionary opportunist' admirably.

The number of initiatives in which he was involved both in Liverpool and on the national stage shows that D'Aeth was an effective and charismatic social entrepreneur. Adept at building alliances, he was in touch with other leading figures such as Thomas Hancock Nunn, the disciple of Canon Samuel Barnett who established a Council of Social Welfare in Hampstead. He was also on good terms with Edward Vivien Birchall, who inspired the foundation in 1911 of the National Association of Guilds of Help and became its first honorary secretary. The association with Birchall, who died in action in France during the First World War, was particularly significant for his legacy of £1,000 that provided the funds that 'sustained the National Council of Social Service in its first precarious years of existence'.[25] From his base in Liverpool, D'Aeth rapidly became an influential figure on the national stage, playing a key role in the foundation of the NCSS in 1915.

These individuals and organizations represented diverse currents within voluntary social service, but there were recurrent themes, and D'Aeth's approach to voluntary social service was typical of his generation. His thought was moulded in the Edwardian upsurge of voluntary social service that preceded the Great War. José Harris has written extensively on the intellectual underpinnings of this movement and its contribution to the growing support for state welfare, which culminated in the establishment of the welfare state. The upsurge in civic awareness and activism of the years before the First World War was marked, she argues, by 'the re-emergence and reformulation of a popular and voluntaristic social-scientific culture that in both personnel and social purpose was strikingly similar to that of the mid-Victorian years'. The language of Victorian Idealist social reform prevailed, but this appearance of continuity was superficial. The Edwardian movement was influenced by Victorian Idealism, 'not necessarily in a formal philosophical or methodological sense, but in more general inspiration and tone'. This unsophisticated idealism sustained an extensive network of voluntary social service organizations. Its adherents viewed themselves as part of the march of progress and saw their practice as 'means to the end of attaining perfect justice and creating the ideal state'.[26]

What united these Edwardian voluntarists was a belief in action as the core of voluntary social service. Edward Prince of Wales's famous outburst when confronted with conditions in the distressed areas in the 1930s that 'something must be done' is typical of this attitude. Harris argues that this emphasis on 'doing something' undermined rigorous examination of consequences. As a result, the conceptualization of state, citizen and society that informed this movement led it to embrace, albeit sometimes reluctantly, state provision of welfare, and this contributed to the erosion of the intellectual framework that sustained it. There were disagreements over the 'precise boundaries of state action', but the most telling feature of the discourse on welfare in the inter-war period 'is the fact that virtually no major social theorist or writer on social policy of this period dissented from the view that the ultimate sphere of "welfare" . . . was or ought to be the institutions of the state'.[27] Voluntary social services were defended in the 1920s 'not on pragmatic grounds, but as a means of enhancing wider corporate consciousness'.[28] Those who advocated social reforms did not see 'themselves as mere technicians . . . many of them believed that they were building a new kind of social and political [order] rooted in a wholly new relationship between the citizen and the state'.[29] Yet this understanding was rarely subjected to detailed examination. Although the 'morally exhortative language' of Victorian and Edwardian social thought provided the veneer of continuity with the earlier Charity Organisation movement, it was located only 'rarely within any clearly stated philosophic framework'.[30]

D'Aeth was a leading figure in this movement. His contribution to the LCVA, and ultimately to the NCSS, was ideological but not in the conventional sense. The Councils of Social Service that this generation of activists inspired were 'less ideologically militant' than the Victorian COS.[31] Like the guilds of help, to which they were close kin, they were 'less inclined to propound a theory of charity than to promote ideas regarding its practice'.[32] But movements that appear to be without significant ideological baggage can be just as revealing of the ideological underpinnings of social and political action as historical periods that appear the least ideological.[33] D'Aeth, like the others, accepted the COS's argument that social service could be improved by co-ordination of voluntary effort, but, like many activists, he recoiled from the Society's dogmatic insistence on clarity of policy as a precondition of co-operation.[34]

D'Aeth was typical of these tendencies in regarding relief work as part of a wider programme for community and civic regeneration, and cultural as well as social welfare projects occupied a central position in his approach.[35] In spite of this superficial similarity, however, his holistic conceptualization of voluntary social service inverted the approach of the COS. The Society saw the conscientious involvement of the active citizen in social welfare work as a preliminary to the foundation of the good society.[36] D'Aeth, in contrast, regarded the good society as immanent in organizations operating in different fields: all that was necessary to release this potential was to bring activists together. D'Aeth's repudiation of ideological preconditions for joint work went beyond co-operation between voluntary organizations, for he also welcomed the extension of state welfare services. D'Aeth saw the Councils of Social Service as acting as a bridge between the state and voluntary social service, hoping that they would be 'representative alike of public and voluntary action'.[37] From his perspective, far from representing a threat to voluntary social service, the greater involvement of governments in the delivery of welfare presented 'great opportunities for co-operation with the state in the administration of new legislation such as the National Insurance Act, the Mental Deficiency Act, and the Probation Act'.[38] A willingness to endorse state welfare made Councils of Social Service politically distinct from the COS. It also smoothed the way for them to become the preferred partner of governments in welfare provision.

D'Aeth's agnosticism about ends was combined with a hard-headed approach to means and under his guidance the LCVA developed two methods of moulding the voluntary sector that were of particular significance for the pattern of growth adopted by the NCSS. The LCVA moved rapidly from simply promoting co-operation between existing organizations to sponsoring new ones. The precedent was set in 1911 when an unsatisfactory record of youth work led to the establishment of the Liverpool Union of Boys' Clubs as an umbrella organization to stimulate the setting up of new schemes. A consequence of sponsoring new more effective organizations was, as the LCVA's Secretary in the 1950s observed, 'the putting to bed of charities which had become out-dated or obsolescent'.[39]

D'Aeth had seen the role of the LCVA in initiating and co-ordinating disparate welfare services as crucial.[40] The LCVA's ability to insert skilled professional staff to administer new initiatives was crucial to its shaping of voluntary provision in the city; the first Honorary Secretary of the Liverpool Union of Boys' Clubs was Warden of the Gordon Working Lads' Institute. The creation of the Liverpool Personal Service Society (LPSS) to co-ordinate casework in the city provided another example. Preparatory work began in 1917, but implementation was delayed by a lack of sufficient funds to appoint a full-time organizer. D'Aeth persuaded one of the city's women's settlements, the Victoria Settlement, to appoint Dorothy Keeling, a former Secretary of the National Association of Guilds of Help, as part-time Warden, allowing the LPSS to employ her part time as its organizer.[41]

The LCVA's capacity to shape voluntary provision in the city rested on its financial dominance.[42] At an early stage in the LCVA's development, Dowdall commissioned D'Aeth to produce a report on the funding of voluntary organizations. As well as equipping D'Aeth with a detailed knowledge of the city's voluntary provision, his survey of 241 agencies with a total income of some £460,991 provided him with a platform to set out his views on obtaining a better return on this expenditure.[43] When, in 1918, an anonymous donor offered D'Aeth £50,000 to set up a scheme for the benefit of Liverpool charities, D'Aeth had an opportunity to put his ideas into practice. The Liverpool Charities Fund he set up soon outstripped the resources at the disposal of the LCRS. Three-fifths of the fund's income was reserved for capital expenditure and new projects, and the remaining two-fifths was distributed automatically to affiliates of the LCVA in direct proportion to their voluntary income. This created a powerful incentive for voluntary groups to ally themselves with the LCVA, but D'Aeth's scheme went further. The distribution favoured organizations that provided annual accounts in the form approved by the LCVA. Those publishing a balance sheet and income and expenditure accounts received the full amount: those publishing a bare statement of receipts and payments received half.[44] Imposing accounting standards armed the LCVA with a powerful mechanism for moulding the internal operation of voluntary organizations, since systems of accounting are not merely descriptive, 'but serve to constitute a realm of facts, to make a world of action visible and hence controllable in economic terms'.[45] The Charities Fund extended the influence of the LCVA, as D'Aeth intended, by prompting the city's voluntary organizations to adopt the sort of 'progressive policies' he favoured.[46]

Haynes at the NCSS

Haynes's approach as leader of the NCSS was moulded on the intellectual and administrative pattern provided by D'Aeth and the LCVA. Indeed, growth on the model of the LCVA had already reached a level of maturity by the time Haynes assumed control at the National Council. The NCSS extended its influence within the voluntary sector by organizing conferences and convening standing committees covering different fields of voluntary work. These brought into contact activists from organizations not directly connected with the NCSS, and continued the strategy proposed by D'Aeth for gaining the confidence of voluntary organizations through joint action.[47] There were a number of subordinate groups and standing conferences that brought together individuals and organizations working in the same fields. The Churches Group, for example, was small but influential, embracing as it did representatives from all the major Christian Churches and from Jewish groups. The Standing Conference of Councils of Social Service provided a forum for representatives of the NCSS's own local, county and regional branches. The Women's Group on Public Welfare and the National Old People's Welfare Committee (later Age Concern) brought together representatives from other voluntary organizations active in fields where the NCSS was keen to expand its operations in the 1940s.[48] The Women's Group had the additional advantage in the post-war years that its members had strong connections to the Labour Party.[49] These standing bodies played an important role in extending the Council's domain of influence, for they often drew in organizations not affiliated to the NCSS. There were seven of these standing committees and conferences in the mid-1940s, each with a full-time official on the staff of the NCSS based in Bedford Square.[50]

The NCSS was adept at creating forums either to meet special circumstances or to bring together disparate organizations in the name of efficiency in the provision of services. The Standing Conference of National Voluntary Organisations (SCNVO) is a good example. Set up at the beginning of the war to co-ordinate wartime relief measures, it drew its membership from a much wider constituency than the NCSS had been able to influence in the inter-war period. Early in the war, the Council's Executive Committee delegated its authority to the Special Emergency Committee of the SCNVO. Although it was thus nominally independent of the NCSS, the Special Emergency Committee's activities were closely monitored from Bedford Square. At the end of 1944, partly on account of the difficulty of arranging meetings in London during the flying bomb phase, it passed its authority to the NCSS Finance and General Purposes Committee.[51] As a result of this process of devolution and the subsequent reversion of authority to the centre, groups that had been drawn temporarily into the orbit of the NCSS became increasingly subject to its direction.

The capacity of the NCSS to provide senior staff with the expertise to organize national and local initiatives also played an important part in its expansion. This was itself the result of its continuing attention to finance, and this was in turn closely connected with its embracing of a working relationship with the state. The rapid growth of the NCSS in the 1930s and 1940s appeared to confirm D'Aeth's vision of the compatibility of voluntary and state social services. The pattern was set with the rural work of the NCSS during the 1920s, continued during the 1930s in its work with the unemployed, and was reinforced during the war when it supervised the establishment of a network of Citizens' Advice Bureaux (CABx). These programmes followed a consistent pattern, and the CABx highlight the main characteristics. The initiative came from the NCSS; indeed, D'Aeth himself had foreseen the need for such an organization during the First World War. Exploratory meetings with representatives of organizations with an interest in advice work were convened under the chairmanship of Sir Wyndham Deedes, a member of the NCSS's Executive Committee, in the winter of 1938–9. Branches were established in the larger cities under the auspices of existing local organizations. Where they did not exist, the NCSS itself took the initiative in finding premises and recruiting voluntary or professional staff, often in co-operation with local authorities. The NCSS also distributed a digest of changing regulations and legislation in the form of its Citizens' Advice Notes prepared by its new information department. Under the supervision of the NCSS, the network of Bureaux grew rapidly, rising from 200 at the start of the war in August 1939 to 926 by the end of the year.[52]

The influence of the NCSS over the development of the CABx was not confined to providing the inspiration and administrative and technical support. It also secured control of the purse strings at an early stage, and this flowed directly from its existing relations with the government. The usefulness of the CABx to the government was twofold. They not only provided an effective channel for disseminating information to the population at large, but also gave the government access to information on the public mood. Even so, the government was slow to offer financial support. As the value of the service became apparent, however, financial backing was forthcoming, and a retrospective grant of £9,459 was made in 1940. By 1944 the annual grant had reached £33,406. As with rural and unemployed work, the NCSS used some of this money to finance the national administration of the scheme. Dorothy Keeling of Liverpool Personal Social Services was drafted into the Council's headquarters to head a CAB department, taking charge of a squadron of travelling officers who supervised work in the localities.[53]

The NCSS found itself once again administering a state grant programme that included funding for its own services. This created the perception of a conflict of interest. The role of the NCSS as a service provider in its own right compromised its qualification to act as a co-ordinating body, since 'the bodies whose activities it sought to co-ordinate might come to regard it as a competitor and rival'. For this very reason, the constitution of the NCSS forbade its making 'national appeals which might have affected adversely the appeals of its constituent organisations', but the inference that it used its relationship with the government to pursue its own ends was hard to escape, and 'suspicion remained'.[54] This suspicion had emerged during the work of the NCSS with the unemployed in the 1930s. An anonymous, but sympathetic, correspondent remarked in a memorandum to the Chairman in 1938 that the NCSS was 'not universally popular' and that there was a widespread belief that the Council in undertaking work with the unemployed, as well as trespassing on the work of others, had 'placed itself in the position of exclusive receiver of grants from HM's Government and the national Trusts'.[55] Similar criticism did not emerge over the CABx, but financial control of this funding programme undoubtedly gave the NCSS powerful means for proselytizing in new localities and for regulating the structures of the organizations that it furnished with grants.

In spite of the misgivings expressed by some supporters, Haynes remained vigilant for further opportunities to extend the influence of the NCSS. In doing so, he demonstrated his own credentials as a social entrepreneur on the model of his mentor, D'Aeth. In 1947 he was instrumental in the establishment of the National Association for Mental Health (now MIND), and he played a leading role in the change of direction at the COS, serving on the Provisional National Council of the new Family Welfare Association.[56] His role in the work of the NCSS following the Lynmouth flood in August 1952 shows that his readiness to take the initiative was not confined to the national stage.[57] Haynes visited the area within a few days of the flooding, making contact with those engaged in the immediate tasks of clearing up after the disaster and helping to set up an emergency Citizens' Advice Bureau in co-operation with the Family Welfare Association. He persuaded the North Devon and West Somerset Relief Fund to pay the salary of a member of the NCSS's staff, Mrs Weeks, who was seconded to the area for a month. Her stay was subsequently extended by a fortnight.[58]

Conclusion: managerialism, voluntarism and the state

Haynes's ideological agnosticism and his emphasis on activism and administration reveal his debt to D'Aeth, but they were not necessarily as empowering of individual citizens as they appeared. The hortatory quality of management merged imperceptibly with the truncated idealism that imbued voluntary social service. The pragmatic approach to social policy measured worth by efficacy, and as a result measurable outcomes tended to usurp the less tangible criteria supplied by an ethical framework. The underlying assumption of both Haynes and D'Aeth was that priority had to be given to bringing individuals and groups together in action. Although they believed that this coming together would engender a dynamic that would ultimately produce a common perspective, this needed no direct intervention to bring it about. The priority was maintaining the conditions for joint action, and this was the role of organization. As a result, the consideration of the wider purposes of organization was increasingly supplanted by the priorities of maintaining the organization itself.

The conception of voluntary organizations elaborated by Haynes is superficially attractive. He presented active involvement in voluntary social service as a means to empower individuals for '[t]he more they can be given responsibility, the fuller will be their citizenship in a free democracy', helping the members of voluntary groups 'to look beyond the confines of its own specialised activities to the work of other groups and thus to the wider life of the community'.[59] Haynes's open-ended approach to questions of organizational form and ideological content is a prospectus for that bringing together of citizens as active 'producers' rather than merely passive 'consumers' of government which is the cherished ideal of apologists for voluntary social action.

The tendency to make a fetish of activism greatly strengthened the influence of professional managers. Action became the predicate of action and the gap in this circular conceptualization of social service was filled, surreptitiously, by organization – the handmaiden of action. To some extent the elaboration of a managerial ethos was an inevitable consequence of organizational development within the voluntary sector. The development of voluntary organizations to carry into effect the wishes of the donor implied a distance in time and space between the donor's gift and its consumption by the object of charity. Gradually this interposition of paid workers between the donor and the beneficiary led to the segregation of the administrative machinery for achieving this from service delivery, and this was personified in a class of employees with distinct functions and interests: the professional managers of voluntary organizations. As a result, professional managers occupied a powerful position within voluntary organizations. This gave them considerable effective power over material resources as well. The functions of the professional managers led them to identify closely with the organizations they managed and this facilitated their assimilation to the voluntary management. This identification could never entirely suppress the different interests of the professional managers and voluntary committee members, but the distinction was blurred as more and more professional managers sat on voluntary committees.

Describing the 'architecture' of the voluntary societies in 1947, the left-wing intellectual Harold Laski gave his impression of the managers of voluntary organizations. 'At the apex of their pyramid', Laski found clustered 'a little handful of sleek, often able, officials who know, almost to a decimal point, the precise degree of deference owed to each member of their committees.'[60] As his comment suggests, Laski was no friend of voluntary social service, but a similarly low opinion of the professional manager was often encountered among the supporters of voluntary social service. Wolfenden's speech on Haynes's retirement echoed Laski's comments. Wolfenden observed that there were 'all sorts of possible variants of the relationship between the chief administrative officer of an organisation and an amateur or part-time chairman'. He noted that the demeanour adopted by the paid official might 'range from superciliousness through public politeness to ostentatious respect, with all sorts of differences between the private feeling and its public expression'.[61] Wolfenden hastened to disassociate Haynes from this style of management, but his comments are a token of the ambiguous attitude to professional administration in voluntary social service.

Haynes's assertion of the importance of managers was not unwarranted. The sheer size and complexity of many large national voluntary organizations called for supervision and direction of some sophistication and the development of management specialization often facilitated further growth. Haynes's own leadership of the NCSS provided a good example. During his first ten years as General Secretary, the Council demonstrated an impressive record of expansion. Its total assets grew from £104,805 in 1940 to £266,385 in 1950, a rise of almost 60 per cent in real terms. At the same time its annual income rose by some 45 per cent in real terms, from £44,312 to £102,735 at current prices.[62] T. H. Marshall attributed the 'amalgamation of voluntary bodies into large national associations with all their liability to bureaucracy and remote control' to the closer collaboration between voluntary and statutory bodies, particularly the increased state funding of voluntary organizations, with its concomitant requirements for accountability.[63] This process was not as one-sided as Marshall thought: there were internal as well as external influences promoting bureaucracy in voluntary organizations. The professionalization of management within the voluntary sector presented a challenge to the voluntary ethos, but its outlook and ambition also increasingly dovetailed with the ideas of sections of the political class.

The ambiguity of the professional managers' position and their identification with the organizations they administered helped to obscure the fact that they entertained a sectional interest in the future direction of voluntary social service. For managers of voluntary organizations, cross-subsidization of different activities was an essential 'long-term strategy . . . for financing the consumption of loss-making activities'.[64]

This meant seeking out sources of finance for an establishment with the resources to pursue the organization's mission on a wider front. These sources of funding need not have been state agencies, as the recent proliferation of profit making charity shops shows. Rather, the priority of action, combined with the managerial imperative of obtaining the resources to finance an organisation as a vehicle for action, precludes contemplation of the philosophical complexities surrounding any particular sources of funding. To put it simply, in the voluntary sector of the 1940s, activists lacked the intellectual tools to object to being co-opted by the state, and this decisively affected the sector's subsequent development.

This was not detrimental to the institutions of the voluntary sector. After a short period of adjustment, voluntary social services flourished in the 1950s and beyond. Nevertheless, the language in which the moral content of charity had been discussed in the nineteenth century was transformed in the course of the twentieth. A discursive tradition that had emphasized that the value of social service accrued to the conscientious individual donor or volunteer was, imperceptibly, superseded by a discourse in which the donor's action was emptied of moral content. This facilitated the projection of something called 'society' as the principal beneficiary of voluntary social service, but society was little more than a rhetorical symbol. In practice, the beneficiary of the public good that inhered in voluntary action was the state. The value of voluntary action was still held to be its role as guarantor of the primacy of civil society. In practice, professionals under the aegis of the state administered its major institutions. George Haynes played an important role in these developments in the 1940s. As a key figure in the bureaucratic layer that encased the voluntary sector, his achievement was to articulate a plausible division of labour between voluntary social service and state welfare within which a formal distinction between voluntary organizations and the state could be affirmed.

Notes

Introduction

1. See, for instance, Benedict Anderson, *Imagined Communities: Reflections on the Origin and Spread of Nationalism* (London: Verso, 1983) and Tom Nairn, *The Enchanted Glass: Britain and Its Monarchy* (London: Radius, 1988).

2. Ireland and more recently Northern Ireland can particularly be seen to militate against the popular idea of Britain as a stable or United Kingdom. Generally on Britain see Linda Colley, *Britons: Forging the Nation, 1707–1837* (New Haven, CT: Yale University Press, 1992). On Britain's less stable past, see Raphael Samuel, *Island Stories: Unravelling Britain* (London: Verso, 1998), and on Wales, Gwyn A. Williams, 'When was Wales?' in *The Welsh in their History* (London: Croom Helm, 1982).

3. See Karl Marx, *The Civil War in France* (Peking, 1977), pp. 66–86.

4. Weber used the term 'ideal type' to describe types of leadership: traditional, charismatic and legal rational or bureaucratic. Its use above coincides with Weber's in the sense that it is a hypothetically constructed entity which allows the state to make judgements as to its actions. See Stanislav Andreski (ed. and trans.), *Max Weber on Capitalism, Bureaucracy and Religion: A Selection of Texts* (London: Allen and Unwin, 1983).

5. Harold Macmillan, 'Speech on British financial situation' at Bedford (20 July 1957).

6. Perry Anderson and Peter Gowan, *The Question of Europe* (London: Verso, 1997).

7. John Locke, *Two Treatises of Government* (London: Everyman Press, 1978).

8. Thomas Humphrey Marshall, *Citizenship and Social Class* (Cambridge: Cambridge University Press, 1950).

9. House of Commons Debates, 5th Series, col. 1818, 7 February 1943. Hogg, Conservative MP for Oxford, made the remark during a debate on the Beveridge Report. Speaking in favour, Hogg said, 'Some of my hon. Friends seem to overlook one or two ultimate facts about social reform. The first is that if you do not give the people social reform, they are going to give you a social revolution. The maintenance of our institutions has been one of the principles of the Conservative Party from time immemorial. Let anyone consider the possibility of a series of dangerous industrial strikes following the present hostilities and the effect it would have on our industrial recovery.'

10. See Jürgen Habermas, *Legitimation Crisis* (trans. Thomas McCarthy) (London: Heinemann Educational, 1976) and David Held, *Introduction to Critical Theory: Horkheimer to Habermas* (London: Hutchinson, 1980).

11. In *Woman's Own* (31 October 1987) Thatcher argued, 'I don't believe in society. There is no such thing, only individual people, and there are families. And no government can do anything except through people, and people must look to themselves first. It's our duty to look after ourselves and then to look after our neighbours.' Margaret Thatcher, *The Downing Street Years* (London: HarperCollins, 1993), p. 626.

12. S. J. D. Green and R. C. Whiting (eds), *The Boundaries of the State in Modern Britain* (Cambridge: Cambridge University Press, 1996).

13. Becky Conekin, Frank Mort and Chris Waters (eds), *Moments of Modernity: Reconstructing Britain 1945–1964* (London: Rivers Oram, 1999); Abigail Beach and Richard Weight (eds), *The Right to Belong: Citizenship and National Identity in Britain 1930–1960* (London: I. B. Tauris, 1998); Harriet Jones and Michael Kandiah (eds), *The Myth of Consensus? New Views on British History, 1945–1964* (Basingstoke, Macmillan, 1996); Nick Tiratsoo (ed.), *From Blitz to Blair: A New History of Britain since 1939* (London: Weidenfeld and Nicolson, 1997); and Jim Obelkevich and Peter Catterall (eds), *Understanding Post-war British Society* (London: Routledge, 1994).

Chapter 1   Controlling the Fire: British Communism and the Post-war Consensus

1. Simone De Beauvoir, *Les Mandarins* (London: Collins, 1957), p. 241.

2. *The British Road to Socialism* (London: CPGB, 1951), p. 14.

3. Doris Lessing, *The Golden Notebook* (London: Joseph, 1974), p. 383.

4. K. Newton, *The Sociology of British Communism* (London: Allen Lane, 1969), p. 160.

5. J. A. S. Grenville, *The Collins History of the World in the Twentieth Century* (London: HarperCollins, London, 1994), p. 358.

6. P. Ginsborg, *A History of Contemporary Italy: Society and Politics 1943–1988* (Harmondsworth: Penguin, 1990), pp. 84 and 88.

7. *The British Road to Socialism*, p. 14.

8. According to J. W. Durcan, W. E. J. McCarthy and G. P. Redman, *Strikes in Post-war Britain: A Study of Stoppages of Work Due to Industrial Disputes* (London: Allen and Unwin, 1983), these were the two most strike-ridden years of the post-war period. The authors noted that 'the number of days lost' in 1969 'exceeded five million for the first time since 1957', p. 66.

9. Harry Pollitt, 'The 20th Congress of the CPSU and the role of Stalin', *World News*, 3:18 (5 May 1956), p. 279. E. P. Thompson, 'Winter wheat in Omsk', *World News*, 3:30 (30 June 1956), p. 408.

10. 'Leninism' and 'Marxism-Leninism' were not epithets used during Lenin's lifetime, but were utilized in the creation of the personality cult that Party members like Stalin consciously constructed around the dead Bolshevik leader.

11. P. Wright with Paul Greengrass, *Spycatcher* (Richmond, Victoria: Heinemann, 1987), pp. 54–6.

12. Ibid., p. 56.

13. See A. Zhdanov, 'Report on the international situation to the Cominform' (22 September 1947) in M. Rush (ed.), *The International Situation and Soviet Foreign Policy* (Columbus, Ohio: Charles E. Merrill, 1970), pp. 124–39. The offensive abroad was characterized by Christopher Mayhew's Communist

Information Department, which under Ernest Bevin's ministry evolved into the Information Research Department (IRD).

14. P. Weiler, *British Labour and the Cold War* (California: Stanford University Press, 1988), p. 228.

15. W. Wyatt, 'The case against the ETU leaders', *New Statesman*, 55:1349 (18 January 1958), p. 63.

16. Ibid.

17. The key figure in this process was Sam Watson, the Durham miners' leader. See B. Brivati, *Hugh Gaitskell* (London: Richard Cohen, 1997), p. 186 and J. Campbell, *Nye Bevan* (London: Richard Cohen, 1997), p. 290.

18. Brivati, *Hugh Gaitskell*, p. 186.

19. Ibid., p. 366.

20. Ibid., p. 354. In the ETU, from 1955, the General President, General Secretary, Assistant General Secretary and more than half of the union's Executive Council were Communists.

21. Lenin, *Left-wing Communism, an Infantile Disorder* (Moscow, 1935), p. 84. These groups included the British Socialist Party (BSP), the Socialist Labour Party (SLP), the Workers' Socialist Federation, which did not join, and the South Wales Socialist Society. They were also joined by shop-steward movements from South Wales and Scotland, the left-wing of G. D. H. Cole's Guild Socialists (the Guild Communists) and later by revolutionary-inclined elements within the Independent Labour Party (ILP). The Communist Unity Convention finally inaugurated the Communist Party of Great Britain on 31 July 1920.

22. Communist Unity Convention, 'Official Report' (31 July and 1 August 1920), p. 59. Marx Memorial Library.

23. Lenin, *Left-wing Communism, an Infantile Disorder*, pp. 82 and 79.

24. Dennis Ogden, interviewed by author, 3 November 1997. Ogden worked, throughout the 1950s, at the Foreign Languages Press in Moscow. He was the first Briton to hear Khrushchev's secret speech. He later became the Party's Moscow Correspondent.

25. Details in V. Serge, *Russia Twenty Years After* (New York: Pioneer, 1937), pp. 3, 24–5 and 186–90.

26. See A. Zhdanov, 'Report on the international situation to the Cominform', pp. 124–39.

27. H. Pollitt, 'Report to Closed Session of the 24th Congress CPGB' (1 April 1956), Communist Party Archive, Museum of Labour History, Manchester (henceforward Manchester), CP/Cent/Cong/09/09.

28. A. Hutt, 'Review of Daily Worker Circulation' [Report to EC] (22 June 1956) p. 5, Manchester, CP/Ind/misc/Hutt/2/1. 1956 figure: K. Newton, *The Sociology of British Communism*, p. 160. 1948 figure: *Daily Worker* (1 May 1948). The figure stands out as incongruous. Newton gave figures for 1947 and 1950 as 38,579 and 38,853 respectively. The drop in membership between 1948 and 1957 was around 30 per cent, with a drop of around 20 per cent between 1956 and 1957.

29. G. Matthews, *All for the Cause: The Communist Party 1920–1980* (London: CPGB, 1980), p. 22. Matthews was Assistant Secretary of the Party in the 1950s and 1960s and succeeded J. R. Campbell as editor of the *Daily Worker*.

30. E. Hobsbawm, interview with G. Stedman Jones, '1956', *Marxism Today* (November 1986), p. 17.

31. W. Thompson, *The Good Old Cause: British Communism 1920–1991* (London: Pluto, 1992), pp. 91–113.

32. *The British Road to Socialism* (London: CPGB, 1958).

33. Morris Schaer, interviewed by author, 9 July 1997. Throughout the 1950s and 1960s, Schaer was a shop-steward in the ETU and remained a Communist.

34. N. Branson, *History of the Communist Party of Great Britain*, Vol. 2, *1941–1951* (London: Lawrence and Wishart, 1997), p. 239.

35. W. Thompson, *The Good Old Cause*, p. 93.

36. Morris Schaer, interviewed by author, 9 July 1997.

37. Dennis Ogden, interviewed by author, 3 November 1997.

38. Ruth Fisher, written reply to author, 30 November 1997.

39. Ibid.

40. W. Campbell, *Villi the Clown* (London: Faber, 1981). A. Macleod, *The Death of Uncle Joe* (Woodbridge: Merlin, DATE), p. 268.

41. Bob Leeson, written response to author, 5 November 1997. Leeson had written for the magazine *World Youth*, and was a prominent member of the Young Communist League. He stayed in the Party after 1956, working in the features department of the *Morning Star* until the early 1980s.

42. Max Morris, interviewed by author, 16 March 1998. Max Morris was on the Executive Committee of the CPGB during the 1950s. He was a leading figure in the NUT and edited the *Educational Bulletin*.

43. B. Ramelson, 'Problems of Unity', *World News Discussion Supplement* (23 February 1957), p. 18, Manchester, CP/Cent/Cong/10/05.

44. Wolf Wayne, interviewed by author, 10 February 1999. Wayne was a member of Amalgamated Engineering Union throughout the 1950s and 1960s.

45. Jim Layzell, interview with Louise Brodie (5 September 1995). British Library National Sound Archive (henceforward NSA), C739/01-05 C1 F4901-5.

46. Ibid.

47. Wolf Wayne, interviewed by author, 10 February 1999.

48. L. Marks to *World News*, 3:23 (9 June 1956), p. 369. Anthony Ryle to *World News*, 3:22 (2 June 1956), p. 346.

49. Trotsky, *Stalin* (New York, 1946), p. 15. Stalin 'Author's preface', *Collected Works*, vol. 1 (Moscow, 1946), p. XIX. E. H. Carr quoted a letter from Stalin to German Communist Party leader Maslow in 1925, in which Stalin described litterateurs such as Lunarcharsky and Bogdanov 'who have passed over to a secondary role', *Socialism in One Country*, vol. 1 (Harmondsworth: Pelican, 1970), p. 199.

50. Lenin, *What is to be Done?* (Moscow: Co-operative Publishing Society of Foreign Workers in the USSR), p. 25.

51. H. Pollitt, 'The 20th Congress of the CPSU and the role of Stalin' in *World News*, 3:18 (5 May 1956), p. 280.

52. Ralph Russell, interviewed by author, 26 May 1998.

53. Brian Pearce, interviewed by author, 1 February 1999. Brian Pearce was a member of the Communist Party Historians Group, along with figures such as E. P. Thompson, Eric Hobsbawm and A. L. Morton. He left the Party following 1956.

54. Morris Schaer, interviewed by author, 9 July 1997.

55. Alison MacLeod, interviewed by author, 15 October 1997. Alison MacLeod was television critic at the *Daily Worker*. She left the Party in 1956. Her experiences of this period are recorded in her book, *The Death of Uncle Joe*.

56. R. Samuel, 'The lost world of British Communism: Part One', in *New Left Review*, 154 (November–December 1985), p. 32.

57. Mike Power in P. Cohen, *Children of the Revolution: Communist Childhood in Postwar Britain* (London: Lawrence and Wishart, 1997), p. 177.

58. Wolf Wayne, interviewed by author, 10 February 1999.

59. Jim Layzell, interview with Louise Brodie, 5 September 1995.

60. M. Jackson, *Strikes: Industrial Conflict in Britain, USA and Australia* (Brighton: J. Spiers, 1987), p. 81.

61. Durcan, McCarthy and Redman, *Strikes in Post-war Britain*, p. 64.

62. Ibid., p. 62. The total number of strikes during the period was 608, and the total number of days lost to strike action was 3,407.

63. *The Economist*, vol. 175 (18 June 1955), editorial, p. 1013.

64. Ibid.

65. J. Lloyd, *Light and Liberty: The History of the EETPU* (London: Weidenfeld and Nicolson, 1990), p. 397.

66. F. Foulkes, cited in C. Rolph, *All Those in Favour?* (London: André Deutsch, 1962), p. 200.

67. Lloyd, *Light and Liberty*, p. 378.

68. Wolf Wayne, interviewed by author, 10 February 1999.

69. See L. Panitch, *Social Democracy and Industrial Militancy: The Labour Party, the Trade Unions and Incomes Policy 1945–1974* (Cambridge, 1976), p. 4. Panitch quoted Samuel Beer, who described the post-war corporatist economy as one where 'government and producers' groups' were in 'intimate and continuous relationship'.

70. F. W. S. Craig, *British Parliamentary Election Results 1918–1949* (Glasgow: Political Reference Publications, 1969), pp. 624, 52, 148, and *British Parliamentary Election Results 1950–1970* (Chichester: Parliamentary Research Services, 1983), pp. 646, 41, 163.

71. *The British Road to Socialism* (1951), p. 14.

72. Ibid.

73. J. Klugmann, *From Trotsky to Tito* (London: Lawrence and Wishart, 1951), p. 9.

74. H. Gordon Skilling, 'Stalinism and Czechoslovak political culture', in R. C. Tucker (ed.), *Essays in Historical Interpretation* (New Brunswick, Va: Transaction, 1977), p. 273.

75. Ibid., p. 4.

76. Branson, *History of the Communist Party of Great Britain*, Vol. 2, p. 239.

77. CPGB figures in Newton, *The Sociology of British Communism*, p. 160. Craig, *British Parliamentary Election Results 1949-1973*. A. Sked and C. Cook, *Post-war Britain: A Political History* (Harmondsworth: Penguin, 1990), p. 85.

78. Notes towards 'Report of Electoral Commission' (19–20 September 1953), Manchester, CP/Cent/EC/03/06. 'H. Pollitt' is underlined at end.

79. Ibid.

80. Political Committee, CPGB (2 October 1953), Manchester, CP/Cent/PC/02/20.

81. Lenin, *Left-wing Communism, an Infantile Disorder*, p. 59.

82. Communist Unity Convention, 'Official Report', p. 59. MML.

83. J. Mahon, *The Party of Socialism* (London: CPGB, 1955), p. 8.

84. Marx, 'General rules of the International Working Men's Association', in Marx and Engels, *Selected Works*, Vol. 1 (Moscow, 1958), p. 386.

85. Lessing, *The Golden Notebook*, p. 144.

86. Cohen, *Children of the Revolution*, p. 26.

87. Max Morris, interviewed by author, 16 March 1998.

88. Panitch, *Social Democracy and Industrial Militancy*, p. 245.

89. Morris Schaer, interviewed by author, 9 July 1997.

90. D. King, J. Ryan and T. Deutscher, *Trotsky* (Oxford: Basil Blackwell, 1986), p. 280.

91. Cited in ibid.

92. C. Milosz, *The Captive Mind* (London: Secker and Warburg, 1953), p. xii.

93. Ibid., pp. 14–15.

94. M. Rosen, interview with Phil Cohen, *Children of the Revolution*, p. 62.

95. D. and G. Cohn-Bendit, *Obsolete Communism, the Left-wing Alternative* (Harmondsworth: Penguin, 1969), p. 147.

96. Ibid., p. 150.

97. Ralph Russell, interviewed by author, 26 May 1998.

98. A. Palmer, 'Learning to read', *Educational Bulletin*, 6:1 (September 1953), p. 9.

99. Statement of 'Teachers for Peace', *Educational Bulletin*, 5:3 (January to February 1953), p. 3.

100. Communist Unity Convention, 'Official Report', p. 59. MML.

101. Lessing, *The Golden Notebook*, p. 148.

102. Mr Justice Winn 'Judgement' (ETU 'Conspiracy' Trial between ETU leadership and John Byrne and Frank Chapple, 28 June 1961), p. 5, Manchester, CP/Misc/ETU/3/13. J. Beeching, 'Unity is not a tactic', *World News*, 3:44 (3 November 1956), p. 702.

Chapter 2   'Sheep May Safely Gaze': Socialists, Television and the People in Britain, 1949–64

Thanks to Janet Thumim for comments and Nick Tiratsoo for help with sources.

1. See Lawrence Black, *Old Labour, New Britain: A Study of the Political Culture of the Left in 'Affluent' Britain, 1951–1964* (Basingstoke: Macmillan, forthcoming).

2. Labour Party, *Your Personal Guide to the Future Labour Offers You* (London: Labour Party, 1958). For a classic indictment, R. H. Tawney, *The Acquisitive Society* (London: G. Bell, 1921).

3. Mark Abrams and Richard Rose, *Must Labour Lose?* (Harmondswoth: Penguin, 1960). See also C. A. R. Crosland, *The Future of Socialism* (London: Jonathan Cape, 1956).

4. John Gollan, *What Next?* (London: Communist Party (CPGB), 1959). *Labour Party Annual Conference Report* (*LPACR*) (London: Labour Party, 1959), pp. 151–5. Richard Crossman, *Labour in the Affluent Society* (Fabian Tract 325, 1960), p. 15.

5. Stephen Swingler, 'Educate socialists now', *Labour's Northern Voice* (December 1959).

6. John Kenneth Galbraith, *The Affluent Society* (London: Hamish Hamilton, 1958). Anthony Sampson, *Anatomy of Britain* (London: Hodder and Stoughton, 1962), pp. 108–9.

7. Mervyn Jones, *Chances: An Autobiography* (London: Verso, 1987), p. 134. Report of the Labour Women's Conference (1960), pp. 15–16.

8. C. A. R. Crosland, *The Conservative Enemy* (London: Jonathan Cape, 1962), p. 130.

9. Raymond Williams, *The Long Revolution* (Harmondsworth: Penguin, 1961, 1980 edn), p. 328. Ralph Samuel, 'Bastard capitalism', in E. P. Thompson (ed.), *Out of Apathy* (London: Stevens and Sons, 1960), p. 55. Raphael Samuel, 'The quality of life', in *Where? Five Views on Labour's Future* (Fabian Tract 320, November 1959), pp. 34–5.

10. Richard Hoggart, *The Uses of Literacy* (Harmondsworth: Penguin, 1957, 1969 edn), p. 243. Stuart Hall, 'The supply of demand', in Thompson, *Out of Apathy*, pp. 55, 73–5.

11. Donald Sassoon, *One Hundred Years of Socialism* (London: Fontana, 1996), p. 195. Trevor Blackwell and Jeremy Seabrook, *A World Still to Win: The Reconstruction of the Post-war Working Class* (London: Faber and Faber, 1985), pp. 93, 107.

12. *Tribune* (16 October 1959). Wyatt in *Reynolds' News* (11 October 1959).

13. Chris Waters, *British Socialists and the Politics of Popular Culture 1884–1914* (Manchester: Manchester University Press, 1990).

14. Labour Party, *Leisure for Living* (London: Labour Party, 1959), pp. 9, 29.

15. This was the story told in H. H. Wilson's seminal study, *Pressure Group: The Campaign for Commercial Television* (London: Secker and Warburg, 1961). See Peter Black, *The Mirror in the Corner: People's Television* (London: Hutchinson, 1972) and Sampson, *Anatomy of Britain*, pp. 604–9. Among more recent cultural accounts see John Corner (ed.), *Popular Television in Britain: Studies in Cultural History* (London: British Film Institute, 1991) and particularly Corner's 'Television and British society in the 1950s', pp. 1–21. See also Bert Hogenkamp, *Film, Television and the Left in Britain, 1950–1970* (London: Lawrence and Wishart, 2000).

16. Black, *The Mirror in the Corner*, p. 42.

17. John Ramsden, *The Age of Churchill and Eden, 1940–1957* (London: Longman, 1995), pp. 252–4.

18. Sir Robert Fraser in Sampson, *Anatomy of Britain*, p. 610. Black, *The Mirror in the Corner*, p. 56.

19. Attlee's speech (13 June 1953) and opinions reported in *Keesing's Contemporary Archives*, 13064 (1–8 August 1953). Black, *The Mirror in the Corner*, p. 49. Correspondence Gaitskell and Florence Buggs (6 and 8 December 1953) in Hugh Gaitskell Papers, University College London Library, E10.

20. Sampson, *Anatomy of Britain*, pp. 605–7. Reith was later chosen to chair Labour's Advertising Enquiry and was something akin to a latter-day 'rational recreator': see D. L. LeMahieu, 'John Reith (1889–1971): entrepreneur of collectivism', in Susan Pedersen and Peter Mandler (eds), *After the Victorians: Private Conscience and Public Duty in Modern Britain: Essays in Memory of John Clive* (London: Routledge, 1994), pp. 191, 189–206.

21. Black, *The Mirror in the Corner*, p. 54. Christopher Mayhew, *Time to Explain* (London: Hutchinson, 1987), pp. 129–30.

22. Black, *The Mirror in the Corner*, pp. 47, 53–4, 110. Mayhew, *Time to Explain*, p. 128.

23. C. Mayhew, *Dear Viewer . . .* (London: Praeger, 1953), pp. 25, 3.

24. Popular Television Association, *Britain Unites to Demand Competitive TV* (1953). This and the National Television Council's *Britain Unites Against Commercial TV* (1953) in Gaitskell Papers, C86.

25. Mayhew, *Dear Viewer . . .*, pp. 5, 9. Mayhew, *Time to Explain*, pp. 127–8.

26. Mayhew, *Dear Viewer . . .*, pp. 5, 14, 24. Mayhew, *Time to Explain*, pp. 123, 128.

176   *Consensus or Coercion?*

27. Labour Party, *Leisure for Living*, p. 26.
28. P. Gordon Walker, *House of Commons Debates*, Series 5, Vol. 527, col. 2102, 19 May 1954.
29. See Bernard Sendall, *Independent Television in Britain, Volume 1: Origin and Foundation, 1946–62* (Basingstoke: Macmillan, 1984), p. 239.
30. Letter, Pollit to CBS (4 February 1954). CPGB Archive, National Museum of Labour History (NMLH), CP/Ind/Poll/3/12.
31. *Socialist Commentary* (December 1953), p. 275. *The Argus – Journal of the Merton and Morden Labour Party* (August 1953). In Merton and Morden Papers, British Library of Economic and Political Science (BLEPS) 4/3. See also Labour Party, *Record of the Tory Government – Three Wasted Years* (London: Labour Party, 1955), p. 63.
32. Black, *The Mirror in the Corner*, p. 136.
33. Janet Morgan (ed.), *The Backbench Diaries of Richard Crossman* (London: Hamish Hamilton, 1981), p. 331 (entry for 26 May 1954).
34. Mary Allen, 'Future of TV', *Labour Woman* (July 1953), pp. 154–5.
35. Ruth Winstone (ed.), *Tony Benn, Years of Hope: Diaries, Papers and Letters 1940–1962* (London: Arrow, 1994), p. 253 (18 November 1957).
36. Doris Lessing, *The Four-gated City* (New York: MacGibbon and Kee, 1969), p. 140.
37. Tom Harrisson, *Britain Revisited* (London: Gollancz, 1961), p. 208. The comments of socialists are Joan Smith, 'Give up soap box for radio', *Labour Organiser*, 32:376 (August 1953), p. 145 and John Heardley Walker in *Weekly Tote Bulletin* (11 May 1959). Merton and Morden Papers, BLEPS 4/1.
38. Harrisson, *Britain Revisited*, p. 209.
39. Labour Party, *Leisure for Living*, pp. 36–7.
40. Hugh Jenkins, 'Entertainment – is it necessary to do anything to do about it?' *Co-operative Party Monthly Letter* (July 1957), p. 19. J. B. Priestley, 'Tele-viewing', in *Thoughts in the Wilderness* (London: Heinemann, 1957), p. 194.
41. Labour Party, *Leisure for Living*, pp. 33, 6.
42. Lindsey Mountford, 'TV versus the soapbox', *Revolt*, 4 (1955). Eric Heffer papers, NMLH, box 'Socialist Revolt'.
43. Allen, 'Future of TV', p. 155.
44. *Weekly Tote Bulletin* (11 May 1959, 13 August 1962). Merton and Morden Papers, BLEPS 4/1. Mountford, 'TV versus the soapbox'.
45. *Socialist Commentary* (July 1960), p. 29.
46. Harry Hopkins, *The New Look: A Social History of the Forties and Fifties in Britain* (London: Secker and Warburg, 1963), p. 403. Danny Blanchflower, 'Darker cricket', *New Statesman* (1 March 1963). A Conservative opponent, Beverley Baxter MP, felt that to minimize TV addiction it should be kept as dull as possible and thus defended the BBC monopoly; Black, *The Mirror in the Corner*, p. 64.
47. On *1984* see the *Manchester Guardian* (29 December 1954) and Black, *The Mirror in the Corner*, p. 21; also Jason Jacobs, *The Intimate Screen: Early British Television Drama* (Oxford: Oxford University Press, 2000).
48. *Daily Worker* (6 June 1956, 27 January 1956).
49. Quoted in Hogenkamp, *Film, Television and the Left*, p. 91.
50. Hoggart, *The Uses of Literacy*, p. 169. Hopkins, *The New Look*, p. 229. Kit Coppard, 'Two television documentaries', *New Left Review*, 3 (May–June 1960), p. 53. Black, *The Mirror in the Corner*, pp. 112–13.

51. Francis Hope, 'TWTWTWTWTWTWTWTWTW', *New Statesman* (29 March 1963), p. 467.

52. W. Stephen Gilbert, *The Life and Work of Dennis Potter* (London: Hodder and Stoughton, 1995), pp. 98–100, 327.

53. *Daily Herald* (31 August 1962).

54. *Daily Herald* (11 April 1960, 18 April 1960).

55. William Pickles, 'Political attitudes in the television age', *Political Quarterly*, 30:1 (January–March 1959), p. 63. It is perhaps symptomatic of Pickles' disinterest in television that these were both radio programmes.

56. See the New Left's 'TV supplement' – 'Some proposals' and 'Tasks for education' in *New Left Review*, 7 (1961), pp. 48, 43. This was a collaborative effort between Kit Coppard, Tony Higgins, Paddy Whannel and Raymond Williams.

57. Alma Birk, 'Visit to Hollywood', *Labour Woman* (January 1956), p. 5.

58. Frank Allaun, 'We don't need the films', *Forward* (24 September 1955).

59. Hopkins, *The New Look*, p. 412. Christopher Mayhew, *Commercial Television – What is to be Done?* (Fabian Tract 318, 1959), p. 15.

60. *Daily Herald* (9 April 1960).

61. Mayhew, *Commercial Television – What is to be Done?*, p. 15.

62. Alma Birk, 'Let's talk it over', *Labour Woman* (January 1958), pp. 6,12 (August 1958), pp. 111–12.

63. 'TV supplement', pp. 43, 39–40. For a modern parallel see David Blunkett's comments on the values encouraged by the popular ITV show *Who Wants to be a Millionaire?*, *Guardian* (30 November 2000).

64. Labour Party Research Department (LPRD), Re. 499, 'The financing of a third television programme' (February 1959). Hopkins, *The New Look*, pp. 331, 400.

65. LPRD, R. 482, Anthony Wedgwood Benn, 'Joint Committee on the Future of TV – TV policy draft proposals' (February 1955). See also Benn in *Socialist Digest* (March 1955).

66. LPRD, R. 482, 'Joint Committee on the Future of TV – TV policy draft proposals', in which Benn argued that both the BBC and ITA should be 'under the supreme control of the Postmaster General'. See also *Socialist Digest* (March 1959) on Benn's proposals to decentralize the BBC structure.

67. See Tony Benn, *Out of the Wilderness: Diaries 1963–1967* (London: Hutchinson, 1987), p. 440. Robert Chapman, *Selling the Sixties: The Pirates and Pop Music Radio* (London: Routledge, 1992), pp. 35–7, 179.

68. Mayhew, *Commercial Television – What is to be Done?*, pp. 2, 4, 7, 9–10.

69. Ibid., pp. 12, 22, 10. *News Chronicle* (10 March 1959).

70. LPRD, Re. 468 'Sub-Committee on TV and Radio' (November 1958).

71. Mayhew, *Commercial Television – What is to be Done?*, pp. 22, 24. LPRD, Re. 500, 'Summary of Recommendations (Third Programme)' (February 1959).

72. Untitled (8 April 1959) in CPGB Press Statements CP/Cent/Stat/1/10. The CPGB did not see the BBC as without political bias and was uneasy at its failure to deal with trade unions.

73. Mayhew, *Commercial Television – What is to be Done?*, pp. 22, 24.

74. Raymond Williams, 'An educated democracy', *Socialist Commentary* (October 1959), pp. 8–10.

75. *Daily Sketch* (6 October 1959), *Daily Worker* (7 October 1959) and on Conservative attempts to portray Labour as the party of state bureaucracy and

178   *Consensus or Coercion?*

controls, see Ina Zweiniger-Bargielowska, *Austerity in Britain: Rationing, Controls and Consumption, 1939–55* (Oxford: Oxford University Press, 2000).

76. *Report of the Committee on Broadcasting* (Chair Sir Harry Pilkington), Cmnd 1753 (1962), p. 245.

77. Black, *The Mirror in the Corner*, p. 154. Hogenkamp, *Film, Television and the Left*, p. 68. See also Richard Hoggart, *An Imagined Life: Life and Times Volume III, 1959–91* (Oxford: Oxford University Press, 1993), pp. 59–71, and for similar reactions to the *Mirror*'s see Corner, 'Television and British society in the 1950s', pp. 9–10. Michael Kenny discusses the New Left's influence on the report in *The First New Left: British Intellectuals after Stalin* (London: Lawrence and Wishart, 1995), pp. 103–8.

78. *Daily Telegraph* (4 April 1962). Correspondence Mayhew to Gaitskell (3 May, 5 July, 24 October 1962), GP C316. Mayhew, *Time to Explain*, p. 131. Black, *The Mirror in the Corner*, pp. 156–7.

79. Gaitskell to Mayhew (29 October 1962), GP C316.

80. Tony Crosland, 'Pilkington and the Labour Party', *Socialist Commentary* (August 1962), pp. 5–8. Also Crosland, 'The mass media', *Encounter* (November 1962).

81. On 'Americanization' I have benefited from reading Richard Weight's unpublished paper, '"Death to Hollywood": the cultural politics of anti-Americanism in post-war Britain', delivered to the 1998 Institute of Contemporary British History Summer Conference, London.

82. Crosland, *The Future of Socialism*, pp. 524, 527, 521–9. Jim Northcott, *Why Labour?* (Harmondsworth: Penguin, 1964), pp. 91–2, 176.

83. LPRD, Rd. 412, 'Joint Working Party on TV and Radio – The Government and the Pilkington Report' (February 1963).

84. 'TV supplement', p. 48. Mayhew, *Commercial Television – What is to be Done?*, pp. 9–10.

85. LPRD, Rd. 412, 'Joint Working Party on TV and Radio – The Government and the Pilkington Report' (February 1963).

86. Sampson, *Anatomy of Britain*, pp. 609–10. Nor (for Fraser's past) did it please Conservatives – see Low's *Manchester Guardian* cartoon reproduced in Sendall, *Independent Television in Britain*, p. ii.

87. Sampson, *Anatomy of Britain*, pp. 612–16. See also Clive Jenkins, *Power Behind the Screen: Ownership, Control and Motivation in British Commercial Television* (London: MacGibbon and Kee, 1961) and Labour Research Department, *Money and Men Behind TV* (London: LRD, 1959).

88. Bert Baker, *The Communists and TV* (London: CPGB, 1965), p. 5, complained that the *Sunday Telegraph* was permitted to advertise.

89. Reported in 'Lopsided TV', Lowestoft Labour Party, *Contact*, 4 (September 1958).

90. Mayhew, *Commercial Television – What is to be Done?*, p. 17. Sampson, *Anatomy of Britain*, p. 611. LPRD, Rd. 412, 'Joint Working Party on TV and Radio – The Government and the Pilkington Report' (February 1963).

91. CPGB, *Forging the Weapon* (London: CPGB, 1961), p. 31. Priestley, 'The popular press', in *Thoughts in the Wilderness*, p. 193.

92. An 'ITA grandee', quoted in Hoggart, *An Imagined Life*, p. 67. Priestley, 'The popular press', p. 191.

93. Labour Party, *Leisure for Living*, p. 38.

94. Joseph Trenaman and Denis McQuail, *Television and the Political Image:*

A Study of the Impact of Television on the 1959 General Election (London: Methuen, 1961), pp. 93–4. On *Dotto*, 'TV supplement', 'Use and abuse', *New Left Review* 7, pp. 39–40. *Socialist Commentary* (February 1959), p. 11, suggested that the BBC and ITV should shut down from 6 p.m. on polling day.

95. See Robert Pearce, 'Introduction' in Pearce (ed.), *Patrick Gordon Walker: Political Diaries, 1932–1971* (London: The Historians Press, 1991), p. 35. Martin Rosenbaum, *From Soapbox to Soundbite* (Basingstoke: Macmillan, 1997), pp. 140, 285–6.

96. Winstone (ed.), *Tony Benn: Diaries, Papers and Letters 1940–1962*, pp. 290, 276 (entries for 27 October 1958 and 7 May 1958).

97. Richard Hoggart, 'Pictures of the people', *Observer* (15 November 1959).

98. Labour Party, *Voice of the People* (London: Labour Party, 1956).

99. See Ross McKibbin, *Classes and Cultures: England 1918–1951* (Oxford: Oxford University Press, 1998).

100. Cited in Black, *The Mirror in the Corner*, p. 35.

101. On this theme see also Steven Fielding, ' "To make men and women better than they are": Labour and the building of socialism', in Jim Fyrth (ed.), *Labour's Promised Land: Culture and Society in Labour's Britain, 1945–1951* (London: Lawrence and Wishart, 1995).

102. Corner, 'Television and British society in the 1950s', pp. 10–11.

103. Hoggart, *An Imagined Life*, p. 71. Hopkins, *The New Look*, p. 413.

Chapter 3   Functionalists, Federalists and Fundamentalists: Labour and Europe, 1945–50

Thanks are due to Lawrence Black and Zoë Doye for their valuable comments on earlier drafts of this chapter.

1. Kevin Featherstone, *Socialist Parties and European Integration: A Comparative History* (Manchester: Manchester University Press, 1988), p. 41.

2. Michael Newman, *Socialism and European Unity: The Dilemma of the Left in Britain and France* (London: Junction Books, 1983), p. 188.

3. Donald Sassoon, *One Hundred Years of Socialism: The West European Left in the Twentieth Century* (London: Fontana, 1997), p. 739.

4. Andrew Thorpe, *A History of the British Labour Party* (Basingstoke: Macmillan, 1997). For example, Thorpe's analysis of the Wilson governments of the 1960s and 1970s proceeds from this premise: see pp. 157ff.

5. Kenneth O. Morgan, *Labour in Power: 1945–1951* (Oxford: Oxford University Press, 1986), pp. 389ff.

6. For Bevin, see Alan Bullock, *Ernest Bevin: Foreign Secretary 1945–51* (London: Heinemann, 1983). Whether there was a longer history to Labour's 'Americanism' is examined by Lawrence Black in a forthcoming article, 'Labour revisionists and the Cold War after 1951', *Contemporary British History*, vol. 15, no. 3. The relationship between the western European left and 'Atlanticism' has been examined in Sassoon, *One Hundred Years*, ch. 9, pp. 209–40.

7. See, for example, Morgan, *Labour in Power*, p. 276; Peter Hennessy, *Never Again: Britain 1945–1951* (London: Vintage, 1993), pp. 333ff.

8. Of course, to speak of 'left' and 'right' raises definitional problems. However, for want of a better term of reference and for consistency, 'left' is used to represent the large section of the parliamentary party who favoured greater

nationalization and a socialist foreign policy (third force). For an examination of some of these issues of definition, see Mark Minion, 'Left, right or European? Labour and Europe in the 1940s: the case of the Socialist Vanguard Group', *European Review of History*, vol. 7, no. 2 (2000), pp. 229–48.

9. Peter Weiler, *British Labour and the Cold War* (Stanford, CA: Stanford University Press, 1988), p. 1; John Saville, *The Politics of Continuity: British Foreign Policy and the Labour Government, 1945–46* (London: Verso, 1993), p. 60; Jonathan Schneer, *Labour's Conscience: The Labour Left 1945–51* (London: Unwin Hyman, 1988), p. 20.

10. John Grahl, 'A fateful decision? Labour and the Schuman Plan', in Jim Fyrth (ed.), *Labour's High Noon: The Government and the Economy, 1945–51* (London: Lawrence and Wishart, 1993).

11. For the 'European' debates within two of Labour's pressure groups, see Mark Minion, 'Left, right or European?' and Mark Minion, 'The Fabian Society and Europe during the 1940s: the search for a "socialist foreign policy"', *European History Quarterly*, vol. 30, no. 2 (2000), pp. 237–70.

12. It should be noted that conscious examinations of what it meant to be British in terms of an evolving pro-European stance were few and far between. This omission should be placed alongside Labour's avowed 'internationalism'.

13. Steven Fielding, Peter Thompson and Nick Tiratsoo, *'England Arise!' The Labour Party and Popular Politics in 1940s Britain* (Manchester: Manchester University Press, 1995), p. 214. For a more prosaic examination of the concerns of the returning armed forces, see Barry Turner and Tony Rennell, *When Daddy Came Home: How Family Life Changed Forever in 1945* (London: Pimlico, 1996).

14. Labour Party, *Report of the 44th Annual Conference* (hereafter LPRAC) (London: Labour Party, 1945), p. 96.

15. David Howell, *British Social Democracy: A Study in Development and Decay* (London: Croom Helm, 1980), p. 145.

16. Drucker cited in Alan Ware, *Political Parties and Party Systems* (Oxford: Oxford University Press, 1996), pp. 20–1. LPRAC 1945, pp. 89–92, 107 and 115–19.

17. Foot made this speech in the Commons: see *House of Commons Debates*, 5th series, vol. 413, cols 338–40, 20 August 1945 (hereafter 413HC DEB., 5s).

18. A copy of this letter can be found at the National Museum of Labour History, Manchester: Labour Party Archives (LPA). International Department, Box 4 File 'Foreign Policy, 1946'.

19. Schneer, *Labour's Conscience*, p. 56.

20. 430HC DEB., 5s, 526, 18 November 1946.

21. Schneer, *Labour's Conscience*, pp. 59–60. The 'rebels' tag appeared in *Daily Telegraph*, 14 November 1946. For the wider support for Crossman's position, see the papers of Morgan Phillips (Labour's General Secretary, 1944–61): LPA, Papers of Morgan Phillips (hereafter MPP), Coventry Borough Labour Party to Phillips, 27 November 1946; Eton and Slough District Labour Party to Phillips, 15 December 1946.

22. Crossman, Foot, Mikardo *et al.*, *Keep Left* (London: New Statesman, 1947). The other signatories were Geoffrey Bing, Donald Bruce, Harold Davies, Leslie Hale, Fred Lee, Levy, R. W. G. Mackay, J. P. W. Mallalieu, Ernest Millington, Stephen Swingler, George Wigg and Woodrow Wyatt. Six 'Keep Lefters' had been party to the 'Open Letter', respectively: Bruce, Crossman, Davies, Foot, Mackay and Mallalieu.

23. Ibid., p. 38.

24. Labour Party, *Cards on the Table: An Interpretation of Labour's Foreign Policy* (London: Labour Party, 1947), pp. 17–18. Bevin's official biographer classed this document as the best statement of the Foreign Secretary's policy during 1945–7: see Bullock, *Ernest Bevin*, p. 398.

25. LPRAC 1947, especially pp. 106–7 and 160–5.

26. For Marshall's speech, see Martin McCauley, *The Origins of the Cold War, 1941–1949* (Harlow: Longman, 1995), p. 139. For the wider implications, see Walter LaFeber, *America, Russia and the Cold War, 1945–1992* (New York: McGraw-Hill, 1993), pp. 59–60.

27. It should be noted that terms such as 'functional' and 'federal' are, of course, often defined and redefined in contradictory ways. For a recent examination of such debates, see Michael O'Neill, *The Politics of European Integration: A Reader* (London: Routledge, 1996).

28. John Young, *Britain, France and the Unity of Europe, 1945–51* (Leicester: Leicester University Press, 1984), pp. 14 and 63–5. The Dunkirk Treaty promised mutual aid and was the seminal moment in post-war European military-defence structures, leading to the North Atlantic Treaty two years later.

29. *Tribune*, 13 June 1947; *New Statesman and Nation* (hereafter *NS&N*), 14 June 1947.

30. British Library of Political and Economic Science (hereafter BLPES). R. W. G. Mackay papers (hereafter RWGM): 8/3, memo, Mackay, Silverman, Hynd and Shawcross, 'Federalist approach' (n.d., *c.*December 1947/January 1948); ibid., 13/1, memo 'Opening speech' of Dr Erik Arrhén (Chairman of the Swedish Parliamentary Committee) speaking at Gstaad, Switzerland (8 September 1947).

31. 441HC DEB., 5s, 1580–1, 6 August 1947; *NS&N*, 9 August 1947. See also R. W. G. Mackay, *Federal Europe* (London: Michael Joseph, 1940).

32. RWGM: 13/4, memo 'Members of Europe Group' (n.d.); 13/1, 'PLP Europe Group'·to all PLP members (n.d.); 8/3, minutes of formation meeting of Europe Group, 2 December 1947. For an examination of the PLP Europe Group, see Stefano Dejak, 'Labour and Europe during the Attlee governments: the image in the mirror of R. W. C. [*sic*] Mackay's "Europe Group", 1945–50', in Brian Brivati and Harriet Jones (eds), *From Reconstruction to Integration: Britain and Europe since 1945* (Leicester: Leicester University Press, 1993), pp. 47–58.

33. BLPES, RWGM 8/3, minutes of meeting, 2 December 1947.

34. Ibid., minutes of meetings, 16 December 1947; 10 February 1948. Emphasis added.

35. 446HC DEB., 5s, 383–409, 22 January 1948.

36. For local branch sentiments in relation to the Czech coup, see LPA. MPP, Aberdeen North DLP to Phillips, 9 March 1948; Ealing West DLP to Phillips, 20 March 1948.

37. Cited in Morgan, *Labour in Power*, p. 274.

38. RWGM 8/3, Mackay, Shawcross, Silverman and Hynd, 'Federalist approach' (Paper A), (n.d.). Extracts of this, Papers B and C and conclusions drawn by Shawcross can also be found in Walter Lipgens and Wilfred Loth (eds), *Documents on the History of European Integration, Volume 3: The Struggle for European Union by Political Parties and Pressure Groups in Western European Countries, 1945–1950* (Berlin: de Gruyter, 1988), pp. 685–91.

39. Ibid., Crawley, 'The functional approach' (Paper B), (n.d.). Crossman does not appear to have played any part in drafting Paper B, as had been intended.

However, his support for a functional approach was evident in his journalistic writings: see, for example, *NS&N*. The issue of whether in fact there was an impending economic crisis in Europe has been questioned most famously by Alan Milward, *The Reconstruction of Western Europe 1945–51* (London: Routledge, 1984).

40. Ibid., Manning and Warbey, 'The fundamentalist approach' (Paper C), (n.d.).

41. For an examination of the EPU, see Walter Lipgens and Wilfred Loth (eds), *Documents on the History of European Integration, Volume 4: Transnational Organisation of Political Parties and Pressure Groups in the Struggle for European Unity, 1945–1950* (Berlin: de Gruyter, 1991), pp. 112–85. For Mackay's involvement, see RWGM 7/1, 7/2, 8/1, 12/1 *passim*.

42. John Grantham has examined the wider implications of the Hague Congress for Labour in 'British Labour and the Hague "Congress of Europe": national sovereignty defended', *Historical Journal*, vol. 24, no. 2 (1981).

43. LPRAC 1948, p. 172. Contributions in support of USSE were made by a number of delegates: see ibid., pp. 173–7. Brockway had announced his resignation from the ILP in *Socialist Leader* (the ILP's weekly newspaper) on 18 January 1947. See also his article in *Labour Forum*, vol. 1, no. 5 (1947), pp. 17–19.

44. Ibid., pp. 177–9.

45. Morgan, *Labour in Power*, pp. 56ff.

46. For more on the division of Germany and its place within the early days of the Cold War, see Anne Deighton, *The Impossible Peace: Britain, the Division of Germany and the Origins of the Cold War* (Oxford: Oxford University Press, 1990).

47. University of Warwick, Modern Records Centre (MRC). Victor Gollancz papers, MSS.157/3/UE/64 'Report of Wimbledon Conference, 26 Sept. 1948'.

48. Ibid., transcript of Warbey's speech.

49. Sydney Silverman, William Warbey *et al.*, *Stop the Coming War: A Plan for European Unity and Recovery* (London: SEG, 1948). The other signatories were listed as A. J. Champion, Harold Davies, William Dobbie, John Haire, Arthur Skeffington-Lodge, Manning, Lyall Wilkes, Ernest Millington, Maurice Orbach, Ben Parkin, Charles Smith, Barnett Stross, Stephen Swingler and Wilfred Vernon.

50. See, for example, *Tribune*, 9 July 1948, 3 September 1948, 10 September 1948 and 1 October 1948. *NS&N*, 24 July 1948, 9 October 1948, 13 November 1948.

51. *Tribune*, 26 November 1948. Crossman was responding to the General Secretary of the National Union of Bank Employees, Hugh Jenkins, who had raised a number of criticisms about *Keep Left*: see *Tribune*, 19 November 1948.

52. The following editorials in *Tribune* are indicative: 'The Atlantic Pact', 18 March 1949; 'A pact made in Moscow', 25 March 1949; 'Socialists and the Atlantic Pact', 20 May 1949.

53. 464HC DEB., 5s, 2011, 2127–30, 12 May 1949.

54. Ibid., 2037–43, 12 May 1949. Warbey had made similar points earlier that year: see 462H.C. DEB., 5s, 2538, 18 March 1949.

55. Labour Party, *Labour Believes in Britain* (hereafter *LBIB*) (London: Labour Party, 1949).

56. Ibid., pp. 3, 24. As the Italian socialist Ignazio Silone, has remarked: 'There is nothing the Socialists nationalise as quickly as socialism', cited in Stephen

Padgett and William E. Paterson, *A History of Social Democracy in Post-war Europe* (London: Longman, 1991), p. 244. For an examination of the ideology behind *LBIB*, see Martin Francis, 'Economics and ethics: the nature of Labour's socialism, 1945–51', *Twentieth Century British History*, vol. 6, no. 2 (1995), pp. 22–43.

57. Newman, *Socialism and European Unity*, p. 123. For the disciplinary effects of the Cold War, see Geoff Eley, 'Socialism by any other name? Illusions and renewal in the history of the west European left', *New Left Review*, no. 227, January/February 1998.

58. *LBIB*, pp. 26–7.

59. For example, see LPRAC 1949, pp. 193–4, 196 and 212.

60. Schneer, *Labour's Conscience*, p. 76. Schneer makes this comment in relation to the affirmative vote for the North Atlantic Treaty, but the analogy still remains.

61. For a fuller examination of the discussions that led to COE, see Morgan, *Labour in Power*, pp. 393–8. For the Labour government's position on the function of the bodies of the COE, see Bevin's speech in the Commons: 467HC DEB., 5s, 1592–4, 21 July 1949.

62. BLPES. Hugh Dalton papers (hereafter HDP) 9/7, Dalton to Attlee, 10 September 1949. The other members of Labour's delegation were the MPs Fred Lee, Margaret Herbison, (Arwyn) Lynn Ungoed Thomas and William Nally; the party's Chief Whip, William Whiteley; and Healey.

63. Ibid.

64. Ibid., 9/8, 'Labour Party papers for Strasbourg', Committee on General Affairs, contribution by some British members of Consultative Assembly, 28 November 1949.

65. RWGM 8/1, Mackay to Crossman, 10 September 1949. Previously Dalton had described Mackay as a 'doctrinaire' for advocating a federal parliament: see LPRAC 1948, p. 177.

66. *Tribune*, Healey, 'The Strasbourg Assembly', 22 July 1949, 'Syrups and figs', 9 September 1949; *NS&N*, 13 August 1949; *Coventry Evening Telegraph*, Edelman, 'What Strasbourg means to us', 22 September 1949.

67. Copy in RWGM 8/1, Silverman and Warbey, SEG to Labour members of Strasbourg delegation, 28 July 1949.

68. LPA. Jo Richardson papers. 'Keep Left Group', minutes, 25 July 1948 (*sic*). Although the year was recorded as 1948, the meeting took place in 1949.

69. Ibid., minutes, 31 August 1949, 26–9 September 1949. The new group comprised Castle, Crossman, Harold Davies, Hale, Mikardo and Wigg from the original inception; and Sir Richard Acland, Donald Bruce, Tom Horabin, Marcus Lipton, Stephen Swingler and Tom Williams of the 'new blood'.

70. Ibid., minutes, 8 March 1950.

71. Sir Richard Acland *et al.*, *Keeping Left: By a Group of Members of Parliament* (London: New Statesman, 1950), especially pp. 19, 26 and 27.

72. For a wider examination of the Attlee government's response, see Grahl, 'A fateful decision?', pp. 148–61; Bullock, *Bevin*, pp. 778–89; Morgan, *Labour in Power*, pp. 417–21. Although the plan was named after Schuman, his colleague Jean Monnet played the crucial role in realizing the ECSC: see John Gillingham, 'Jean Monnet and the ECSC: a preliminary appraisal', in Douglas Brindley and Clifford Hackett (eds), *Jean Monnet: The Path to European Unity* (Basingstoke: Macmillan, 1991), pp. 130–45.

73. *Tribune*, 12 May 1950, 19 May 1950; *NS&N*, 13 May 1950.
74. Labour Party, *European Unity* (London: Labour Party, 1950). HDP 9/14, Healey to Dalton, 3 May 1950.
75. Ibid., pp. 6–7.
76. For example, *Tribune*, 16 June 1950; *NS&N*, 'Britain's answer to M. Schuman', 17 June 1950; LPA. MPP, Epping DLP to Phillips, 13 July 1950; Epson and Ewell CLP to Phillips, 12 July 1950.
77. 476HC DEB., 5s, 2122–30, 27 June 1950.
78. Ibid., 1997, 26 June 1950.
79. For Labour's subsequent debates during the 1950s to 1980s, see Newman, *Socialism and European Unity*, pp. 156 ff.
80. For examinations of the tensions between national identity and European integration/unity in the post-war years, see: Anthony D. Smith, 'National identity and the idea of European unity', *International Affairs*, vol. 68, no. 1 (1992), pp. 55–76; and William Wallace, 'Rescue or retreat? The nation state in western Europe, 1945–93', *Political Studies*, vol. 42 (1994), pp. 52–76.

Chapter 4   The Pigmentocracy of Citizenship: Assimilation, Integration or Alienation?

1. For the purposes of this chapter, black migrants will be defined as British subjects from the English-speaking Caribbean unless otherwise stated.
2. T. H. Marshall, *Citizenship and Social Class* (Cambridge: Cambridge University Press, 1950). Marshall describes a national community as real and tangible when it is bounded within a geographical area and defines itself in relation, or in opposition, to other national communities (nations). But this is not to say that the people who make up a national community view themselves as a solid cohesive community. All post-industrial national communities are fragmented, containing subcultures or stratification by class, ethnicity or race. A national community can only be represented as a cohesive amorphous mass on a nationalistic level.
3. Ibid., pp. 71–2. He defines citizenship as comprising three elements: civil, political and social. The civil element is composed of the rights necessary for individual freedom, and is most directly associated with the rule of law and a system of courts. The political part of citizenship consists of the right to participate in the exercise of political power, and is associated with parliamentary institutions. The social element of citizenship is made up of a right to the prevailing standard of life and the social heritage of the society. These rights are significantly realized through the social services and the educational system.
4. In the United Kingdom there are no clearly defined laws of citizenship, indicating the rights, duties and obligations attached to the individual and the state. There is no constitution or basic list of rights and obligations that can form the foundation of citizenship law. Because of the absence of a written constitution and the fact that the constitutional theory in Britain does not envisage a British nation or a sovereign people, the decision of who belongs and who does not has remained the prerogative first of the ruling classes and the monarchy, and then, after 1945, of the state.
5. T. K. Oommen, *Citizenship, Nationality and Ethnicity* (Oxford: Polity Press, 1997), p. 19.

6. R. Plant, 'So you want to be a citizen?', *New Statesman* (6 February 1998), p. 30.

7. *Encouraging Citizenship: A Report by the Commission on Citizenship* (London: HMSO, 1990). The commission states that citizenship requires a sense of community and horizontal comradeship (i.e. everybody within a nation being perceived as equal participants within that nation), in order to create a national community and identity. The sense of horizontal comradeship is imagined because, as in Benedict Anderson's notion of an 'imagined community' (*Imagined Communities*, London: Verso, 1983), even the smallest nation or community will never know most of their fellow members, meet them, or even hear of them, yet in the minds of each lives the image of their communion.

8. P. Gilroy, *There Ain't No Black in the Union Jack* (London: Routledge, 1987).

9. A. Dummett and A. Nicol, *Subjects, Citizens, Aliens and Others: Nationality and Immigration Law* (London: Weidenfeld and Nicolson, 1990), pp. 161–71.

10. D. Hiro, *Black British, White British* (London: Grafton Books, 1971), p. 201. He states that *laissez-faire* policies towards labour mobility collapsed (especially with regard to black immigration) during the early 1960s when the Commonwealth Immigrants Act of 1962 effectively controlled the numbers of black immigrants allowed into Britain.

11. C. Harris, 'Post-war migration and the industrial reserve army', in Winston James and Clive Harris (eds), *Inside Babylon: The Caribbean Diaspora in Britain* (London: Verso, 1993), p. 21.

12. Zig Layton-Henry, *The Politics of Immigration* (Oxford: Blackwell, 1992), p. 72

13. Ibid., p. 29

14. Harris, 'Post-war migration and the industrial reserve army', p. 21.

15. Ibid., p. 22.

16. HO 213/244, Murray, J. *et al.* to Prime Minister, 22 June 1948, in Harris, 'Post-war migration and the industrial reserve army', pp. 25–6.

17. Layton-Henry, *The Politics of Immigration*, pp. 13–14. Layton-Henry argues that the less profitable and more labour-intensive sectors of the British economy, such as public transport, the Health Service, the textile industry and metal manufacture, were eager to recruit New Commonwealth workers because these sectors of the economy could not successfully compete for British workers with more profitable sectors, such as the car industry, telecommunications and insurance.

18. Dummett and Nicol, *Subjects, Citizens, Aliens and Others*, p. 178.

19. B. Carter, C. Harris and S. Joshi, 'The 1951–55 Conservative government and the racialization of black immigration', in Winston and Harris (eds), *Inside Babylon*, pp. 65–6.

20. Dummett and Nicol, *Subjects, Citizens, Aliens and Others*, p. 19.

21. Until 1962 the migration of black workers into Britain could not be effectively limited, only discouraged, because the British government did not have the legal power to stop the migration of black workers from the West Indies to Britain. They were entitled to migrate because of their status as British subjects, until that status was devalued with the Commonwealth Immigrants Act of 1962.

22. Layton-Henry, *The Politics of Immigration*, p. 40.

23. Ibid. p. 32.

24. These anti-black riots were not the first in Britain during the post-war period. R. Glass, *Newcomers: West Indians in London,* (London: Allen and Unwin, 1960), details anti-black rioting in Liverpool from 31 July to 2 August 1948, and another race riot in Deptford, London, on 18 July 1949. There were also two days of interracial violence in Camden Town in August 1954. Such attacks on black people were significant because they received widespread media coverage and coincided with the public outcry about the increasing number of black immigrants.

25. Clive Harris, 'Post-war migration', in Winston and Harris (eds), *Inside Babylon*, p. 25. Harris interprets a letter sent by eleven Labour MPs to Clement Attlee on 22 June 1948 as racializing Caribbean migrants as the other; as a distinct and separate race which, if allowed to enter Britain in large numbers, would threaten the country's racial purity.

26. Dummett and Nicol, *Subjects, Aliens, Citizens and Others*, pp. 179–80.

27. Ibid., pp. 182–3. The determining factor as to who was free from control and who was not was based on the issuing of passports. A distinction was made between passports issued by colonial governments and passports issued by British embassies in the colonies. Passports issued by embassies would not be subject to control because the people holding these passports would be of British descent, whereas colonials issued with a passport from colonial offices, together with citizens of independent Commonwealth countries, whose passports were issued by their own governments, would be subject to control.

28. Ibid., p. 184.

29. A. Sivanandan, *A Different Hunger: Writings on Black Resistance* (London: Pluto, 1982), p. 108. Sivanandan states that only immigrants who were issued with employment vouchers were allowed to settle. The Commonwealth Immigrants Act (1962) created three types of voucher: 'A' vouchers were available to people who had jobs to come to, 'B' vouchers to those who had skills or qualifications that Britain might find useful and 'C' vouchers to unskilled workers. By 1964 'C' vouchers had been phased out. Since the majority of the unskilled came from the West Indies, the deletion of 'C' vouchers further restricted the entry of black migrants.

30. Gilroy, *There Ain't No Black in the Union Jack*, p. 46.

31. Robert Miles, *Racism after Race Relations* (London: Routledge, 1993), pp. 140–3.

32. The real issue behind their growing militancy was not addressed by the Conservative government: namely, that for assimilation to be successful there has to be a general acceptance by the host population of the group being assimilated. Without this acceptance the group being assimilated will react against this non-acceptance in usually violent and militant ways.

33. The first organization set up after the 1962 Act was the Commonwealth Immigrants Advisory Council (CIAC), to advise the Home Secretary on immigrant welfare and integration. This was replaced by the National Committee for Commonwealth Immigrants (NCCI) in 1965, set up under the Race Relations Act. The NCCI and the Race Relations Board worked to try and promote racial harmony, and to ensure that the policies of the Race Relations Act (the main purposes of which were to outlaw discrimination in public places and to penalize incitement to racial hatred) were implemented.

34. Black migrants were considered the 'other'. They were regarded as culturally, intellectually and physically inferior, and not the right sort of people for assimilation or integration into white British society.

35. LAB 13/42, memorandum, Recruitment of Colonial Subjects for Employment in Great Britain, May 1948, in Harris, 'Post-war migration and the industrial reserve arrhy'.

36. The Enlightenment, also known as the 'Age of Reason' began in the 1600s and lasted until the late 1700s. The period was characterized by the pursuit of culture and science over nature over religion. Enlightenment philosophers believed that the scientific method could be applied to the study of man's nature. This entailed the ordering of the human race based on race and culture. Works by Kant in 1775 and Blumenbach in 1776 attempted to order mankind on the basis of biology and level of civilization. According to Blumenbach there were five races belonging to a single species: Caucasian, Mongolian, Ethiopian, American and Malay. He stratified these groups with the Caucasian in first place and the Ethiopian in last place. Kant, on the other hand, detailed four separate races with white Aryan at the top and black African at the bottom. Both scholars assumed the Caucasians to be civilized, ideal stock, and all other races to be inferior to this ideal.

37. Miles, *Racism after race Relations*, p. 111.

38. E. J. Rose *et al.*, *Colour and Citizenship: A Report on British Race Relations* (Oxford: Oxford University Press, 1969), p. 23.

39. A. Geddes, *The Politics of Immigration and Race* (Baseline Books, 1996), p. 14.

40. Black migrants came from many different islands within the Caribbean and were normally bound by island loyalties. However, their experience in Britain, firstly all being lumped together, not taking into account island differences and prejudices, and secondly enduring racism and discrimination, saw the formation of a localized black community who would band together against racial oppression.

41. Sivanandan, *A Different Hunger*, p. 107. He states that black migrants in Britain rejected British culture because British culture rejected them as being non-British. Some black migrants, and especially their descendants, rejected western culture altogether and practised Rastafarianism, which was seen as subversive and a direct threat. Throughout the late 1970s and early 1980s, Rastafarianism gained popularity among black youths due to further exclusion, until the late 1980s when its popularity began to decrease.

42. Ibid.

43. S. Castles and G. Kosack, *Immigrant Workers and Class Structure in Western Europe* (Oxford: Oxford University Press, 1973).

44. Miles, *Racism after Race Relations*, pp. 165–6. In contrast, Miles argues that it was not black migrants who were unassimilable; it was the racist beliefs of British citizens resident in Britain about these migrants that hampered the assimilation process.

45. Sivanandan, *A Different Hunger*, p. 115. The speech by Roy Hattersley was referring to the unassimilability of migrants from the Asian continent, particularly Pakistanis. He used the example of West Indian migrants to illustrate how assimilation could occur if there was something in common, such as language and religion.

46. Address given by the Home Secretary, the Rt Hon. Roy Jenkins, MP, on 23 May 1966 to a meeting of Voluntary Liaison Committees (London: NCCI, 1966).

47. Rose *et al.*, *Colour and Citizenship*, p. 24.

48. The introduction of the term 'ethnic' during the 1960s and 1970s represented a movement away from the concept of race, which still perpetuated notions

of biological differences. Ethnicity defined the differences between people and communities firmly on the basis of culture and practices, and not on colour. Some scholars have argued that ethnicity has merely replaced race because the term 'ethnic minority' has been used only to describe black minorities in Britain.

49. Sivanandan, *A Different Hunger*, p. 117.

50. Ibid., p. 118.

51. J. Rex and S. Tomlinson, *Colonial Immigrants in a British City: A Class Analysis* (London: Routledge, 1979).

52. S. Small, *Racial Barriers* (London: Routledge, 1994), p. 165. Small describes the policies of integration as colour blind because the government and the opposition throughout the post-war period held the view that the mention of race or racism only exacerbated problems and incited racialized animosities. Therefore if the language of race and racism disappeared, so would race and racism themselves. Left-wing governments generally thought that the primary problems confronting black people were class based and the idea of racism contradicted this view. Right-wing governments argued that positive discrimination and the notions of race inhibited the free workings of the market, especially where the policies of equal opportunities were concerned. The commitment to a meritocracy rather than positive action would ensure the free play of the market.

53. These tools include language (migrants not able to speak or write English are disabled from gaining access to information or completing the necessary forms) and cultural knowledge (knowledge of the processes involved that are specific to the British system, which will enable them to 'work the system' to their advantage).

54. N. Foner, *Jamaica Farewell* (London: Routledge, 1979), pp. 48–50.

55. Hiro, *Black British, White British*, pp. 52–4.

56. G. Peach, *West Indian Migration to Britain: A Social Geography* (London: Oxford University Press for IRR, 1969), pp. 83–91.

57. Small, *Racial Barriers*, p. 171.

58. E. Thomas-Hope, 'Hope and reality in the West Indian migration to Britain', *Oral History*, vol. 8, no. 1 (1980). Thomas-Hope states that the main aspiration of many West Indian migrants was to better themselves, find work and eventually return 'home' a success.

59. Author's interview with Kay, June 1998. She emigrated to England in 1961 at the age of 23, and returned to the Caribbean in September 1999.

60. M. Chamberlain, *Narratives of Exile and Return* (London: Macmillan, 1997), p. 75.

61. Interview with Kay, June 1998.

62. Interview with Kay, June 1998.

63. M. Keith and M. Cross, 'Racism and the postmodern city', in M. Keith and M. Cross (eds), *Racism, the City and the State* (London: Routledge, 1993), p. 21.

64. During my own initial research in 1998, in the form of questionnaires, almost all of the black migrants questioned thought that they would be accepted into British society.

65. Winston James, 'Migration, racism and identity formation: the Caribbean experience in Britain', in James and Harris (eds), *Inside Babylon*, pp. 244–6. Harris states that it was the English who helped black migrants to feel 'black' or to feel West Indian. But these identities, especially the description 'black', were soon appropriated by black migrants to describe all non-white people in their struggle against oppression in Britain.

66. L. Garrison, *Black Youth, Rastafarianism and the Identity Crisis in Britain* (London: ACER Project, 1979), p. 39. He states that Rastafarianism proved very attractive for black British youths because it promoted a positive self-image encompassed in spirituality. Rastafarianism also emphasized cultural separation.

Chapter 5   From 'Colour Blind' to 'Colour Bar': Residential Separation in Brixton and Notting Hill, 1948–75

1. D. Hinds, 'The island of Brixton', *Oral History Journal*, vol. 8, no. 1 (spring 1980), p. 49.

2. All references to black or black Caribbean people throughout this chapter refer directly to 'black' people born in the Caribbean and British Guyana and their descendants. This chapter does not include reference to Britain's Asian community, except where statistics or comments do not allow separation of the two.

3. See particularly the 'immigrant-race' school, including the work of Sheila Patterson, *Dark Strangers: A Sociological Study of the Absorption of a Recent West Indian Migrant Group in Brixton, South London* (London: Tavistock, 1963). It was only after migrant 'choice' was considered that this changed. Two more recent works that do this and go beyond, to consider the diversity of individual migrant experience are Margaret Byron, *The Housing Question: Caribbean Migrants and the British Housing Market*, Research Paper no. 49, University of Oxford, and Mary Chamberlain, *Narratives of Exile and Return* (New York: St Martin's Press, 1997).

4. Ruth Glass and H. Pollins, *Newcomers: The West Indians in London* (London: George Allen and Unwin/Centre for Urban Studies, 1960), p. 3, and Patterson, *Dark Strangers*, p. 3. One academic strand was to replace the idea of 'race' with 'ethnic' relations, distinguishing groups by cultural difference. However, analysis of the social, political and cultural construction of racialized relations allows a wider analysis of events.

5. Diagram in A. Sivanandan, *A Different Hunger: Writings on Black Resistance* (London: Pluto, 1982), p. 112; Paul Gilroy, *Ain't No Black in the Union Jack* (London: Routledge, 1987), p. 22.

6. Robert Miles, *Race and Migrant Labour* (London: Routledge and Kegan Paul, 1982), p. 4.

7. Gilroy, *Ain't No Black in the Union Jack*, p. 27.

8. W. James and C. Harris (eds), *Inside Babylon: The Caribbean Diaspora in Britain* (London: Verso: 1993), p. 3, and Gilroy, *Ain't No Black in the Union Jack*, p. 27.

9. Stuart Hall quoted in James and Harris (eds), *Inside Babylon*, p. 4.

10. Introduction, in Rick Halpern, *Down on the Killing Floor: Black and White Workers in Chicago's Packinghouses 1904–54* (Chicago: University of Illinois Press, 1997); see also R. Kelley, '"We are not what we seem": rethinking black working-class opposition in the Jim Crow South', *Journal of American History*, June 1993, p. 97.

11. Peter Alexander and Rick Halpern (eds), *Racializing Class, Classifying Race: Labour and Difference in Britain, the USA and Africa* (Basingstoke: Macmillan, 2000).

12. Peter Fryer, *Staying Power: The History of Black People in Britain* (London: Pluto, 1984), p. 295.

13. Ceri Peach, *West Indian Migration to Britain: A Social Geography* (London: Oxford University Press: London, 1968), pp. 66–7.

14. Milner Holland, *Report of the Committee on Housing in Greater London* (Cmnd 2605, London: HMSO, 1965), p. 11; Select Committee on Race Relations and Immigration, *Housing* (London: HMSO, 1971), p. 31. It was predicted that London boroughs would have a shortage of 100,000 houses by 1974, as compared with families wanting separate homes. A further 150,000 of those that did exist would be unfit.

15. There are few statistics available on minorities in Britain until the 1980s, although in the 1971 census place of birth is established, which gives some idea of numbers and location; surveys before this provide approximate results (R. Skellington, *'Race' in Britain Today*, 2nd edn, London: Sage, 1996, p. 22. Some estimates are available of figures prior to 1971 from contemporary surveys, such as by Sheila Patterson, Pearl Jephcott, Ruth Glass and Ceri Peach, and some local authority estimates. However, the accuracy of these figures is variable and fear of officials asking questions has meant that many are under-estimates, especially of overcrowding.

16. Glass and Pollins, *Newcomers*, p. 38.

17. T. Lee, *Race and Residence: The Concentration and Dispersal of Immigrants in London* (Oxford: Clarendon Press, 1977), p. 62. London ward-level concentration Location Quotient value over 2.0 (even distribution 1.0); 1961, 64.5 per cent of 'West Indians'; 1966, 64.6 per cent; 1971, 57.5 per cent.

18. Lee, *Race and Residence*, p. 19.

19. Margaret Byron and Ceri Peach, 'Caribbean tenants in council housing: "race", class and gender', *New Community*, vol. 19, no. 3 (April 1993), pp. 407–23 at p. 421; 'Government policy on housing and race relations', *New Community*, vol. 1, nos 1 and 2 (winter 1997–8), pp. 112–17 at p. 115.

20. Lee, *Race and Residence*, p. 17. At borough level, the proportion of the total population that was Caribbean born in 1971 was at its highest, 6.5 per cent, in Hackney and Brent; Lambeth and Haringey were next with 5 per cent (ibid., p. 16). At ward level, the proportion of the population is higher; however, only 18 of 654 wards in the Greater London area had more than 10 per cent of its population born in the Caribbean, and only 7 wards more than 15 per cent (ibid., p. 23). However, in areas of high concentration the smaller areal unit considered one finds a more heavily concentrated black population, with some streets containing mostly black Caribbean people (ibid.). In considering the levels of concentration, it is worth noting that these figures do not include those black Caribbean people born in Britain, and because of the young age of the migrant population it was likely that these figures would have risen (Byron and Peach, 'Government policy on housing and race relations', p. 115).

21. E. Pilkington, *Beyond the Mother Country: West Indians and Notting Hill White Riots* (London: I.B. Taurus, 1988), p. 55.

22. Patterson, *Dark Strangers*, p. 56.

23. E. Burney, *Housing on Trial: A Study of Immigrants and Local Government* (London: Oxford University Press, 1967), p. 119. Census data on racial or ethnic groups were realized to be an under-estimate, in part because black people born in Britain were not included at this time. Also many were not listed to vote because of fear of officials, and wanting to hide the reality of numbers in multi-occupied housing from officials.

24. Glass and Pollins, *Newcomers*, p. 41.

25. Isolyn Robinson in a booklet of interviews: *The Windrush Legacy: Memories of Britain's Post-war Caribbean Migrants* (London: Black Cultural Archives, 1998), p. 27.

26. Pilkington, *Beyond the Mother Country*, p. 55.

27. Pearl Jephcott, *A Troubled Area: Notes on Notting Hill* (London: Faber and Faber, 1964), pp. 23, 25.

28. *The Windrush Legacy*, p. 44.

29. Lee, *Race and Residence*, p. 8.

30. Select Committee of Race Relations and Immigration, Session 1976–7, *The West Indian Community* (London: HMSO, 1977), p. x.

31. Byron and Peach, 'Caribbean tenants in council housing', p. 410.

32. Lee, *Race and Residence*, figures for Greater London, p. 35.

33. Nancy Foner, *Jamaica Farewell: Jamaican Migrants in London* (London: Routledge and Kegan Paul, 1979), p. 49.

34. Lee, *Race and Residence*, p. 118. Owner occupants are people, or households, that have bought their own home and in some cases rent out rooms.

35. Ibid., p. 36.

36. Public Records Office, Kew (henceforward PRO), LAB 26 226, Colonial Office Working Party on the Recruitment of West Indians for UK Industries, July 1949.

37. This refers to the work of Patterson, *Dark Strangers*, and Glass, *Newcomers*, who trace the development of black concentrated settlements in Brixton and Notting Hill, referring to a process by which the black migrant population were assimilated, or integrated into the society at large, seeing the latter as the goal for social policy.

38. J. Cullingworth, *Council Housing: Purposes, Procedures and Priorities*, the Ninth Report of the Housing Management Sub-committee of the Central Housing Advisory Committee, Ministry of Housing and Local Government (London: HMSO, 1969), paragraph 142.

39. Peach, *West Indian Migration to Britain*, p. xvi.

40. Scholars of the 1950s and 1960s spend time establishing the reality of a British ghetto. Claudia Jones, in an editorial for the *West Indian Gazette*, picked up on the prominence given to Martin Luther King's warning of a British ghetto developing when he visited Britain in 1964. She noted that of all the press coverage of his visit, most was concerned with the '"ghetto" quote', *West Indian Gazette*, vol. 6, no. 4 (November 1964).

41. Glass, *Newcomers*, p. xii.

42. 'Dr King's racial warning to Britain', *The Times*, 7 December 1964, p. 6.

43. *De facto* segregation refers to a separation of a racial group, in this case through socio-economic and political forces. This separation is not, however, written law (*de jure* segregation).

44. Much work has been done on the American ghetto – see, for example, Kenneth Kusmer, *A Ghetto Takes Shape: Black Cleveland 1870–1930* (Chicago: University of Illinois Press, 1976); A. Spear, *Black Chicago: The Making of a Negro Ghetto 1890–1920* (Chicago: University of Chicago Press, 1969). However, the words 'ghetto' and 'slum' (referring to a rundown area including houses unfit for human habitation) have often been used interchangeably in Britain, creating misconceptions: for example, describing 'the area of London where deprivation is very acute (ghettos)', *Grassroots*, vol. 4, no. 1 (14 July 1975), p. 8.

45. Glass, *Newcomers*, p. 41.

46. Gilroy, *Ain't No Black in the Union Jack*, p. 167.

47. H. Cayton and S. Drake, *Black Metropolis* (London: Jonathan Cape, 1946), pp. 8–12 and quoted in Peach, *West Indian Migration*, p. 83.

48. Peach, *West Indian Migration*, pp. 87, 83.

49. Rex quoted in S. Smith, *The Politics of Race and Residence: Citizenship, Segregation and White Supremacy in Britain* (Cambridge: Polity, 1989), p. 57; S. Small, *Racialised Barriers: The Black Experience in the United States and England in the 1980s* (London: Routledge, 1994), p. 8.

50. Pilkington, *Beyond the Mother Country*, p. 48.

51. PRO, CAB 134 1210, 17 May 1956.

52. Higher rents would mean that more money would be invested in improving the property.

53. Milner Holland, p. 165.

54. L. J. Sharpe, 'Brixton', in N. Deakin (ed.), *Colour and the British Electorate 1964* (London: Pall Mall Press/Institute of Race Relations, 1965), p. 16.

55. N. Deakin, *Colour Citizenship and British Society: An Abridged and Updated Version of the Famous Report* (London: Panther/Institute of Race Relations, 1970), p. 153.

56. Described by Lambeth Borough Council, Rex and Tomlinson, *Colonial Immigrants in a British City: A Class Analysis* (London: Routledge and Kegan Paul, 1979), pp. 130–1.

57. Foner, *Jamaica Farewell*, p. 48.

58. H. Flett in R. Ward (ed.), *Race and Residence in Britain: Approaches to Differential Treatment in Housing* (Birmingham: Economic and Social Research Council, 1984), p. 83. The Cullingworth Committee refers to the 1969 report by the Central Housing Advisory Committee, *Council Housing Purposes, Procedures and Priorities*.

59. Flett, ibid., p. 85.

60. Foner, *Jamaica Farewell*, p. 49.

61. Flett in Ward (ed.), *Race and Residence*, p. 84. Housing associations also rehoused people throughout the period. In my interview with Loretta McKnight, she stated that she chose to stay in Notting Hill. Interview with Loretta McKnight, May 1997.

62. Sharpe in Deakin (ed.), *Colour and the British Electorate*, p. 23.

63. Milner Holland, p. 426.

64. *Hustler*, 8 June 1968, figures from 1967 Notting Hill Summer project, p. 5.

65. Rex and Tomlinson, *Colonial Immigrants*, p. 131.

66. Sharpe in Deakin (ed.), *Colour and the British Electorate*, p. 21.

67. Milner Holland, p. 111.

68. C. and M. Phillips, *Notting Hill in the Sixties* (London: Lawrence and Wishart, 1991), p. 108

69. In Notting Hill much redevelopment was in private, rather than public hands, which resulted in the gentrification of the area, homes being built for more prosperous residents for a profit. Kensington remained a Conservative-run council. In 1968 the Housing Committee Chairman summed up the local government perspective: 'our view is that it is quite wrong to deflect money into an area which is quite capable of pulling itself up by its own bootstraps'. Jan O'Malley, *The Politics of Community Action: A Decade of Struggle in Notting Hill* (Nottingham: Russell Press, 1977), p. 16.

70. Interview with A. Sivanandan, June 1997.

71. *The Windrush Legacy*, p. 27.

72. Milner Holland, p. 201. Although conditions for the local white population were not ideal, the greater overcrowding in black Caribbean homes exacerbated the problem: for example, one-quarter of black households in London shared cooking facilities, compared to 2 per cent of households for the rest of the population. Deakin, *Colour and Citizenship and British Society*, p. 69.

73. Foner, *Jamaica Farewell*, p. 48.

74. Deakin, *Colour, Citizenship and British Society*, p. 71.

75. Milner Holland, p. 22.

76. Smith, *The Politics of Race and Residence*, p. 39; see also Deakin, *Colour, Citizenship and British Society*, chapter 8; W. W. Daniel, *Racial Discrimination in England: Based on the PEP Report* (London: Penguin, 1968), chapter 3.

77. Glass, *Newcomers*, p. 49.

78. Pilkington, *Beyond the Mother Country*, p. 56.

79. Glass, *Newcomers*, p. 49.

80. Patterson, *Dark Strangers*, pp. 52–3.

81. *The Windrush Legacy*, p. 20. Sydney White was housed by the League of Coloured Peoples in Brixton in 1947.

82. Baron Baker in *The Windrush Legacy*, p. 18.

83. Sam King in *The Windrush Legacy*, p. 8.

84. *The Windrush Legacy*, p. 19.

85. Quoted in Hinds, 'The island of Brixton', *Oral History Journal*, vol. 8, no. 1 (spring 1980), p. 51.

86. E. Scobie, *Black Britannia* (Chicago: Johnson Publishing Co., 1972), p. 198. In the arena of housing the 'colour bar' was allowed to flourish, more perhaps than in other parts of the black experience. For example, whereas for the work environment experience of racism was seen as a national issue, it was seen as a matter for the landlord to decide with whom he was prepared to live. Glass, *Newcomers*, p. 66.

87. 'So sorry, no coloured, no children', *West Indian Gazette*, vol. 3, no. 2 (September 1960), p. 5.

88. Foner, *Jamaica Farewell*, p. 47.

89. In the contemporary period, references were made to 'coloured' people, meaning black Caribbean, Asian and African people. Through most of the period covered in this chapter there was little official distinction between the different groups.

90. Dipak Nandy, *New Statesman*, 21 April 1967, p. 533.

91. Ibid.

92. Smith, *The Politics of Race and Residence*, p. 39; see also Deakin, *Colour, Citizenship and British Society*, chapter 8; W. W. Daniel, *Racial Discrimination in England: Based on the PEP Report* (London: Penguin, 1968), chapter 3.

93. 'So sorry, no coloured, no children', p. 5.

94. Hinds, 'The island of Brixton', p. 49.

95. Dipak Nandy, *New Statesman*, 21 April 1967, p. 533.

96. Foner, *Jamaica Farewell*, p. 47, results of PEP 1967.

97. PRO, CK 1 1, *Report of the Race Relations Board for 1966–7*, p. 19.

98. Ibid.

99. Smith, *The Politics of Race and Residence*, p. 52.

100. *The Windrush Legacy*, p. 8.

101. Sivanandan, *A Different Hunger*, p. 6.

102. Sam King in *The Windrush Legacy*, p. 8.

103. Select Committee on Race Relations and Immigration, Session 1970–1, *Housing* (London: HMSO, 1971), Vol. 1, p. 38.

104. Connie Mark in *The Motherland Calls: African Caribbean Experiences* (London: Ethnic Communities Oral History Project, henceforward ECOH, London, 1992).

105. Milner Holland, pp. 190–1. The word 'coloured' in this report referred to people of black Caribbean, Asian and African origin, following the colloquial usage of the word in the 1950s and 1960s.

106. Ibid.

107. Peach, *West Indian Immigration*, p. 84.

108. Smith, *The Politics of Race and Residence*, p. 37.

109. Interview with Pamela Stewart, May 1997.

110. Flett in Ward (ed.), *Race and Residence*, p. 85.

111. Interview with Loretta McKnight, May 1997.

112. Foner, *Jamaica Farewell*, p. 4.

113. Interview with Loretta McKnight, May 1997.

114. Ceri Peach, 'The force of West Indian island identity in Britain', in C. Clarke *et al.* (eds), *Geography and Ethnic Pluralism* (London: George Allen and Unwin, 1984), p. 224.

115. Ibid., pp. 224–5.

116. Interview with Pamela Stewart, May 1997.

117. Phillips, *Notting Hill in the Sixties*, p. 49.

118. This is not to suggest that a homogenous white community existed, but parts of the local white population were joined on the opposite side of the racial divide to the black population. During the 1950s it is argued that the government actually promoted this attitude by asserting that 'Britishness' was an ideal, but one that only 'white' people could make a claim to. Bob Carter *et al.*, 'The Conservative government and the racialization of black immigration', in James and Harris (eds), *Inside Babylon*, p. 57. The nature of 'whiteness' is the source of current historical debate; it is questioned whether we can really talk about 'white' as a single category, considering the variety of people that are subsumed under this label. See particularly D. Roediger, *The Wages of Whiteness: Race and the Making of the American Working Class* (London: Verso, 1991).

119. Glass, *Newcomers*, p. 40.

120. Interview with A. Sivanandan, June 1997.

121. Sheila Patterson, 'The recent West Indian immigrant group in Britain', *Race*, vol. 1, no. 2, p. 35.

122. Select Committee on Race Relations and Immigration, Session 1970–1, *Housing* (London: HMSO, 1971), Vol. 1, p. 50.

123. Hinds, 'The island of Brixton', p. 50.

124. *West Indian Gazette*, vol. 5, no. 4 (July 1962), p. 3. The Mangrove, owned and run by Frank Critchlow, later became infamous as a central point of black protest against police racism in 1971.

125. Isolyn Robinson on Brixton from *The Windrush Legacy*, p. 27.

126. Phillips, *Notting Hill in the Sixties*, p. 49.

127. Connie Marks in *The Motherland Calls*, p. 4.

128. Jephcott, *A Troubled Area*, p. 86.

129. Interview with Margaret Payne, January 2000.

130. *'Sorry no Vacancie': Life Stories of Senior Citizens from the Caribbean* (London: ECOH, 1992), p. 20.

131. Glass, *Newcomers*, p. 267.

132. *The Windrush Legacy*, p. 37.

133. The gendered nature of the experience of racism in Britain is an issue in itself and is the subject of scholarly discussion and debate – see particularly a whole issue of *Feminist Review* that is dedicated to the topic, *Feminist Review*, 17, autumn 1984.

134. Milner Holland, p. 194.

135. The phenomenon caused headlines, such as 'No Nigs at the Black Horse', *New Statesman*, 5 March 1960, p. 324.

136. Phillips, *Notting Hill in the Sixties*, p. 47.

137. Hinds, 'The island of Brixton', p. 50.

138. Times News Team, *The Black Man in Search of Power* (London: Thomas Nelson, 1968), p. 140.

139. Peach, *West Indian Migration*, p. 89.

140. Ibid.

141. Ibid.

142. Hinds, 'The island of Brixton', p. 49.

143. *West Indian Gazette*, vol. 3, no. 2 (September 1960), p. 1.

144. *West Indian Gazette*, vol. 5, no. 2 (July 1962), p. 3.

145. Michael Abdul Malik, *From Michael DeFreitas to Michael X* (London: Deutsch, 1968), p. 68.

146. Ibid., p. 104.

147. Some types of tenancy remained under controls after 1957, to be phased out at a later date.

148. 'Rachmanism and you', *West Indian Gazette*, vol. 5, no. 9 (October 1963), p. 6.

149. From the transcript of Barry Carmen interview no. 60 for the BBC, 1958, Institute of Race Relations (IRR) Archive.

150. Carmen interview no. 61, 1958, ibid.

151. Phillips, *Notting Hill in the Sixties*, p. 47.

152. Interview with A. Sivanandan, June 1997.

153. Pilkington, *Beyond the Mother Country*, p. 116.

154. Ibid., p. 117.

155. Carter *et al.* in James and Harris (eds), *Inside Babylon*, pp. 69–70.

156. PRO, CAB 124 1191, *Sunday Times*, 14 November 1954, 'Colonial immigrants'.

157. PRO, CAB 134 1210, Cabinet Committee on Colonial Immigrants, April/May 1956.

158. Fenner Brockway tried to pass a bill that would legislate against racial discrimination, prepared in 1954. The first Race Relations Act was not passed until 1965, but this only covered discrimination in 'places of public resort'; it was not until 1968 that housing and employment were included, but so were many exceptions. Fryer, *Staying Power*, p. 383; Sivanandan, *A Different Hunger*, p. 117. Dean suggests that the 1958 Nottingham and Notting Hill disturbances were 'a turning point in securing legislation'. Dennis Dean, 'The Conservative government and the 1961 Immigration Act', *Race and Class*, vol. 35, no. 2 (1993), p. 64.

159. Black migration was limited by a voucher system based on employment. Migrants who had a job to come to (voucher A) and those with useful skills (B) were able to enter the country; it was harder to obtain voucher C, for unskilled workers, and this was removed by the 1965 White Paper. Sivanandan, *A Different Hunger*, pp. 108–9. The fact that Irish immigrants were precluded from the system reiterated the racist nature of the legislation. The government believed that controlling numbers was necessary if integration was ever to take place. Dean, 'The Conservative government and the 1961 Immigration Act', p. 69.

160. Sivanandan, *A Different Hunger*, p. 110.

161. Fryer, *Staying Power*, p. 384.

162. Select Committee on Race Relations and Immigration, Session 1970–1, *Housing*, Vol. 1, p. 50; PRO, C K 1 1, *Report of the Race Relations Board for 1966–7*.

163. L. Bridges, 'The Ministry of Internal Security: British urban social policy', *Race and Class*, vol. 16, no. 4 (1975), p. 376; Sivanandan, *A Different Hunger*, pp. 119–21.

164. 'Brixton's farewell to Rev. D.I.G. Shewing', *West Indian Gazette*, vol. 5, no. 10 (May 1963), p. 9.

165. Pilkington, *Beyond the Mother Country*, p. 84.

166. 'Racism in the GNC', *Backayard News Sheet*, 1973, p. 4.

167. Pilkington, *Beyond the Mother Country*, p. 143.

168. Marika Sherwood, *Claudia Jones: A Life in Exile* (London: Lawrence and Wishart, 1999), p. 94.

169. When I interviewed Sivanandan (June 1997) he stated that in these years he was unaware of much of the organization that took place as family and work came first, leaving no time for such activity.

170. Sharpe in Deakin (ed.), *Colour and the British Electorate*, p. 15.

171. Scobie, *Black Britannia*, p. 236.

172. *The Windrush Legacy*, p. 51.

173. Malik, *From Michael DeFreitas to Michael X*, p. 76.

174. Scobie, *Black Britannia*, p. 234.

175. Black activity surrounding this event forced recognition of their concerns in a number of government departments. Dean, 'The Conservative government and the 1961 Immigration Act', p. 65.

176. Sivanandan, *A Different Hunger*, p. 16.

177. Ibid., p. 20; Scobie, *Black Britannia*, p. 291.

178. *Black Eagles Pamphlet, Black People's News Service*, BPM, March 1970.

179. *Dashiki and Homeless Black Young People: Dashiki Annual Report 1973/4* (London: Zulu Publications, 1974).

180. Scobie, *Black Britannia*, p. 277.

181. In the black press, constant mention is given to youth groups that black organizations set up to help black youths and educate them in 'black' history. The Black Liberation Front, for example, set up a youth league. Vince Hines, *Britain, the Black Man and the Future* (London: Zulu Publications, 1972).

182. Both a younger generation of black people and particularly black women were influenced by these groups and ideas. Examples are Brixton Black Women's Group and the Organization for Women of African or Asian Descent (OWAAD). Many of the founding members, such as Gerlin Bean, started their organizational activity within groups set up around the ideas of Black Power.

Chapter 6   Local Government, Rates and Rents: The Policies of the London County Council and Three Borough Councils

1. For further discussion on this topic, see, for instance, H. Drucker, *Doctrine and Ethos in the Labour Party* (London: Allen and Unwin, 1979) and D. Coates, *The Labour Party and the Struggle for Socialism* (Cambridge: Cambridge University Press 1975). S. Goss, *Local Labour and Local Government: A Study of Changing Interests, Politics and Policy in Southwark from 1919 to 1982* (Edinburgh: Edinburgh University Press, 1988) provides an excellent view from the local level.

2. G. D. H. Cole, *Short History of the British Working Class Movement, 1789–1947* (London: Allen and Unwin, 1948), p. 289. The quote cited here comes from Volume III of the original work, first printed in 1927.

3. John Gyford, *The Politics of Local Socialism* (London: Allen and Unwin, 1985), p. 3.

4. Clement Attlee, 'Local government and the Socialist Plan', *Socialist League Forum Lecture No. 7* (London: Socialist League, *c.*1930s), p. 5, quoted in Gyford, *The Politics of Local Socialism*, p. 3.

5. Gyford, *The Politics of Local Socialism*, p. 3.

6. Goss, *Local Labour and Local Government*, p. 148.

7. Sidney Webb, for instance, saw municipal socialism as a 'democratic organisation on the basis of the association of consumers for the supply of their own needs'. Sidney Webb, 1910, quoted in Sir Adolphus Ward, Sir George Prothero and S. Leathes (eds), *The Cambridge Modern History* (Cambridge: Cambridge University Press), Vol. XII, pp. 730–65.

8. John Mason, 'Partnership denied: the London Labour Party on the LCC and the decline of London government 1940–65', in Andrew Saint (ed.), *Politics and the People of London: The London County Council 1889–1965* (London: Hambledon Press, 1989), p. 253.

9. Leader of the LCC, 1934–40.

10. Gyford, *The Politics of Local Socialism*, p. 4.

11. *House of Commons Debates*, 5th Series, vol. 564, col. 689, 7 February 1957.

12. See, for instance, Ken Young and Nirmala Rao, *Local Government since 1945* (Oxford: Blackwell, 1997).

13. Until the Local Government Act (1948), local authorities determined their own rate valuation, e.g. how much the borough was worth, based on the rental values of the properties within their jurisdiction. In 1948, the Labour government transferred this power to the Inland Revenue.

14. Notably this was to do with problems surrounding valuation and the mechanics of how the government would calculate this. That Acts were passed in 1953 and 1955 in an attempt to plug the holes left in the 1948 Act was merely an indication of the troubles besieging the Inland Revenue at this time.

15. K. Young and N. Rao, *Local Government since 1945*, p. 138.

16. Ibid.

17. Minister of Housing and Local Government.

18. *The Economist*, 10 September 1955.

19. 'Smoothing the ratepayer', *The Economist*, 16 April 1955. See also Young and Rao, *Local Government since 1945*, p. 137.

20. Young and Rao, *Local Government since 1945*, p. 131.

21. Whether or not local government found this situation favourable, the danger of this 'dependence' was noted by politicians. Butler felt that if the financial foundations of local government were to stay as they were, there was danger of 'the atrophy of local government and its degeneration into little more than an agent of the Central Government', CAB 129/84, 'Local government finance: memorandum by the Lord Privy Seal', 14 December 1956, paras 22, 19; cited in Young and Rao, *Local Government since 1945*, p. 125.

22. *House of Commons Debates*, 5th Series, vol. 564, col. 623, 7 February 1957.

23. *The Economist*, 7 January 1956, p. 60.

24. Labour MP for Kettering.

25. *House of Commons Debates*, 5th Series, vol. 564, cols 645–8, 7 February 1957.

26. Cabinet Minutes, 29 January 1957.

27. CAB 129/84: 'Local government finance: memorandum by the President of the Board of Trade', 19 December 1956, quoted in Young and Rao, *Local Government since 1945*, p. 139.

28. Tony Travers, *The Politics of Local Government Finance* (London: Allen and Unwin, 1986), p. 12.

29. For instance, Mr Mitchison proclaimed: 'What about the local authorities? . . . They are being called upon increasingly to pay more and more for what they have to provide . . . and the Minister is going to put on their backs £219 million for the benefit of the banks, the brewers, Unilever and all the rest. That is really what this Bill comes to' (*House of Commons Debates*, 5th Series, vol. 564, col. 646, 7 February 1957).

30. 'Logic for ratepayers', *The Economist*, 6 August 1955, and 'Storm over rates', 24 March 1956.

31. Indeed, it would be interesting to explore in more depth the relationship between industrial (de)rating and the Labour government's 1945–51 nationalization policy.

32. *Labour Party Annual Report*, 1956, pp. 29–30.

33. *The Economist*, 28 January 1956.

34. Ibid.

35. *Labour Party Annual Report*, 1956, pp. 29–30.

36. D. Mathieson, 'Holborn and St Pancras South Labour Party 1947–63: an analysis of one CLP and the post war consensus' (unpublished Ph.D. thesis, Huddersfield Polytechnic, February 1989, Camden Local Studies and Archives Centre, Holborn Library), pp. 52–3.

37. Published by the Labour Publishing Society, Ltd. Editorial Board: Tom Braddock, Jack Stanley and Gerry Healy with John Lawrence as editor.

38. See Mathieson, 'Holborn and St Pancras South Labour Party'.

39. *Socialist Outlook*, vol. 3, no. 5 (May 1951), National Museum of Labour History, Manchester Labour Party Archives.

40. *Socialist Outlook*, 21 May 1954. The NEC then turned against *Socialist Outlook* in October 1954, although Bevan, Foot and Lee all defended it, concerned that *Tribune* might be next to feel the wrath of the NEC. As Gerry Healy and Jack Stanley argued: 'The decision of the NEC of the Labour Party to declare

ineligible for membership of the Party persons "associated with" or "supporting" SOCIALIST OUTLOOK is unprecedented in the History of the Labour movement of this country' (*Socialist Outlook*, 13 August 1954).

41. Peggy Duff, *North London Press*, 25 January 1957. Ironically, at around the same time, the LCC began implementing a policy based on rent increases in respect to floor level. On 21 February 1956 the Housing Committee decided to raise the rents on certain estates according to the view and on 20 November 1956 they extended the policy to further estates. *London County Council Printed Minutes 1956*, 21 February 1956, p. 78.

42. Peggy Duff, *Left, Left, Left: A Personal Account of Six Protest Campaigns 1945–65*, (London: Allen and Busby, 1971), p. 90.

43. *North London Press*, 25 January 1957 (Camden Local Studies and Archives Centre, Holborn Library, London).

44. The effects of the new valuation lists in 1956 were beneficial to local authorities with regard to public perceptions of the rates. If the valuation of a property rose, rate poundages were likely to fall.

45. *St Pancras Borough Council Printed Minutes 1955*, Vol. 72, 16 March 1955, p. 156, and *St Pancras Borough Council Printed Minutes 1956*, Vol. 73, 14 March 1956, p. 152.

46. *St Pancras Borough Council Printed Minutes 1956*, Vol. 73, 19 December 1956, p. 668.

47. *North London Press*, 21 June 1957.

48. *North London Press*, 15 July 1958.

49. Ibid.

50. *St Pancras Borough Council Printed Minutes 1958*, Vol. 75, 30 July 1958, p. 424.

51. *St Pancras Borough Council Printed Minutes 1957*, Vol. 74, 20 March 1957, p. 160.

52. Mathieson, 'Holborn and St Pancras South Labour Party', p. 153.

53. *North London Press*, 11 October 1957.

54. *North London Press*, 28 July 1957.

55. *North London Press*, 22 March 1957.

56. Ibid.

57. *North London Press*, 7 June 1957.

58. Duff, *Left, Left, Left*, p. 90.

59. Ibid., p. 91.

60. Mathieson, 'Holborn and St Pancras South Labour Party', p. 145.

61. This legislation removed the rent controls of all properties with a rentable value above £40, with the exception of properties not exceeding £40 in value with controlled tenants. Where tenancies were controlled, it was obviously in the interests of the landlords to remove their sitting tenants to allow for decontrol. The Rent Act confused the issue of derequisitioned houses: if owners did allow former tenants to become licensee, there was no guarantee in the Rent Act against rent decontrol, giving the rent position of licensees an ambivalent status.

62. *St Pancras Borough Council Printed Minutes*, Vol. 75, 19 March 1958, p. 163.

63. Ibid.

64. Duff, *Left, Left, Left*, p. 91.

65. Mathieson, 'Holborn and St Pancras South Labour Party', p. 168, and *North London Press*, 28 February 1957.

66. Duff, *Left, Left, Left*, p. 95.

67. Ibid.

68. *North London Press*, 7 March 1958.

69. Mathieson, 'Holborn and St Pancras South Labour Party', p. 168.

70. *Labour Party Annual Report*, 1958, p. 19. John Lawrence went on to join the Communist Party (*Sunday Pictorial*, 23 November 1958).

71. *North London Press*, 8 August 1958.

72. Mathieson, 'Holborn and St Pancras South Labour Party', pp. 163–4. The *North London Press* reports that the amount was £800 (*North London Press*, 14 November 1958).

73. *St Pancras Borough Council Printed Minutes 1858*, Vol. 75, 12 November 1958, pp. 630–932.

74. Letter sent out to members by the Secretary of the St Pancras South Constituency Labour Party, quoted in O. Cannon and J. R. L. Anderson, *The Road from Wigan Pier: A Biography of Les Cannon* (London: Victor Gollancz, 1973), p. 171.

75. Bernie Holland, interviewed by Roy Gore and Louise Brodie, November 1997 (National Sound Archive, British Library, Call mark – C609/85/01-04 – F6013-6).

76. *Labour Party Annual Report*, 1958, p. 19.

77. Ibid.

78. *Lambeth Borough Council Printed Minutes 1956–57*, 30 January 1957.

79. *Islington Borough Council Printed Minutes 1957–58*, 15 November 1957, pp. 243–4.

80. *North London Press*, 27 December 1957.

81. *North London Press*, 30 May 1958.

82. *Islington Borough Council Printed Minutes 1957–58*, 21 February 1958, p. 389, and *North London Press*, 28 February 1958.

83. *North London Press*, 8 August 1958.

84. *North London Press*, 31 October 1958.

85. *Lambeth Borough Council Printed Minutes 1955–56*, p. 940.

86. Under the scheme, rent paid by the tenants was one-fifth of the income of the husband and wife, ignoring child allowance, plus an addition of 2s 6d for each wage earner over the age of 15 and 5s over the age of 21. In October 1956, members amended the scheme slightly. *Lambeth Borough Council Printed Minutes 1955–56*, p. 940.

87. *London County Council Printed Minutes 1955*, 25 October 1955, pp. 522–3.

88. *London County Council Printed Minutes 1958*, 21 October 1958, pp. 636–7.

89. Braddock was on the original editorial board of *Socialist Outlook*.

90. See Mason, 'Partnership denied', pp. 260–1, for a fuller account of this.

91. Letters to *Tribune*, 14 November 1958, and *Manchester Guardian*, 2 February 1959.

92. LCC Alderman Donald Soper, Francis Williams, former editor of the *Daily Herald*, and others attacked the 'intolerant behaviour on the part of some Labour Councils' and claimed that 'the LCC has become in some ways the worst of all offenders', *Tribune*, 14 November 1958, cited in Mason, 'Partnership denied'.

93. *Evening Standard*, 25 November 1959.

94. Ibid.

95. N. P. Hepworth, *The Finance of Local Government* (London: Allen and Unwin, 1970; 7th edn 1984), p. 24.

96. J. Stephens (Bristol, South), *The Labour Party Annual Report*, 1955, p. 124.

Chapter 7　Planned Communities: The Social Objectives of the British New Towns, 1946–65

1. New Towns Committee, *Interim Report* (London: HMSO, 1946).

2. Ibid.

3. New Towns Committee, *Second Interim Report* (London: HMSO, 1946), p. 3.

4. New Towns Committee, *Final Report* (London: HMSO, 1946), p. 5.

5. Ibid., pp. 10–11.

6. Ibid.

7. Ministry of Health, *Design of Dwellings* (London: HMSO, 1944).

8. Ibid., p. 8.

9. Aneurin Bevan, 'Conference on housing layout in theory and practice. Part I', *Journal of the Royal Institute of British Architects*, vol. 55, no. 9 (1948), p. 382.

10. Lewis Silkin, 'Conference on housing layout in theory and practice. Part II', *Journal of the Royal Institute of British Architects*, vol. 55, no. 10 (1948), p. 431.

11. James Dahir, *The Neighbourhood Unit Plan* (New York: Russell Sage Foundation, 1947), p. 5.

12. Ibid., p. 7.

13. Ibid., p. 17.

14. Ibid., pp. 19–20.

15. Ibid.

16. *House of Commons Debates*, 5th Series, vol. 422, col. 1089, 8 May 1946.

17. Ministry of Health, *Design of Dwellings*, p. 61.

18. Ibid., p. 61.

19. New Towns Committee, *Final Report*, p. 16.

20. Bevan, 'Conference on housing layout in theory and practice. Part I', p. 382.

21. Public Record Office, Kew (henceforward PRO): HLG 90/208, *The Planning of Residential Neighbourhoods*, January 1947.

22. Ibid., p. 6.

23. Gordon Campleman, 'Some sociological aspects of mixed-class neighbourhood planning', *Sociological Review*, vol. 43, no. 10 (1951), p. 196.

24. Peter H. Mann, 'The socially balanced neighbourhood unit', *Town Planning Review*, vol. 29, July 1958, p. 96.

25. Ibid., p. 97.

26. J. E. MacColl, 'The social implications of the new town', *The Fortnightly*, December 1947, pp. 429–36.

27. Ibid., p. 434.

28. Ibid.

29. Ibid.

30. Campleman, 'Some sociological aspects of mixed-class neighbourhood planning', p. 195.

31. Bertram Hutchinson, *Willesden and the New Towns* (London: HMSO, 1947), p. 2.

32. Mann, 'The socially balanced neighbourhood unit', p. 98.

33. Ruth Glass, *The Social Background to a Plan* (London: Routledge, 1948), p. 132.

34. Ruth Glass, 'Urban sociology in Great Britain', in R. E. Pahl (ed.), *Readings in Urban Sociology* (London: Pergamon Press, 1988), p. 71.

35. Hemel Hempstead Development Corporation, *Hemel Hempstead Master Plan* (London: HMSO, 1947), paras 71–9.

36. Hemel Hempstead Development Corporation, *Annual Report* (London: HMSO, 1962).

37. Brian Heraud, 'Social class and the new towns', *Urban Studies*, vol. 5, no. 1 (1968), p. 39.

38. Hemel Hempstead Development Corporation, *Annual Report* (London: HMSO, 1962).

39. *The Times*, 29 June 1953.

40. Stevenage Museum Oral History Project (henceforward SOHP): Transcript, A090/2.

41. SOHP: Transcript, A090/2 .

42. Hertford Public Record Office (henceforward HPRO): Stevenage Development Corporation, meeting 204, minute 112, 28 February 1956.

43. HPRO: HHDC/CNT/HH/Box 209/ Misc. 37, Hemel Hempstead Development Corporation Papers, Housing Policy, 1 October 1952.

44. HPRO: HHDC/CNT/HH/Box 209/ Misc. 37, Sheepshanks to Wells, 22 August 1952.

45. HPRO: HHDC/CNT/HH/Box 209/ Misc. 37, Hemel Hempstead Development Corporation Papers, Housing Policy, 1 October 1952.

46. Alan Duff, *Britain's New Towns* (London: Pall Mall, 1961), p. 72.

47. Heraud, 'Social class and the new towns', p. 53.

48. Ibid., p. 49.

49. Ibid.

50. Norman Dennis, 'The popularity of the neighbourhood community idea', in Pahl (ed.), *Readings in Urban Sociology*, p. 84.

51. James Johnson, *Suburban Growth: Geographical Processes at the Edge of the City*, (London: Wiley, 1974), p. 2.

Chapter 8   Reconstituting the Family: Education for Parenthood and Maternity and Child Welfare, 1945–60

1. See for example, J. Dale and P. Foster, *Feminists and State Welfare* (London: Routledge & Kegan Paul, 1986), and E. Wilson, *Women and the Welfare State* (London: Tavistock, 1977). In addition, Denise Riley in *War in the Nursery: Theories of the Child and Mother* (London: Virago, 1983) argues that the closure of the day nurseries was not a deliberate attempt to send mothers back to the home, but certainly indicates that state policy did have this effect.

2. However, within sociology there is a growing body of work on women's caring roles within the family, e.g. Jean Gardiner, *Gender, Care and Economics* (Basingstoke: Macmillan, 1997).

3. See, for example, A. Oakley, *The Captured Womb: A History of the Medical Care of Pregnant Women* (Oxford: Blackwell, 1984).

4. J. Lewis, *Women in Britain since 1945: Women, Family, Work and the State in the Post-war Years* (Oxford: Blackwell, 1992), p. 11.

5. Ibid., p. 14.

6. See, for example, D. Dwork, *War is Good for Babies and Other Young Children: History of the Infant and Child Welfare Movement in England 1898–1918* (London: Tavistock, 1987).

7. C. Hardyment, *Dream Babies: Child Care From Locke to Spock* (London: Cape, 1983), p. 235.

8. And still is. For example, 'Family life is the foundation on which our communities, our society and our country are built', Jack Straw, Foreword, *Supporting Families: A Consultation Document* (HMSO, 1998).

9. Robert Sutherland, 'Health education and the health visitor', *Woman Health Officer*, vol. XX, no. 2 (February 1947), p. 15. With thanks to The Wellcome Institute for the History of Medicine for providing access to *Woman Health Officer*, the official journal of the Health Visitors' Association: SA/HVA.

10. PRO: MH55/1571, Advisory Committee on Mothers and Young Children, Personnel and General Purposes Sub-committee, report on *Existing Arrangements for the Teaching of Parentcraft and How This Might Be Extended and Developed*, 1944, p. 3.

11. Ibid.

12. Ibid.

13. PRO: MH55/1571, Letter from the National Federation of Women's Institutes to the Interdepartmental Committee on Parentcraft, 17 June 1944.

14. Elizabeth Tyleden, 'Confidence in the ante-natal period', *Woman Health Officer*, vol. XXIV, no. 12 (December 1951), p. 314.

15. PRO: MH55/1751, Interdepartmental Committee on Home-Making, *Draft Interim Report*, 1945, p. 3.

16. For example, as evidenced by the large number of studies conducted in the 1950s on the impact of married women working. For example, see Pearl Jephcott, *Married Women Working* (London: Allen and Unwin, 1962) and Ferdinand Zweig, *Women's Life and Labour* (London: Gollancz, 1952).

17. Hence a number of sociological studies were implemented, primarily focusing on working-class communities. For example, M. Young and P. Wilmott, *Family and Kinship in East London* (London: Routledge and Kegan Paul, 1957) indicated a change in the working-class family and community rather than an overall decline in these institutions *per se*.

18. For example, through publications such as John B. Watson, *Psychological Care of Infant and Child* (New York: Norton and Co., 1928) and Frederick Truby King, *Feeding and Care of Baby* (London: Macmillan, 1913).

19. John Bowlby, *Forty-four Juvenile Thieves: Their Characters and Home Life* (London: Baillière, Tindall and Cox, 1946).

20. John Bowlby, *Maternal Care and Mental Health* (Geneva: World Health Organization, 1951).

21. John Bowlby, *Child Care and the Growth of Love* (London: Penguin, 1953).

22. See, for example, the work of D. W. Winnicott, in particular *The Child and the Family: First Relationships* (London: Tavistock, 1957), and A. Freud and D. Burlingham, *Infants Without Families: Reports on the Hampstead Nurseries*

1939–45 (London: Hogarth Press, 1974). In addition, inter-war psychoanalysis was already beginning to emphasize the mother's role rather than Freud's father figure, as evidenced in the work of Helena Deutsch and Melanie Klein. For further information, see Janet Sayers, *Mothering Psychoanalysis: Helene Deutsch, Karen Horney, Anna Freud, Melanie Klein* (London: Penguin, 1991).

23. Hardyment, *Dream Babies*, p. 223.

24. Ibid. and D. Richardson, *Women, Mothering and Childrearing* (London: Macmillan, 1993), p. 28.

25. Hardyment, *Dream Babies*, p. 223.

26. Ibid.

27. PRO: MH55/1571, Advisory Committee on Mothers and Young Children, Personnel and General Purposes Sub-committee, report on *Existing Arrangements for the Teaching of Parentcraft and How This Might Be Extended and Developed*, 1944, p. 3.

28. PRO: MH55/1571, Interdepartmental Committee, *Draft Interim Report*, 1945, p. 1.

29. PRO: MH55/1540, Letter from Miss Z. Puxley, Assistant Secretary, Ministry of Health, to Mrs Wright, Chairman of the Personnel and General Purposes Sub-committee, Advisory Committee on Mothers and Young Children, 4 August 1943; MH55/946, Letter from Miss Z. Puxley to Mr Fife Clark, Public Relations Officer, Ministry of Health, 24 November 1944.

30. Dr D. Odlum, *You and Your Children* (London: HMSO, 1951).

31. PRO: MH55/947, Letter from Mr Fife Clark, Public Relations Officer, Ministry of Health, 1 June 1945.

32. Robert Sutherland, 'Health education and the health visitor', p. 4.

33. Simon Yudkin, 'The care of the toddler', *Woman Health Officer*, vol. XXIV, no. 10 (October 1951), p. 264.

34. Dr Solomon, 'The emotional needs of the under five', *Woman Health Officer*, vol. XXV, no.3 (March 1952), p. 62.

35. L. G. Housden, *The Teaching of Parentcraft* (London: Methuen, 1951), p. 10.

36. A. Binney (ed.), 'Development of a health personality: report of a summer school discussion group', *Woman Health Officer*, vol. XXXI, no.11 (November 1958), p. 412.

37. For example, in R. S. Illingworth, 'Elasticity in infant feeding', *Woman Health Officer*, vol. XXV, no. 1 (January 1952).

38. 'Editorial comment', *Woman Health Officer*, vol. XXXI, no. 11 (November 1958), p. 398.

39. D. H. Geffen, 'Science of breast feeding', *Woman Health Officer*, vol. XXI, no. 2 (February 1948), p. 12.

40. Anne Cuthbert, 'The anxious mother', *Woman Health Officer*, vol. XXX, no. 1 (January 1957), p. 17. For example, in H. Gavron, *The Captive Wife: Conflicts of Housebound Mothers* (London: Routledge and Kegan Paul, 1966).

41. Miss Amis, 'Maternity and child welfare: report of the annual conference organised by the National Association of Maternity and Child Welfare', *Woman Health Officer*, vol. XXIV, no. 8 (August 1951), p. 207.

42. PRO: MH55/946, Minutes of the first meeting of the Joint Ministry of Health and Ministry of Education Committee on Parentcraft, 30 August 1944.

43. Miss Amis, 'Maternity and child welfare', p. 208.

44. G. M. Francis, 'The International Child Welfare Congress. Part II. Random points from Papers', *Woman Health Officer*, vol. XXXI, no. 11 (November 1958), p. 409.

45. Housden, *The Teaching of Parentcraft*, p. 16 (my italics).

46. Ibid., p. 121 (my italics).

47. The Wellcome Institute for the History of Medicine: SA/HVA/D.6/1, *Ten-minute Talks: Mother*, 1947, p. 30.

48. PRO: MH55/1571, Draft Circular, Ministry of Health, June 1944.

49. Sutherland, 'Health education and the health visitor', p. 4.

50. However, the introduction of the welfare state saw the extension of their role to the care of the whole family while also developing their work in M&CW clinics.

51. Jane Lewis, 'Mothers and maternity policies in the twentieth century', in Jo Garcia *et al.*, *The Politics of Maternity Care: Services for Childbearing Women in Twentieth Century Britain* (Oxford: Oxford University Press, 1990), p. 21.

52. Means-testing had increasingly been used to provide such services before the introduction of the National Health Service.

53. Oakley, *The Captured Womb*.

54. Unlike the more 'technical' aspects of maternity, such as gynaecology and obstetrics, which were male dominated.

55. Cuthbert, 'The anxious mother', p. 17.

56. Dr Elizabeth G. Gore, 'The psychology of infant feeding', *Woman Health Officer*, vol. XXVII, no. 8 (August 1954), p. 215.

57. Ibid.

58. The Wellcome Institute for the History of Medicine: SA/HVA/D.6/1, *Ten-minute Talks: Mother*, 1947, p. 1.

59. Lucy D. James, 'Health visiting today', *Woman Health Officer*, vol. XXXII, no. 9 (September 1959), p. 325.

60. 'Editorial comment', *Woman Health Officer*, vol. XXXIII, no. 10 (October 1960), pp. 363–6.

61. 'Editorial comment', *Woman Health Officer*, vol. XXXI, no. 11 (November 1958), p. 398. The same was said of pregnant women: see Tyleden, 'Confidence in the ante natal period', *Woman Health Officer*, vol. XXIV, no. 12 (December 1951), p. 314.

62. PRO: MH55/1571, Advisory Committee on Mothers and Young Children, Personnel and General Purposes Sub-committee, report on *Existing Arrangements for the Teaching of Parentcraft and How This Might Be Extended and Developed*, 1944, p. 3.

63. E. Wilson, *Only Halfway to Paradise: Women in Postwar Britain 1945–1968* (London: Tavistock, 1980), p. 189.

64. Anna Davin, 'Imperialism and motherhood', *History Workshop*, vol. 5 (1978), p. 54.

65. Ibid., p. 53.

66. See J. Lewis, *The Politics of Motherhood: Child and Maternal Welfare in England 1900–1939* (London: Croom Helm, 1980).

67. PRO: MH55/1571, Note of Interview with Dr L. G. Housden by members of the Interdepartmental Committee on Parentcraft Instruction, 22 February, 1945.

68. Amy Burne, 'The family', *Woman Health Officer*, vol. XXVII, no. 1 (January 1954), p. 13.

69. 'Centre news', *Woman Health Officer*, vol. XXI, no. 11 (November 1948), p. 21.

70. J. Stanley Coleman, 'The place of the husband in confinement', *Woman Health Officer*, vol. XXVIII, no. 5 (May 1955), p. 146.

Chapter 9　The Organization Man: George Haynes at the National Council of Social Service

1. Margaret Thatcher, *Woman's Own*, 31 October 1987; Margaret Thatcher, *The Downing Street Years* (London: HarperCollins, 1993), p. 626.

2. Karl Marx, *Capital: A Critique of Political Economy*, Vol. 1 (London: Lawrence and Wishart, 1954), p. 78. For a useful discussion of this issue see James Heartfield, 'Marxism and social construction', in Suke Walton (ed.), *Marxism, Mysticism and Modern Theory* (London: Macmillan in association with St Antony's College, Oxford, 1996), p. 16.

3. Hansard, *House of Lords Official Report 1948–9*, 5th Series, vol. CLXIII, col. 76.

4. Ibid., col. 96. Samuel and Beveridge were not lone voices in the late 1940s. Abigail Beach, ('The Labour Party and the idea of citizenship, *c*.1931–1951', unpublished Ph.D. thesis, University of London, 1996), for example, has described the importance of voluntary social service in the Labour Party's conception of citizenship. Steven Fielding, Peter Thompson and Nick Tiratsoo (*'England Arise': The Labour Party and Popular Politics in 1940s Britain* (Manchester: Manchester University Press, 1995)) agree, asserting that the incoming Labour government set out to inspire a generation of active citizens and that voluntary and community organizations were a central part of their conception of how this could be achieved.

5. Frank Prochaska, *Royal Bounty: The Making of a Welfare Monarchy* (New Haven and London: Yale University Press, 1995), p. 239.

6. NCSS Executive Committee (EC) 25/4/40; NCSS EC 20/9/40, in London Metropolitan Archive (LMA) 4016/IS/01/031 (2); NCSS Finance and General Purposes Committee (FGP) 26/2/46; NCSS FGP 26/3/46, in LMA/4016/IS/01/048 (1); Margaret Brasnett, *Voluntary Social Action: The History of the National Council of Social Service 1919–1969* (London: National Council of Social Service, 1969), pp. 95–6.

7. Brasnett, *Voluntary Social Action*, p. 84.

8. Joan S. Clarke, 'The National Council of Social Service', in Lord Beveridge and A. F. Wells (eds), *The Evidence for Voluntary Action* (London: George Allen and Unwin, 1949), p. 253. Also National Council of Social Service *Annual Reports*, 1939–60.

9. Clarke, 'National Council', p. 253.

10. Sir John Wolfenden, 'George Haynes: a tribute', *Social Service Quarterly*, vol. XL, no. 4 (1967), pp. 139–40; Brasnett, *Voluntary Social Action*, pp. 95–6.

11. *Family Welfare Association Annual Report 1956–57*, p. 24. The Charity Organisation Society, a vigorous opponent of collective welfare since its inception in 1869, became the Family Welfare Association in 1946 under Astbury's leadership. The change of name reflected the change in direction masterminded

by Astbury. David Owen, *English Philanthropy 1660–1960* (Cambridge, MA: Harvard University Press, 1964), p. 246.

12. G. E. Haynes, 'The future purposes and organisation of the National Council of Social Service', appended to Annual General Meeting 14/12/44 in LMA/4016/IS/01/007(1).

13. Haynes, 'Future purposes', pp. 1–3.

14. See, for example, Harris, 'Political thought' and Jane Lewis, 'Women, social work and social welfare in twentieth century Britain: from (unpaid) influence to (paid) oblivion', in Martin Daunton (ed.), *Charity, Self-interest and Welfare in the English Past* (London: UCL Press, 1996), p. 215.

15. Haynes, 'Future purposes', p. 3.

16. Ibid., pp. 8–9.

17. Ibid., p. 7.

18. Mike Whitlam, 'At the top: the role of the chief executive', in Chris Hanvey and Terry Philpot (eds), *Sweet Charity: The Role and Workings of Voluntary Organisations* (London: Routledge, 1996), p. 163. Whitlam's insight is based on his own experience as Chief Executive of both the British Section of the Red Cross and the Royal National Institute for the Deaf. See also John Clarke and Janet Newman, *The Managerial State* (London: Sage, 1997), pp. 29–33.

19. Haynes, 'Future purposes', p. 9.

20. Sir George Haynes, 'Prospects for human welfare', First Dorothy King Memorial Lecture delivered at McGill University, 23/10/64, in LMA/4016/IS box 178.

21. Haynes, 'Prospects'.

22. H. R. Poole, *The Liverpool Council of Social Service, 1909–59* (Liverpool: Liverpool Council of Social Service, 1960), pp. 49–51.

23. Owen, *English Philanthropy*, pp. 460–8; Poole, *Liverpool*, pp. 7–8, 14.

24. Charles Leadbetter, *The Rise of the Social Entrepreneur* (London: Demos, 1997), pp. 78–80.

25. Brasnett, *Voluntary Social Action*, p. 18.

26. Harris, 'Political thought and the welfare state 1870–1940: an intellectual framework for British social policy?', *Past and Present*, vol. 135 (1992), pp. 121–6.

27. Harris, 'Intellectual framework', p. 134.

28. Ibid., p. 135.

29. José Harris, 'Political ideas and the debate on State welfare, 1940–45', in Harold L. Smith (ed.), *War and Social Change: British Society in the Second World War* (Manchester: Manchester University Press, 1986), p. 234.

30. Harris, 'Political thought', p. 24.

31. Pat Thane, *Foundations of the Welfare State* (London: Longman, 1996), p. 161.

32. Jane Lewis, *The Voluntary Sector, the State and Social Work in Britain: The Charity Organisation Society/Family Welfare Association since 1869* (Aldershot: Edward Elgar, 1995), p. 69.

33. Michael Freeden, 'The stranger at the feast: ideology and public policy', *Twentieth Century British History*, vol. 1, no. 1 (1990), pp. 9–34.

34. Brasnett, *Voluntary Social Action*, pp. 13–14.

35. F. G. D'Aeth, 'The Social Welfare Movement', *The Economic Review* (Oxford Christian Social Union), vol. XXIV (1914), pp. 404–14.

36. Sandra M. Den Otter, *British Idealism and Social Explanation: A Study in*

Late Victorian Thought (Oxford: Clarendon Press, 1996), introduction; Stefan Collini, 'The idea of "character" in Victorian political thought', *Transactions of the Royal Historical Society*, 5th Series, vol. 35 (1985), pp. 29–50.

37. D'Aeth, 'Social Welfare Movement', p. 408.

38. Brasnett, *Voluntary Social Action,* pp. 6–18.

39. Poole, *Liverpool*, p. 19.

40. D'Aeth, 'Social Welfare Movement', pp. 408–9.

41. Poole, *Liverpool*, pp. 32–3.

42. Owen, *English Philanthropy*, pp. 460–4.

43. Frederic G. D'Aeth, *Report to the Chairman of the Liverpool Council of Voluntary Aid on the Charitable Effort in Liverpool* (Liverpool: [LCVA], 1910), p. 18.

44. Poole, *Liverpool*, pp. 43–4.

45. Michael Power, *The* Audit Society: *Rituals of Verification* (Oxford: Oxford University Press, 1997), p. 94.

46. Poole, *Liverpool*, p. 44.

47. D'Aeth, 'Social Welfare Movement', p. 408.

48. Clarke, 'National Council', p. 252; NCSS *Annual Reports,* 1937–60.

49. Fielding, Thompson and Tiratsoo, *'England Arise'*, p. 21.

50. Clarke, 'National Council', p. 254.

51. EC 24/10/40; EC 14/12/44, in LMA/4016/IS/01/031(2)

52. Brasnett, *Voluntary Social Action,* pp. 99–101.

53. Ibid., pp. 101–3.

54. Ibid., pp. 125–6.

55. Anonymous Memo to Chairman, 6/4/38, 'Ourselves as others see us – as we are and as we might be', in LMA (uncatalogued), box 139.

56. EC 29/5/47 in LMA/4016/IS/01/32 (1).

57. For a colourful account of the disaster and subsequent relief work, see Eric E. Delderfield, *The Lynmouth Flood Disaster: The Full Story* (Exmouth: Raleigh Press, 1953)

58. FGP 23/9/52; FGP 28/10/52 in LMA/4016/IS/01/050 (1).

59. Haynes, 'Future purposes', p. 3.

60. Harold Laski, 'The cuckoo call', *The New Statesman and Nation*, 29 November 1947.

61. Wolfenden, 'George Haynes', p. 139.

62. NCSS Annual Reports, 1939/40–1950/1.

63. T. H. Marshall, 'Voluntary action', *Political Quarterly*, vol. XX, no. 1 (1949), p. 32.

64. Estelle James, 'How nonprofits grow: a model', in Susan Rose-Ackerman (ed.), *The Economics of Nonprofit Institutions: Studies in Structure and Policy* (New York: Oxford University Press, 1986), p. 188.

Index